GOLDILOCKS

Christian Jay Ashliman

ISBN 979-8-9866190-0-2 *(Paperback)*
ISBN 979-8-9866190-1-9 *(Hardcover)*
ISBN 979-8-9866190-2-6 *(eBook)*
ISBN 979-8-9866190-3-3 *(Audiobook)*

Cover Art Design © by Regan Ferreira
Title/Author Design © by Whitney Deelstra

More about the author found at *https://www.cashliman.com*

PREMONITION

There once was a bright, wide ocean-blue-eyed baby boy with golden wisps of hair that grew out the top of his head. He climbed trees and scraped his knees, played in the sand with sticks and toy trucks and cut his fingers up on all the wonderful things a baby boy does. He was tough, that baby boy, and sucked the blood from his little cuts—wiped them on his shirt sometimes, too. He was sturdy and adventurous, crafting little wooden bows with shoe strings, shooting little wooden-shaft arrows at make-believe monsters, winning the day, winning the dame, beating the creatures that rose from the deep ides of his mind. He swung little swords, chopped little axes, and fought the armies that dared stand against his little imagination. He smiled a lot, laughed even more. That little boy laugh, with those little boy teeth.

He loved to run and lived to explore. So one day, he set out into the woods. Verdant and thick, the woods that sat on the edge of town were his for the taking, his to discover. He was excited, and the blood running through his veins was bubbling and warm. His tummy was nervous, but he chose to go, chose to see what hid in the mystic, dark trees. He journeyed for days on end, walking his little boy feet down a thousand little trails. The woods grew cold at night, stiffening up his limbs and joints, making it harder to go on. But he went on, all the same. Days turned to months, turned to years and beyond. The little boy with his little sparkling eyes grew weary, grew scared, jaded by the woods. He longed for the battles and monsters he could fight across the stage of his mind, the creatures he could shoot his little bow and arrow at, swing his little wooden sword at, just like he used to. But they never came and his journey kept getting darker and colder, kept getting harder all the same.

One day on his travels through the deep, dark woods, he came upon a little cottage with a cobblestone chimney and a big, ornate door. He approached, tapping his swollen knuckles against the entryway. Tap, tap, tap. Three little knocks echoed inside, but no rushing footsteps came to let him in. Tap, tap, tap. Three more, and no one came. How strange, he thought, a cute little cottage, smoke pluming out the chimney, and no one's home. The little boy pushed against the round, cold-rolled steel knocker, and the door swung open wide. The sweet and succulent smells of boiling stew wafted out past his nose, and before he could stop himself, he leapt inside. It had been years since he smelled a meal as rich as this one.

The cottage was wondrous, warm, and inviting. On an oversized oak table sat three little bowls, each one filled with a sweet-smelling stew. It was meaty and spiced, filled with all his favorite goodies. He had to have a taste, just one spoonful, maybe even half a bowl. He climbed up in the first chair, sturdily planted in front of the first sizzling dish of soup. The chair was too tall, too awkward to sit in correctly. The boy's feet dangled above the ground, swinging back and forth as he picked up the spoon and filled it with the warm and bubbly stew. Steam was rising from the bowl, gathering on the boy's forehead as he peered down at the meal. The spoon rose to his lips, touched his tongue, and he shouted—too hot! It was too hot, too hot to enjoy. He threw the spoon back on the tabletop and leapt out of the massive chair.

Maybe one of the other bowls would taste a little better. He stumbled around the table, finding another chair set before another bowl of stew. He sat down, but this chair was too short—the boy's bruised knees rose above his hips, and his bum thumped against the ground. But he snatched up the spoon, dipped it in the stew, and shoved it in his mouth. Too cold! It was far too cold, as if ice had been tossed in the mix. Frozen stew was no good! He leapt out of the chair and rounded the table once more.

He sat in the third and final chair, which supported him perfectly. His feet sat flat on the ground, his rump hung a few inches above the floorboards, and it all felt juuuust right. He smiled and grabbed at the last clean spoon, filled it with stew, and took his bite. Juuuust right, it was. Warm and waiting, big and delicious, the stew in this last bowl was perfect. Just what he had been waiting for, walking for, journeying for all this time. The salt and seasoning, potatoes and meat, it was all juuuust right. He took another bite, then another, and before he could stop himself, he had cleaned out the bowl, drinking every last drip and drop. He leaned back, let out a burp, patted his stomach, and smiled a big, toothy grin. His tummy was warm and everything was perfect.

All this eating was making the boy tired. It had been months, years even since he last saw a soft, cozy, warm bed. That's what he wanted now. Surely the cottage had one of those, maybe even three of them. He walked up the creaking stairs, and before him, sure enough, sat three beds, each one with a blanket and pillow set perfectly across their frames. He crawled into the first bed he saw, but it was too short. His feet hung over the edge, and his toes wiggled in the chilly evening air. He hopped out of that bed and into the next one. His rump slammed against the baseboard, sounding off a knock that echoed through the cottage. This one was far too hard— there was scarcely any padding in it at all! He threw off the sheet and vaulted from the middle bed over to the last one. It sprang him back, bouncing him in the air before cradling the boy softly. Juuuust right, this one was. It was perfect—soft and warm, it reminded him of home, of the times when he was younger, when his mom would tuck him in and plant a little kiss on his golden hair-covered head. He smiled a big, toothy grin, closed his eyes, and fell fast asleep.

Then the bears came home.

PART ONE

Juuuust Right

Chapter 1

Songs of Death

If you're reading this, don't.

I don't give a shit about how I feel. That's what I tell myself, always telling myself, every day as one hour slips into twenty-four. That's what I tell myself, every day with the same vigor, the same mental posturing. The same physical hesitation. Why do I stop and sit and watch, why do I stretch my thoughts across the chasms of time, attempting to reason out the meaning behind this madness? I don't give a shit about how I feel—and neither should you.

And this is all madness, here in the deep woods of Oregon. Sitting crisscross-applesauce on top of an upside-down kayak strapped to the roof of my car. It's all trees and bark, fallen pine needles, and a graveyard of shattered ambition. All the things I want for my life, dormant under rows of headstones, unused, waiting, sleeping. Begging for engagement. All the things I want for my life, warring against all my reluctance and laze. A road trip crusade, barreling for the perfect moment to get down off this perch and make something happen. Maybe I just need to stop reading this, stop bleeding this, start breathing it and move my hands and feet for it. For all the wonder I want in my life. So I tick the miles on my odometer up and up. But that's never enough.

And that was all back in Oregon, after college, after a spring of incubating in May, when wanderlust was rooted deep in my soul, and I thought that was enough. That was after my academic mentors moved on, and the rot of Las Vegas and the sand dunes of California spoke gently in my ear. It was June and the blood had done its letting. But May and April and even March had some stories to tell, because spring is a time of radiant growth. And us humans grow, but it doesn't feel so magnificent all the time. It doesn't look like sunbeam daisies or peacock feathers. It's gross, uncomfortable, messy—the massacre of an old self for the violent birth of a new one. This is that story. But we aren't in the woods in Oregon yet, when floating heads and long dead baby bones became my living eulogy. When the bloodbath of spring scabbed over into summer in twenty-nineteen. That part comes, and it's all madness because it has to be.

My eyes blinked open, wildly darting around the room. That damn noise, the alarm going off, my god-forsaken alarm—only, no. That's not my usual alarm, that's my ringtone. It's got to be my ringtone. I know my alarm chime, it's welded to my DNA and makes me jump when I hear it on a stranger's phone in public. That's not this sound—this sound is the ringtone. Phone's ringing, vibrating loud, screaming to be picked up. Fine.

I leaned over, letting the mountain of blankets I was burrowed in tumble off my body. Who the hell is calling me right now? It's gotta be six or seven in the morning. I snatched the wailing phone off my nightstand, eyeing the time before answering—8:02 a.m. Mom was calling, ringing in from across the country where it was 10:02 a.m. I sighed, conceding there would be no return to the warm, fuzzy lair I had just been slumbering in. Up and at 'em. I jammed my thumb into the screen, answering the call.

"Happy birthday to you, happy birthday to you, happy birthday dear Christian, happy birthday, to youuuu!" She sang through the speaker, loud enough that I recoiled, hovering the phone five or six inches away from my ear. That's right, it was that day today. Another one of those. Too early to be dancing and singing, I rubbed my forehead.

"Did I wake you up? I woke you up, didn't I?" she said, reading the several seconds of dead air on my end, while I composed a smile.

"Yeah, you did. But that's okay, I need to get up anyways. It's already eight o'clock," my sleepy voice groaned back. No sense in lying, she'd sound that one out before I'd finish the sentence. "Thanks for calling and singing, though. The tradition lives on!" I remarked with a smile. And I was smiling, always smiling when I got that birthday song.

My conversations with mom always went on past the hour mark, sometimes even stretching past two. These talks were the exception to the rule, the rule that I tend not to enjoy phone conversations all that much. Tend to keep them short and sweet. But not with her. Those talks could go on and on. And this one was, as nine o'clock slipped into nine-thirty, nearing ten.

"What do you want to do after you graduate?" she asked in no minced words. The question that taints and tarnishes the mind of every undergrad, every young person, every human being at some point their life. What are you going to do with all this time, all this youthful energy, all this pent-up ambition? There's this big thing, this big oyster that's sitting wide open, jaws wide open, ready for you to engage—what are you going to do? You just went to school for six years, what's next? I hated the question, hated it because it was all I thought about, all I drank about, all I smoked, dreamed, and ate about. An annoying little court-jester, dancing around me, singing, shrieking, slapping my shins, jingling his little bells— you're absolutely clueless, you're absolutely clueless, you're absolutely, positively clueless! It didn't feel so positive, more like absolutely, eternally, existentially clueless.

"I don't know," I refrained, the same answer every time she asked. "I think I want to leave Utah for a while, travel or come visit you maybe, I'm just not sure. There's a lot of options, and none of them seem obviously right."

"Well, there's a good chance that none of them will be absolutely or obviously right. But I like that you're leaning towards getting out of Utah for a while. I keep thinking that you need to separate yourself from that place for a bit," she advised. She always advised, and whether I wanted to listen or not, her advice was usually right. Women get this weird, sage-style wisdom once they grow into motherhood. They know they have it, too. Sometimes not so humble about applying it like Neosporin to every worldly wound, but all the same, their advice mends.

She went on, "I think you should just jump. Ya know, leap and see where you land. You never know what's out there until you go out and look." More ointment for the confused and idle soul. I was pacing around my room, wearing tracks in the frilly carpet beneath my toes.

On that twenty-fourth day of March, on my twenty-fourth birthday, I was given a little brown book. Leather-backed, with a little stretchy cord used to cinch the pages closed. On the spine, there was a loop of more stretchy material, where I could secure a pen for easy access. I don't know how many pages were in the book, I never counted. They didn't have numbers, letters, or designs of any sort— just row after row of pinstriped lines that covered each and every page. It was the best book I never read.

But the first page of my little brown book had been filled with scribbles and I was proud. I was journaling again, writing again, emptying out my question-filled brain on those pinstriped lines. As I wiggled my wrist and fingers, wielding my little silver pen, the frustration spilled out, and was replaced with a clearing high. The first page was filled, line upon line, all the way down to the final, most southern edge. And I was proud. But now it was time to start page two, and I was lacking the special sauce. No topic, no thought, just a blank slate. But habits need nurturing, I knew that. I'd just gone through six years of school to get my four-year degree in psychology, and they always say that habits need nurturing, need reinforcing. They need some encouragement. One data point isn't enough to make something conclusive; you need more. I need more—more pages, more evidence that this little habit of emptying the dumpster-fire burning inside my skull was worth continuing. Because the high of piecing the puzzle together—that was worth it.

The world was tilted over, angled ninety degrees to the left. Beads of sweat gathered in the crook of my elbow, where the side of my cheek was resting. Music drummed in the background, repeating over and over phrases from catchy, repetitive tunes. Stuck in my head, side-scrolling, normally left to right, side to side. Now up and down and down and up again, the words wedged like a doorstop, sung by some one-off artist no one's ever heard of. But I'd listened to this on repeat for the past two months and the hippy voice was emoting the possibilities of life: travel, exploration, where to go and what to do.

My silver pen jotted quickly across the pinstriped lines rowing page two of my little brown book. Scribbling the sounds, the letters, the lyrics—maybe if I could see them in real time, get them out into the physical world, away from my eardrums, away from the backs of my eyelids, maybe then they would stop being stuck like glue to my refraining brain. The voice wailed, telling me and the planet that there's always been a way. But the words stopped short of an answer and broke into instrumental jives as I was caught in the web of what he meant.

There has always been a way to what? Always been some way—some way to make a choice, to live outside the confines of this room, to live outside in the world. Maybe I just like spilling ink, and maybe on page two, I'm learning that the hard way. I'm writing, scrawling something down the lines, those pinstriped lines. A giant ellipsis, waiting and watching for more wisdom to flood the room so I can write that into fiction, too. But this isn't fiction, this is page two, and I'm scribbling another data point, building up that habit. More drumbeats and background singers, more fluttering guitar strings, more scripture of the song to fill my pages up, so I have a well-rounded page two. Evidence.

The voice was bleeding out my speakers, swooning about a song born on the wind, how the cycle of life has no end, no place to begin. I had heard it three-hundred times, but today was different. Today the world was at a ninety-degree angle, with page two of a hand-twitching habit in the making. Here it is, here and now—I'm proud because I'm doing something, making some space inside my brain and page two is filling up just like page one did, and I'm doing something. Something better than sitting and stewing. My song, my tune, my book, my little leather-backed journal with manilla-colored pages. It's born at the tip of my pen, the part of my weapon that spills black and mighty, dark and bloody and real. Lyrics, to-do's, comic drawings of sword fighting armies, archers rowed atop the northern pinstriped line, blasting their little arrows down upon hordes of demons and devils, little dagger-wielding grumbling goblins. Cartoons and quotes, wrecking balls slamming all around the page—I'm spilling ink all over this thing and I'm proud.

Could have been five hundred pages left to fill, no end in sight, but a beginning that was staked, a beginning that was real—nowhere? Not a chance, I have a start right here, right on page one, when I leaked ink all over the hem about jumping, leaping and seeing where I'll land. What a rush, what a high that would be—is right now. To just jump and live in the world, to be of the world. I wanted that.

I jolted out of a post-euphoric melt. Head still resting in the crook of my arm, pen still caught between my fingers, my eyes peeled open at an unknown sound somewhere else in the house. My face was pasted to the side of my arm, with a slimy pool of drool gathering in the crook of my elbow. Unsticking my cheek, I licked up the saliva. What an animal. The world reoriented from its ninety-degree tilt, blood rushing from one half of my head, filling in the spaces of the other. Straight up and down, it was dark outside the window now, bright in my room. Music wasn't playing anymore, and a blob of my congealed spit had escaped the confines of my drool-pool, smearing across some of my cartoon drawings.

The next morning I had a meeting with Bill. He was the kind of guy who could say something at any moment, and you wished you had been able to record it because it was advice you might need in five years. Maybe it was because Bill was my teacher that I held him in such high esteem. He told us we could call him Billy if we wanted, but that felt too equalizing. He was my teacher, my mentor, not my younger friend. It always seemed his quirky-ness was his best trait. The way Bill looked at the world around him, the way he perceived it all, took it all in, and then explained, in wonderful teacher-wisdom terms, how it all works. Or how it all should work. And how it all should work, according to Bill, seemed fine by me.

I walked into my meeting with Bill, little brown book in hand, and my little silver pen fit snug in its stretchy loop. I was nervous, but not to the point of inducing acute anxiety. Meeting one-on-one with someone you admire is a nerve-wracking pre-game, gulping shot after shot of faulty expectations and sinister what-ifs. Prior to entering his classroom on the fourth floor of the library, I could feel my heart beat a little harder with each step up the stairs. It was late in the semester and the weather was nice outside, so I walked up four flights of stairs as my only exercise for the day, rather than ride the awkwardly silent elevator. If you thought spoken words weren't allowed in libraries, this elevator would give you a run for your money. Not a peep, a how-do-you-do, hardly a smile, and never a sound. Passing four floors, in utter silence, as if we were about to storm the beaches of scholastic Normandy—nervous, pigeon-toed, and staring straight ahead. So I climbed the steps instead. And after opening the door to Bill's classroom and starting our conversation? No problem. No hesitation, no worry, no nervousness. But Bill was that kind of guy, he made you feel comfortable.

I scribbled furiously, playing the part of an in-court stenographer. I just wanted to get the meat on the counter—I'd weigh the life of it later over a cup of coffee and some alone-time. Bill was talking, charting off in some wildly important direction. He was entering that phase in discussion when you started cataloging the words. I was throwing myself months, years into the future, looking back and knowing this moment might come in handy. These words might be useful. And they were. He was listing hard, going off about what I'd done this final semester, what he'd seen me do, what he saw I could do. Where I could go. He was begging me, pleading with me to jump, take a leap and see where I land. I scribbled, he talked. I scribbled. He paused. I looked up.

"Most importantly, you gotta get over yourself, dude," Bill said. My face was turning hot and red, blood backing behind every pore. Not anger, never anger at Bill. No confusion, no ignorance. Just hot and red and embarrassed because I knew he was right. He was right and there was no other way of putting it and he'd known, and I'd known, known for long enough. But that was the kind of guy Bill was, he'd say it to your red face, your hot face—he'd say it and he'd mean the shit out of it. I nodded, acknowledging a point well made. I thought I got it.

"Once you write something, it's not yours anymore. Those words are out in the world, they exist outside of your mind, outside of your pen—they become everyone else's," he went on, donning a caring, yet strong and insightful tone. More Billy-wisdom, only this time I sat still, pen, wrist, and fingers frozen, breathing in the sounds as he made them. Get over yourself. Get over myself. I need to get over myself. He's said it and I'm hearing it, and he's right. He's got to be right. Just like mothers and their sage-style wisdom, Bill's got life under his belt, Bill writes like a magician and he's preaching to me about me and with me, and he said get over myself.

I was struck by Bill's acute ability to be so in-tune with the fact that I was insecure in letting others view and critique my work. And not just my written work, but anything I created, any success or failure I fielded. What everyone outside that classroom door thought about me was a big deal, had been a big deal, always a big deal. I wore it on my sleeves, dressed in it like my favorite outfit. Did everyone struggle with this? Did he tell every salivating undergrad to get over themselves? Everyone seemed insecure to some extent—but there was a personal way Bill navigated the conversation and explained the ownership and truth of words and why it mattered. To me, it seemed like a group of sounds I needed to hear right at that moment. As if his voice box had tuned the perfect puzzle piece at the perfect moment, in the perfect order, unlocking some new perfected idea. Get over yourself, just try getting right over yourself.

Bill drifted on, "And don't be afraid to just *go there*—to the dark places." Bill had a lot to say about fear. He was persuading me into writing what scares me most—to just go there. He didn't dance around the subject like most people do. He seemed to have an intimate relationship with fear, even with death. His intimacy came from understanding the devilish duo. After starting a conversation with Bill, it didn't take long to know the man had been through things. Seen things, felt things that could never be un-felt. But just as he had said, and more as he had written, he was over himself and *went there* more often than not.

The difference with Bill was somehow, through all his dancing with fear and death, he managed to still see it as dancing. As if the struggles, strife, and wounds from his past were just more magnificent jive-moves he could perform at the drop of a hat. Most people dance with fear and death, and when the song ends, they bow, shake hands, and promptly sprint from the ballroom floor. That is, if they don't slip in their own urine and shat-in pants on the way out.

More than just dancing, Bill might flirt a little too, just to see what would happen. The courage to look and really see what the dance entailed—that's what set Bill apart. He wasn't coarse or bitter, but friendly, open, and incredibly honest right when he needed to be. He was willing. Despair didn't jade him from flaming the fires of ambition and inspiration among the undergrads. Students with eyes so wide, it was a marvel they didn't plop out of their heads and roll down four flights of library stairs. But that was just the kind of guy Bill was. And my eyes were wide as I imagined all of what horrified me and what it would mean to ink it into existence and not care if someone read it. My eyes almost plopped.

Here was Bill, speaking to bright and wide-eyed mounds of clay every day, filling them up with energetic gas, editing their terrible ideas into ones now recognizable as important. Fixing their flagrant mistakes, all while making them feel like it was their idea in the first place. Bill made liberal use of his red pen; he bled all over everyone's work. He'd slit arteries in the pages we turned in for homework and watch the blood gush out from the vital parts. And he'd smile from ear-to-ear and watch you squirm under the criticism, watch you struggle every second with the charge of just getting over yourself. Ready to chop down and bleed it out in all the right ways. Always the right ways, the best ways, because Bill knew best, and what Bill knew seemed fine by me. So I sat red-faced, breathed in the idea of getting over myself, and thought I got it.

College was a long and brilliant ride, filled with its fair share of high-rises and low-blows. It was the biggest collective experience I've ever been through. Not necessarily because of the classes, books, or campus—although those aspects played a role. It was the post-parent, post-home environment that created definitive learning experiences. That time when you're still a kid and act like a kid, but you've got all the freedom and move-about of an adult.

Four years of school is a lot, would be a lot, and that's just the average bachelor's degree. I got my degree, but I decided it was necessary to turn four years into six—a fact I don't let myself regret. At least on good days. Some brilliant minds drop out, and some people who are dense as a thick-battered muffin get doctorate degrees. My first two years were illuminating, all the same. I learned what plastic bottle vodka tasted like, both on the first sip, and the second time it sours back up at 3:30 a.m. And the girls, the constant horniness that permeated every late-night party; everyone had a goal, the goal, the one that ended on a twin mattress with no bed frame. Six years of school because the first two were filled with F's on the grade sheet, in my head, on my bed, everywhere I stumbled. Two years of tales that it would take another book to play out.

Along with Bill's writing class, I took Folklore during my final semester of school. When I say "folklore" around the dinner table at family functions, Grandma nods her head and my younger cousins tilt their confused faces to one side. Just that one simple word ages a person by generations. But there's something catchy about the word. "Folks" has such a comfy feel when you say it, like you're referring to Grandpa on his ole John Deere tractor, or a familiar friend from back home embracing you. Folks make me think of little dinky elves daintily bouncing through the undergrowth of a meadow. Not tall, Legolas-like elves, mind you, but little Keebler-bastards, all sprinting around, running little errands with their little hands and little faces, wearing their tiny, little shoes. There's something so cute, so warm about the scene, like none of it could ever be wrong or out of place. Folks drink their golden tree sap in little wooden mugs, and slam each other's backs, and laugh real loud and when they love, they love hard. Folks are waiting for you, they adore you and cherish you and you're comfortable around them—we like folks. Folklore was oh-so-cozy, fuzzy blankets tucked around my toes, hot cocoa and Keebler-elf-cookies radiating warmth through my fingers, arms, stomach, and throat. And it really was.

It was taught by a wonderful lady by the name of Cassady. She was in her mid-fifties, if I had to guess. She had strikingly blonde hair and the kind of smile you always hoped your teachers would give you. It was a big, toothy grin that reassured you she was on your side, through the thick-shit and thin-cynicism college can become. She didn't have the straightest teeth, or the whitest ones by my recollection. Stained by a million cups of coffee, she was energy, she was always buzzing and smiling. Everything about Cassady had the aura of a life fully lived. She was the perfect folklore teacher, as if she once was one of those little Keebler-elves herself, rushing around the woodland, but never stopped growing and now stood five-foot-nine before a class of salivating undergrads, here to tell us what tree sap tasted like.

She spoke like folklore, buzzed like it, looked like it, and she loved it. And that was just the kind of person Cassady was, always ready to drive the magic school bus to whichever folksy tale was up next.

Her eyes were soft, complementing the welcoming warmth of her smile. It was never scary talking to Cassady, not that I did a whole lot of that anyways. I mostly just listened. Cassady would stand before the class, every Tuesday and Thursday, with that beaming grin and greet everyone as they walked through the door. And if your name slipped her mind, she would mutter, "Oh shoot!" under her breath, as if she had forgotten something way more important than one of a thousand student names, and quickly referred back to her attendance sheet. Then she would profusely apologize and promise that next time she would get it right. And usually, she did.

Cassady was the embodiment of passion for her craft, and I just felt lucky to have a chair to plant my ass in four hours a week and listen. She didn't care so much for the physical items of the world, insomuch as they could help her understand more about the people who used them. Cassady was a master people-person, in the truest sense of the word. Most people throw that combo-slang around implying that they like talking to and helping people—and sure, that was as true for Cassady as it was for the next humanist.

But her people-person skills went deeper—they threaded to the core of what culture is. See, Cassady didn't just enjoy being around people and talking to them. She craved to ask questions, big questions, questions that all the other people-persons would never have even thought of. Cassady found groups, embedded herself, and went to work on them like peeling an onion—layer after layer. She wrote books about it, too. But that was just the kind of person that Cassady was. She wasn't focused on how she felt about things, there was too much going on outside the bus window.

Cassady assigned the class a project, due at the end of the semester. I knew it was coming down the pike, but as undergrads tend to do, I wadded up my little hopeful blip of foresight, and threw it in the trash. Probably should have aimed for the recycling bin, I'd need that later. Projects can wait until the week before their due. It's not easy being a professional procrastinator, but then again, it might just be the easiest thing.

Cassady wanted us to compile a record of some facet of culture, have it recorded either through video, audio, or written word, so it could then be uploaded into the virtual folklore database the university was building. The database was already massive, filled with all kinds of interesting tidbits from random cultures all over the world: tales told by Indian chiefs, depression-era cooking recipes, video instructions on rain dances, and ghost stories. So many ghost stories. I was excited to be able to add something, to be a part of something bigger than myself. The perfect project to round out my final perfect semester.

But March was ticking over into April, and I didn't have long before May would come, and school would end and the death knell would sound on my days as an academic. My days as a sponge, soaking up all the musical notes my teachers could produce. There are moments in time when the stars in the curtain of night seem to connect together like the dot games I used to play in church as a little boy. They're all spaced out and then suddenly a picture appears because I drew the lines and joined the rows and columns of periods into something more than pinstripes. It's people, it's mentality, it's circumstance—it all happens together and they connect and the picture starts to appear. I never knew where the beginning or the end was. It didn't matter, as death brings along with it new life. New sounds, new and exciting songs. And I wanted to sing.

Chapter 2

Life on LSD

Some people live for the holidays. They start playing Christmas music in October. They plan out their Halloween costume in July. They hide their Easter eggs three months early for their little bright-eyed toddlers to find. Three months ago it was winter and they were out digging holes in the ice just to find a good spot to hide that plastic, candy-filled egg. They paint their faces green on St. Patrick's Day, matching up their socks, shoes, and underwear and they run around pinching everyone and pissing everyone off because we forgot and it's a Monday, you asshole. I've got other things on my mind than wearing green undies.

On April Fool's Day they fill three-hundred plastic cups with water and put them one inch apart on the stairs, every step lined with cups of water. No way to get up and out from the basement other than crawling out the side window—unless you want to soak your shoes and the carpet, or dump three-hundred cups of water out, one by one. They Saran wrap the toilet seat so your piss-stream flings off onto every wall. They Saran wrap your entire car and it's April in Utah, so it freezes and you're not going anywhere until you peel off the icy sheets. Saran wrap must get a lot of business around April 1st. And it was April 1st. But I don't play the games.

The most I've done is tie the sink-sprayer open once or twice. But it's a Monday, and I've got better things to do.

It was early, and I was awake. More awake than I'd normally be at this time, but I've got things to do, better things. I was just waiting for the right time—not too early, not too late. Passing the time went easy when I scribbled and scratched down my pinstriped lines with my little silver pen. My favorite, most hated question was parading around my brain again, as it always did. What was I going to do after I graduated? This was April, the last month of school. The end time was approaching, and I needed direction, was craving some direction. The right answer had to exist, somewhere in the gray matter of my mind. But the more I sat, the more I felt around about it, the more I was grasping at straws, filling my fists with nothing but what ifs and possiblys. I hate the question. I hate that little clown dancing his jig around my shins, moving every day a little further from slapping them and a little closer to slicing. And the blood was starting to run. Every minute, hour, and day, as the end time drew nearer. Cutting and cutting and chiming all about how I had no clue, absolutely no clue. And I really didn't.

So I was scribbling, entertaining the idea of road tripping again. Road tripping like I did last year in twenty-eighteen. But that was only a week, a little solo adventure to get out of the house and into the world for a bit. I could do that again, but more than a week? I could do that. Maybe a month. Maybe I'd stay out there, fall in love with it, find someone, find somewhere, find the thing, the purpose for time after school. Time after school was long—from now until death. That's a heavy span and I've gotta fill it. The road was fun, the road was filled with things—time to think, time to figure it all out. I could live out there, in the wild, take from it, educate myself on it. I could do that. Not so sure, not so obviously right. But I might be able to do that. Transfer from university into the school of the world.

I closed my little brown book and slipped my pen in its loop. I shook my head, not so sure. Rubbed my forehead, doubly not so sure. Never sure. I wanted to be sure, wanted to be able to answer that damn question that everyone asked me at every family function, every get together, every phone call. What are you gonna do after you graduate? I used to tell them I was going to be a therapist. Degree in psychology, that seemed right. I would listen to people's problems, listen real long and hard. Sit with my book and my pen and jot notes, watching down my nose as the ink traced out someone's agony, looking through my therapist glasses that would be thick and smart. I'd grow into some of that sage-style wisdom myself and ask just the right questions to those clients and they'd be solved, and their problems would evaporate under a better line of reasoning. That's what I would do, or thought I was going to do during four out of those six collegiate years.

My first year of school I thought a business degree was my thing. My sixth year of school? Everything was mushy and mingled, and if you saw the top of my graduation hat, all would be set right. I walked up and accepted my bachelor's degree in psychology with the words "No 'Effin Clue" painted out across the square cap, big and proud. And it was true. Proud of my indecision, proud of that little clown court-jester doing his slapping and slicing. Smiles, winks, and adoration for the words—but after it was over, I was just screaming into my pillow.

When I saw therapy in action, watched the results, the successes and failures, the patience, the demeanor, the world through those thick-rimmed glasses—I hated it. Didn't want to do it, knew I couldn't do it without calling the client a whiny bitch. That's therapy under my thumb, pour out your first-world problems in complete detail while I nod and listen. And I would listen, I could do that. But afterwards, your prescription is quit being a bitch, go sort yourself out. Now, pay me seventy-five dollars an hour.

It's April though, here we are in April—foolish, cold, confusing April and I've almost got this psych degree. I never liked April. April is tricky here in Utah. It's always tricky. Always leads you on like it's spring, the white sun rising higher and shining brighter, and it's lovely. Then one day, just when April's invested enough in you to make you believe in spring, it dumps two feet of snow on you and it's colder again and winter has played the best fool's joke. And every year, every damn year, I tell myself that this year, this time, I won't fall prey. I'm not gonna believe in spring or summer until May. April can't trick me, I know the seasons, I've lived here long enough to know the joke. Every year I repeat the chorus of winter, laughing at those who believe the weather reports. You think that was the last snow? The one we got at the end of March? Were you born yesterday? This is Utah—northern, cold, frigid, winter-living Utah. April is winter, just like March is and you're a fool for believing otherwise. And when April twenty-fifth rolls around and it hasn't snowed yet, then I start believing in spring, maybe even summer. And all the same, on the twenty-sixth day it dumps two feet of frozen rain and it's fooled me.

So I am a fool and seldom has that ever felt more present than it does right now. A fool because I'm in the end times and I know school gives me cover, gives me a checklist to live up to the old-folk anthem—get an education! And I am, I have been for six damn years! A fact I don't let myself regret—at least on good days. But that's all about to go away, gone and wiped into the past.

What then?

I always thought I could save the vital, messy thinking for the acid. Take some drugs and sit and stare at the wall and the chemicals would do the heavy lifting. Lysergic acid diethylamide—little cheat-sheets that waddled around my mind and flipped over the bins like a toddler looking for new toys. I'd make it all a mess up there, and often enough, I might find something I'd long forgotten. Or better yet, something I never knew was there in the first place.

LSD in a forest always seemed like a good idea. Surrounded by trees, greenery, leaves hugging you up tight. I'd always wanted that, but most of my acid adventures were just four walls and screens broadcasting tie-dye infused YouTube videos with Pink Floyd moaning in the background. I'd get my deep-woods trip, but we aren't to that part in the story yet. Today was just the drug at home. And it would do my heavy lifting, show me that choosing could be as simple as the setting sun every evening.

And the time was almost here, almost right—not too early, not too late in the morning on this April Fool's Day. The sun was still white and the frost on the grass outside was just beginning to melt over into dew. It was beautiful and I was ready to answer some questions and make some headway. Some people live for the holidays, and today was mine. When I could play the fool and stop tainting my sober, wishy-washy mind with questions and leave the answers up to drugs. I suppose that's life on LSD. I finger-tweezed a square of paper onto the veiny meat beneath my tongue.

Chapter 3

Gonna Die Trying

April slogged on.

My right foot pumped off the asphalt, my left planted firmly in the griptape. Down sharp, ninety-degree cornering roads, longboard wheels humming from their rotations against the ground. Logan, Utah is laid out on a grid system, with each perfect little block following the next one. If you zoom out, it looks like graphing paper. I was raised on this graphing paper, brought up to know the crisscrossing veins that pumped people through my city. It's usually not very busy in Logan, unless you decide to brave Main Street at 5:15 p.m. on a weekday, in which case you'll be solving some math-grid equations of your own before too long. The graphing paper made it easy to find things, and easier to back-track if needed. It made it possible for you to call out street numbers, not names, and have a majority of people know exactly where and what you were talking about.

Just like the grid of my city, the cemetery followed suit. Line after line of headstones, all illuminated by the brilliant rays of heavens-glow. Line after line of black asphalt, pumping graveyard visitors through the solemn veins of mourning, leading east, west, north, then south again. Every morning, I found myself racing through long, stretched pine tree shadows—hooded reapers drawn out across the grass, steepened as the morning light peeked over the towering Wasatch mountains. It was a vibrant three minutes of floating above the dead, rocketing down cemetery lanes on my longboard, trying to balance my own overflowing cup of life's-blood, not wanting to part with one single drop, not in this place. The dead were dead, and I was living. I was brimming with life. Every morning, racing through this casket-land, all in an attempt to reach the other side without letting a dead hand grab at my ankles. Until one day, I was rooted down and pulled deep into the earth.

I always thought it so ironic that city planners put the Logan cemetery right in the heart of the college campus experience. Surrounded on all four sides by student housing, a football stadium, a basketball arena, and a physical education building—the cemetery sits as if it's part of the club. Even weirder was that after so many years of traversing its grounds, it really did start to feel like it was part of the club. I don't think I understood that fact until I stooped down into the dirt and had a conversation with the dead.

I was finished with classes for the day, excited to head home, throw my backpack on my bed, don my oversized computer headphones, and play World of Warcraft for another six hours straight. Just like last week and the week before that. Brimming with life. Zipping through campus on my longboard, I leaned left and right, swerving back and forth under a canopy of trees that broke up the spring sunshine into small pockets of golden warmth. The rusted bars of the cemetery fence were visible now, gates swung wide allowing students a shortcut through the paths of the dead. This was my route, my favorite road to take. With the hustle of young adults sprinting to classes, trucks dropping off another week's food to the cafeteria, buses squealing sighs, starting and stopping and starting again—there was a lot of noise. It emanated from the school grounds, especially in the early morning and afternoon hours. But moments after passing through the menacing graveyard gates, there was a gracious blanket of silence. No trucks, no buses, no loud-speaker announcements, no squealing tires or rumbling motorcyclists strutting their stuff. Just silence and the occasional far-off hum of an engine grinding its way through the endless grid.

It started to make sense why this place was part of the club. I was soaring through the air, loud and proud, ripping and roaring as I saw fit, mentally charged with ideas as pure as the white April sun. And suddenly, as I passed through the pointed gates, I was nothing. I was floating in a muffed meadow where only the chirps of counterfeit-spring birds could pull me down to reality. I was nothing amid a vast green and black and gray sea of memories, rocks with dates and little English wisdoms etched into their surface surrounding me. I was nothing, pumping through the veins of this harrowing place with nothing achieved, nothing to etch into the fateful rock I'd own someday.

So I pumped a little harder, swerved a little more, and angled the corners of the cemetery, pointing myself toward home. World of Warcraft wasn't going to play itself, and the dead definitely weren't going anywhere anytime soon. The opposite edge of the cemetery was in view now, my eventual escape from this wrestling bag of mixed emotions and silence. I wouldn't look back, not at the thousands of pillars of salt and stone. I didn't have time to look back, I wasn't curious to look back. I pumped harder and harder in my attempts to break free from the encapsulating burial ground. World of Warcraft wasn't going to play itself. And suddenly, without a word of warning, my head was turned, and I saw the lights, and just like Lot's wife, I turned into a pillar of salt and stone.

My feet weren't my own, my pumps were driven by forces beyond my control and I was confused, but following my feet, all the same. I swung around corners for reasons unknown and came upon a very sacred, very specific little plot of dirt and grass. A rounded headstone with my grandpa's name carved deep into its surface. My grandma's name was there, but there was only one date under her name, no English wisdom chiseled in quite yet. She was still brimming, too. The rock was dark gray, with rough edges around the outside. The surface shined so clear, I could make out my own reflection behind the inscription of dates, names, and epitaphs. Here I was standing before the tombstone of the grandfather I never met, stolen from the world years before I was born, killed by a sinister cancer. I stood, confused at who or what had taken control of my feet, and guided my legs to this spot. It sure as shit wasn't me.

This wasn't the first time I came here, but it was the first time I was led, as Déjà Vu wrung out the rag of my brain. I had run this grid a thousand times, seen this stone a thousand more, and thought, "See ya later, Gramps!" on every occasion. More than once I had been inspired by this silence, wrapped myself in comfort, and whispered inquiries to the body below ground, the one I never met. I was here, with my feet growing roots to the center of the earth, being devoured by the mulching dirt and dust of aged and decrepit souls.

Waves of mud, dead-yellow grass, and bonemeal rose high, beating loud against the pine trees and willows pinstriping the grid. There was no silence anymore, just as I slipped under the surface and posed more questions for the souls laid to rest.

"What am I going to do after I graduate?" I groaned, hoping for a hot new take, an answer more direct than me just road tripping. But I knew, I just needed more encouragement from my elders, just one more person, dead and six feet under, to tell me to leap.

The underground wasn't so scary, as I lounged in my own casket, making conversation with the skeleton in the next one over. Boy, could we talk! For what seemed like hours, we bounced back and forth over the dirt and budding leaves of my life, the direction I was going, the reason behind it all, the sight of the future, the brilliance of the past. He cackled and reeled with laughter, and I reciprocated. Afterall, it's not every day you get to dive into the sod and hang out with your dead grandpa.

We both had a lot to say, a million questions to ask, and no time to get it all out. We rolled around in our graves for a while, letting the mud tarnish our pure-white clothes. He thought it was hilarious to add a little character to his burial gown. Pure and perfect shirts were boring. I added some grime to mine, too. Then, I added a little to his, and he added a little to mine, tossing clods of condensed soil into each other's coffins and cracking up with boisterous laughter the entire time. The roots of my questions, the roots shooting out the bottoms of my heels, burrowing deep through the dirt, they found him, his skull, his memory, his body laying tenderly in its lovely wooden box. They found him, and they drank up the gray matter of his mind and satiated my questions again—leap, just leap and see where you land.

My hand burst through the weeds and tangled grass, shooting into the air like a zombie rising from the dead, ready to feast on my pound of flesh. My fingers clawed inward, grasping for light and oxygen, stained brown from hours of dirt-clod throwing. One hand out, my other one punched through the underside of the surface, now pulling my energized body from the depths below. I rose to my feet, took a step forward, and ran my fingers down the rough marble edge of Grandpa's headstone. There were only two shreds of thought scrolling left to right across the back of my eyelids as I stood close-eyed, breathing deep the spring-time air.

One. Leaving would be entirely necessary for this magnificent, stupid, challenging, laugh-cackling adventure of mine. The mud on my shirt painted quite the story, how leaving would really force my eyes to widen, for me to truly see. Or die trying. It was the simple act of doing it anyway, leaving this place I called home, leaving the comfortable, predictable grid I grew up in, everything positioned in perfect blocks, all cornered at ninety degrees. It was the simple act of moving my toes, my legs, my ass, my arms, fingers, tongue, and head in new ways that weren't going to be so Keebler elf comfy-like, so routinely predictable, that my purpose would finally reveal itself. But that was never going to happen if I didn't at least die trying.

Two. Leaving this two-dimensional graphing paper couldn't be for the sake of learning new ways to solve math equations for other people. My math would have to be done in service to no one besides myself. My math would have to be messy and bleed into the next sheet of paper, with random child-like doodles climbing up the sides and shooting each other's brains out all over the page. My math would only make sense to me, in the most authentic way possible. I wasn't about to leave this place banking on the adoration or acceptance of other people.

Besides, Grandpa had already spelled it out with his muddy finger on the front of my pearly-white, button-up shirt. So I'm gonna leap, or I'm gonna die trying. And maybe I'll splat hard at the bottom of the cliff, but at least I can say I jumped. At least I tried. And maybe that gory image is the one they'll carve on the headstone marking my grave one day. And maybe they'll all laugh or bury their hands in their pockets so deep they almost touch the pavement, and hang their heads—but I'm gonna die trying. I'm gonna let my roots grow into the earth and learn from the ones who came before, the ones I never met. It was as simple as moving my hands and feet and my sobered mind knew it once more, the picture and stars coming into focus.

Someone named Sister Eubank was chiming through my speakers. I don't know what led me there, how her voice ended up being the one I needed that morning. Hell, I didn't even really know who she was. Who cares who someone is when the words coming out of their mouth reach out of my ten-dollar Amazon computer speakers and slap me right across the face. I was aghast, mouth hung wide in wonder. I don't usually prefer being assaulted first thing in the morning. I usually prescribe myself three or four snooze buttons, a hot cup of coffee, a throat-full of Mary-Jane, and three or four hours of virtually blowing the brains out of little random comic doodles on a little digital screen. World of Warcraft isn't gonna play itself. Welcome to every Sunday morning of my adult life, up until this one.

Sister Eubank was keynoting like crazy, throwing all kinds of words out at me—and they were fitting. Then, right at the end, she put together this little zinger that I jotted down with my little silver pen down my little pinstriped lines. And as much as I wanted someone a hundred years from now to find my little brown book and attribute these letters to me, I gave her credit:

I don't know all the reasons why the veil of mortality is so thick. This is not the stage in our eternal development where we have all the answers. It's the stage where we develop our assurance, or sometimes hope, in the evidence of things not seen. Assurance comes in ways that aren't always easy to analyze, but there is light in our darkness.

There is light in our darkness. Dear ole Sister Eubank, you've gone and said it. Aren't those moments of post mind-gasm clarity so brilliantly confusing? Especially when it's something you've always known, just presented and packaged in a new way. A way that induces just enough Déjà Vu for you to realize what you've always known. I mean, of course there's joy in the journey, light in the darkness, a diamond nestled in the bedrock of coal and stone. You know that; I know that. But we don't understand it until we get our little package in the mail, expedited by Amazon slave-labor, plugged into my computer, tuned to the right sound frequency, the right dot com, at the right moment. I get little packages all the time, but I don't like their wrapping. I think they could be prettier, shinier, messier, more perfectly imperfect. But every once in a while, I get a package, shred the wrapping paper, dig into the box, and find a puzzle piece that fits juuuust right.

There are a lot of words that can describe one moment in time. I've found nearly a hundred that seem to do just that. It isn't a foreign concept, it isn't complicated math. It's a second, a blip in the stream of time, pinned against the wall with your last thumbtack. It's the spot when your pen touches the page, your foot presses the gas, your nail strikes a G chord. When the sun finally dips below the horizon, when you shoot to the surface for air. It's that time when you touched the singing kettle by accident, crusting your skin from a fiery burn. When your bones snapped from tumbling too far or when you dropped priceless china to the floor, shattering into a million microscopic shards. It's the time your mother says leap, the time you slipped paper under your tongue. The break in noise when clouds of silence take over, the moment your fingers brush rough headstones. The partition in time when I opened my little brown book, and wiggled my wrist and fingers around.

But I'm obsessed with time and its passing, so I grasp at words that help this stream make sense. And I found one. That was the first time I'd heard the word, and in seven little letters I knew all I needed to know. *Caesura.* I took one of them to look up the meaning. It said, "A metrical pause or break in a verse where one phrase ends and another phrase begins." Read me that definition a thousand times and I won't bat an eye. I won't even know what you're talking about. Why do you keep describing a comma? A semicolon? Who cares. But box up the causal meaning in the letters c-a-e-s-u-r-a, and suddenly it's packaged juuuust right for me. Not too hot, not too cold. Just like Sister Eubank's keynoting, just the words you want to hear at the moment you want to hear them, spoken with the sounds and syllables and a succinctness that moves you. And it did. That space in between, after the end but before the start.

It was past fool's day, in the middle of April, and I was wiping that month all around, soaking in a thirty-one-day caesura. The calm before the craze. I awoke every morning, skipping out the door, speeding through the grid up toward my college campus. Scouring for a parking spot, a second parking lot, sometimes a third. Campus parking is utter and complete bullshit. Finding one God-forsaken rectangle of land to leave my car, mounting my longboard, and flying three inches off the ground toward the cemetery, toward classes, toward a hundred more beautiful and inspiring caesuras. I rested my head in the crook of my elbow often enough, feeling quite full on the meal of material and magic I was main-veining. I raised my hand, I asked a question, then five, then a hundred. I didn't get a hundred-and-six answers, just more questions—exactly what I wanted. Answers were final, questions were the light in all my darkness, and I was ravenous for as many breaks in meter, as many caesuras, as I could possibly get. I wasn't breaking phrases, but hovering between phases of life—six years of school ending and all that wild worldly living out on the horizon. Time to engage! Dear ole Sister Eubank would be so proud.

And in there, smearing all around April, spring pretending to come, I found another word, an opposite word, the one that comes after the time between phases and phrases. The one that arrives once the horizon line is here. More impact with less letters: *OUTSET.*

I scrawled this word out across the manilla page of my little brown book. Not one other pen stroke or dirt smudge accompanied the six letters, drawn in all caps. I used the first line of that mysterious leaf and the remaining vacant bars, row after row of pinstriped lines, were filled with my imagination. A floating nebula of memories, some already having occurred, some yet to transpire, trudged around the beige desert of the page. There was so much sand and sediment seeping into my shoes, grinding in between my raw and wiggling toes, begging me to pause, take my sweet little caesura, contemplate my choice, think myself out of the idle moment. Just think before you leap. Once you splat hard on the rock at the bottom of the cliff, there's no going back, no patching up those pieces of bone and sinew.

But while I slimed around April, the outset desired my soul, and I started getting high off the idea of letting him have it. I could be fifty years old looking back on a life of starts someday. A journey of wondrous caesuras-turned-outsets. Fifty years old and I had moved my body so much that it forgot how to bitch and moan. I moved my arms and mouth and found a lady that was also fifty years old, and with that lady, I made a bunch of little comic-book children that were always so happy to see me. They gathered around my ankles, cheering and bleating like goats anticipating mother's milk. I loved that.

They weren't clowns, they weren't slicing and cutting my shins, they were warm and circulating, little wide-eyed babies, looking up at me. They all had ocean-blue eyes, watching, awaiting my next move. They were wiggling back and forth, shaking and dancing around my feet. Blurry and beautiful, they opened their mouths and caught my salt-filled tears on their little fleshy-pink tongues. They said they tasted better than ice cream. Salt and ice and cream, just like in elementary; six years old when we made our own frosted desserts in Ziploc bags. We surrounded the sugary goodness with massive granules of salt, flash-freezing the substance into an impossibly delicious jelly. A little light in a big bag of salty darkness. Dear ole Sister Eubank would be so proud.

Brain fully drained, blood and putty dripping over the seam of my little brown book, I reawakened in a room that was familiar. Back in my office chair, pressing hard against my ass. The page was blank, row after row of pinstriped lines. At the very top, on the very first line, in very big letters, that were all very much capitalized, spelled:

OUTSET

I already wrote it, I already knew it, I had already heard it before—seeing it slip out of people's dry, cracked, and idle lips time and time again. An avalanche of lessons taught by every rich dad, every seminar on success, every wise old fool that knew the secret. Work hard, every day, all day long, sweat and bleed until you're pale and empty, devoid of energy, lost in ambition. Or at least sit for an hour a day in meditation, just visualizing your goals. That should be good enough! Get high as hell on it, just like Mary-Jane, bubbling up your head into a boiling red balloon, lost in time, magnifying glass so close to your face that everything is always getting blurry. And salt, pillars and pillars of it, flowing from your eyes, white rivers of brine drip-dropping onto the carpet. There were no little comic-book kids dancing around my toes, no little smiles beaming up at my splotchy red-rosy cheeks. Just one simple word, packaged juuuust right into six outstanding characters. And I finally gathered a shred of how Goldilocks really felt.

Chapter 4

My Pound of Flesh

Samuel Taylor Coleridge once opened his mouth on the evening of July 12th, 1827, and said, "Prose equals words in their best order; poetry equals the best words in the best order." His nephew wrote it down, probably having no idea that a hundred-and-ninety-four years later, some schmuck would start Chapter Four with it. And I did.

Since Coleridge's day, thousands and thousands of new English words have been born, writers laboring for years to describe the most specific experiences possible. Today, the sauce is so thick, antonym and synonym lists can stretch out as long as grocery store receipts. It's specific and lovely, when there's a hundred-and-one ways to describe a definitive feeling.

It was the thirtieth day of fool's month, the final twenty-four hours of my wiping, smearing caesura, and college was closing. Classes came to a screeching halt for the last time. Finals were tested, subjects wrapped, and books returned. Students hung their heads in exhaustion from hell-week and snorted coffee and energy drinks just to force their feet forward another step. Another step. Another step. Heads hung so low they could almost lick the sidewalk.

My head was upright, eyes twinkling, teeth showing. They would all be back in the fall, ready to test those finals out again, ready to mentally download as many words in their perfect order as possible. Not me. I was done, complete with my college training. Six years down the line and I had just learned a special little six-figure word. I slowly walked across the vibrant green grass of the Quad, a four-cornered field in the center of campus, where young academics would string up hammocks, throw frisbees, and make out in the shade of towering oak trees. It was beautiful. They would have thought it was beautiful, too, if they quit licking the pavement like a popsicle for just one moment. Their brains were blown out all over their four-inch thick Econ-1800 textbooks. I understood; I knew their ailment. Six years of school, and I might be smiling and walking proud like a gangster, swag in my step, but I still feel empathy for those poor, bogged down and writhing souls.

Across the Quad, spearing high into the lazuli-blue sky, stood the crown-jewel of our campus. They called it Old Main. Rising to a satisfying point, it confidently towered over the other structures surrounding it. At the top, fringing all four sides of the apex, were massive, pure-white A's. It stood for Aggie, but I liked to imagine it as a symbol for excellence. A mascot of belief in achievement. Maybe I had a pair of rose-colored sunglasses on as I made my way slowly across the Quad, gazing up into the cyan ether. Clear eyes, full hearts, can't lose. And college was closing, ending, gone away.

Cyan skies turned sapphire, and I found myself scribbling in my little brown book again. I became consciously aware of words that had accidentally leaked from my pen.

I find that as evening turns to night, my stress turns to paranoia.

Disgusting. There was an avalanche coming, rushing in and already here, and I didn't know how to prepare. I didn't even hear it roaring down the mountain toward me—I'm just deafened by caesuran ear plugs and rosy glasses that hoped for fool's month to go on forever. But here stress is slipping into paranoia, and those two emotions are making harmonious love right on the backside of my eyelids. It looked more like an aggressive kink than love to me, but they begged to differ. They laughed at me, scoffed at my inability. They made out and sucked on each other's ears and tongues and teeth. It was repulsive. I gagged and threw up in my mouth a little as I thought about the rest of time and how I needed to do something with it, needed to fill it up.

School was going away. Magical questions were leaving my life. Wonder was preparing to abandon me to the ethos of my own mind, my own ideas and theories. No longer was there a catalyst of magnificent change, this excuse to burst out of bed in the morning and move. This comfortable veneer to hide behind and leave me believing that as long I'm in school, I'm doing enough. Every year since I was a little comic-kid, I opened my eyes every morning, slipped on my little shoes, pulled my little shirt over my head, and yanked my little underwear and shorts up over my little hips. I was taken to school, force-fed an education, and never had a choice in the process. I didn't want a choice, I just did it anyway, and I loved it. But that was gone now, and my eyes weren't so clear. They were blurry again, and my body was starting to experience sodium withdrawal.

My little hand had always been held, ever so gently. Guided toward growing into something not-so-little anymore. Led to the one moment when I would have to actually choose. To the one wink when I would have to claim an outset of my own and stop existing in the middle of the caesura I thought was so safe and cozy. And that scared the shit out of me. And I was disgusted. I smile wide and bright and watch all the hanging heads and I'm excited, but I know they've got something I don't anymore. As long as I'm in school, I'm doing enough. But I'm not anymore, and as the sky turns from that swirling, magical shade of baby-boy-blue, to a dark and demon-filled gloom of black, I'm paranoid.

Images of me tripping off my cliff and slapping like a bloody pancake onto the jagged rocks below replayed over and over across the cinema of my mind. And that scared the shit out of me. I wanna fly, fly over the dead ones that came before, like I did every day on my way to school, three inches off the ground, longboard wheels listing against the pavement. I wanna fly, but it's dark and that scares the shit out of me.

All I ever wanted was sweating out of every pore, beading down my roasted flesh. I hated the way forward, couldn't see the way forward, wallowing in the pit of my bed. But that's before the leaving time came. I haven't even leaped yet, I'm just stewing in the jumping part. Much to the dismay of Sister Eubank, darkness flooded out every bit of light and that scared the shit out of me.

The yellow and wrapping sun of May came, much to my surprise. Fool's month had bled out and died and I was happier for it. Let it rot. I had eaten sleep for dinner the night before, and awoke with a gnawing gorge in my stomach. The grit and sand and mush that had polluted my mind wasn't nourishing me now, but all the same, another broken moment

44

to be thankful for. I scoffed. Skipping every other line, and again in all caps, I penned:

BE GRATEFUL
SAY IT
ALWAYS

Grandpa died of cancer before I was born. I knew him, but not in the way I knew my mom or Bill or Cassady. That's what made our relationship so spectacular. He once said that he wouldn't take back the cancer if he could, he wouldn't remove the malignancy that ransacked his final years of life. Now, when you hear someone say something as heinous as that, you pause. Who wouldn't pop into a time machine, zooming back to the day, the moment, the exact blip when cancer decided to prey an outset on you? But he wouldn't do it, and I always believed him. So, laying in bed on the first sunflower morning of May, with a shaky hand and Grandpa's dirt clods still covering me head-to-toe, I was grateful for my trials. And I'd say it, and I'd scoff, but I'd still write it and try to believe it, all the same.

I didn't have cancer and I wasn't going to die. After all, I hadn't even tried yet. What I did have was the sexual product of paranoia and stress—a sick, twisted baby growing in my belly. Trying to scrape its way out, trying to convince me I really would die trying. Screaming at me full-bore, tilted on the idea that when left to the big dogs, I wouldn't be able to run with 'em. Never in my twenty-four years as an earthling had I been forced to own my laze and degeneracy. Never forced to understand my own individuality, and defend it. So I was grateful—in an attempt to stare back into the black void, the vast and ever-stretching chasms of time, find a thread of light and be thankful that I had the courage to search in the first place. Dear ole Sister Eubank would be so proud. I scoffed.

It's a strange thing—to be truly grateful for the darkness. To thank God for struggling, to appreciate the chance to count out the salt in your tears. It's not enjoyable, it never will be. But Grandpa understood that without cancer, he wouldn't have loved as hard as he did, wouldn't have enjoyed smearing mud on his cleanly-pressed, pearly-white clothes. He knew that in order to live a life of poetry and prose, to see everything come together in the most sensationally perfect way, you couldn't turn your head away from the shit. The shit made those threads of beaming light shine that much brighter. Just like Bill, he didn't marinate in fear and death's womb. It wasn't his hot tub to soak in. But when his toes dipped under the surface, as everyone's inevitably do, he didn't scream or run away. He didn't live with regret, cursing God for insurmountable odds—he simply sat down, pulled out a pen, and wrote *Be Grateful. Say it. Always.*

In that final semester of college, there were three courses that broke me—creating an environment that was juuuust ordered enough for the goopy oatmeal in my head to fall into some sort of meaningful place. Cassady taught me all about Keebler elves and their folksy little belts and shoes. She showed me how to see the threads in their clothes, the spice in their cookies. She revealed all about the world's folksy forests, even peeling back the stunningly bottomless, lore-ridden undergrowth. Most importantly, Cassady taught me how to truly understand all of it, together, all at once in a Van Gogh rainbow wave of color and consideration.

Bill kindled a lukewarm fire, adding pines and timbers, one after another, raising the heat within my husk so masochistically high that I had no choice but to acknowledge a future filled with getting over myself, sliding my little silver pen out of its little stretchy loop, and gorging black ink all over my little pinstriped lines. If you're reading this, don't. Not for my sake, but for yours—you might get a little blood and blown out brains on your shirt. And I can promise you, club soda and all the salt-filled tears in the world ain't gonna pull that stain.

But there was another grand teacher I had, who put perfect words in the most perfect order I'd ever seen. Her name was Lucy, and she taught me poetry. She didn't even teach it—she breathed it, ate it for breakfast, lunch, and dinner, slept with it intimately, thought about it, bled about it, cried about it—lived for it. Lucy made no bones about what she wrote; she wasn't afraid to dive headfirst into those fear-and-death-filled black pools of despair and even ruminate for a while in them. Let some of the substance seep into bones of her own. Bill and Lucy were best friends, and they'd marinate together sometimes and they'd laugh and cackle and rub dirt on each other and it was wild and lively. Then she'd crawl out, rolling down hills of daisies and daffodils, tarred-and-feathered in a wondrous coat of earthen beauty, lining pages and pages of her own little leather-bound book with the most perfectly ordered characters a word-wizard could cast.

Lucy's brother killed himself. It was twenty-thirteen, and Benjamin was twenty-four years old and he drank himself to death. I didn't know Benjamin. I was just sprouting my little eighteen-year-old wings in that year, having just graduated from high school. But Benjamin was not, he was busy drinking himself to death.

There's this game that the Universe plays on wizards like Lucy. I don't know what little entity up in the midnight stratosphere is pulling levers to play out their wildest abstractions, but they are pulling those levers all the same, sending souls off planet earth and up and up and up through the clouds and gathering rain. If you asked Lucy, she might tell you that there is no ghostly aura pulling those levers, or that there might not be any levers at all. But the sickly game is still played, and in twenty-thirteen, Benjamin pulled his own lever, and he violently joined the rest of the lever-pullers up in the midnight stratosphere. The sickly game was to see just how wizard-like Lucy could be. Just how perfectly she could line those perfect words in the perfect order after something so traumatic and dark was jammed into her life. And she played the game hard. Lever-pullers seem to enjoy the spells and magical lightning that spark from wizard pens after the most crushing pain imaginable has been realized. So they pull levers outside time up there, watching all of us down here turn into pillars of salt, white-knuckling pens, trying to make sense of it all. It's a broken game you gotta play, all the same.

I was going to talk with Lucy, climbing the creaking staircase of the old English building on campus. This relic of a structure sat on the southern side of the Quad, kiddy-corner to the Old Main tower. The stairs creaked and cracked and creaked some more. I wondered if I'd actually make it to Lucy's office or if the age-old boards would give way under my weight, pulling a lever of my own. But my lever was safe for the time being, as I reached the attic space where they housed all the English teachers, writers, readers, and sensation-makers. They were hidden, or hiding, from the rest of the crowded campus.

If I had a choice, I would have staked my office out there, too. It was quiet, sometimes even silent, other than the creaking and cracking of the carpeted steps. It had more character—lower ceilings, warmer lights, skinnier hallways. A horde of Keebler bastards had found this land and claimed it for their own. Up there, where the air was a slight bit singed from peeling paint and the musk of day-old coffee, were my people. My little Keebler elven bastards with their pens and agony.

Lucy and Bill shared an office. It was scarcely big enough for the two of them, but they made it work like a well-oiled machine. Books were stacked to the low-hanging ceiling, rogue papers piled on any horizontal surface that was sturdy enough to bear the weight of three-hundred-and-forty-seven rough drafts of the same poem or piece of prose. Every shred of parchment could have the most brilliant spell-casted, wizard-written experience on it—or it might have a scribbled hit-list of all the darlings one of these authors planned to kill. Edits on edits, revision upon revision—playing with levers of their own up in their little heavenly paint-peeled, coffee-fueled stratosphere. And it really was.

My knuckles thumped the thick oaken door to the Lucy-Bill-Experience-Room, and I was greeted by a balmy, "Come in!" Lucy was sitting in her office chair, legs crossed, waiting for the extraction ceremonies to begin. You remember the folklore project I went on about in Chapter One? Well, here I was to retrieve my pound of flesh. The last perfect project to cap off my last perfect semester.

In all the space Lucy and Bill didn't have in their creaking tree-top escape, they somehow managed to fit a full-length couch against the back wall. That's where I planted down, and it was comfy and cozy and old as the days are long and it reminded me of the frilly carpet lining the floor of my room back home—and it probably had a whole lotta Keebler toots pounded into it, too. I pulled out my voice recorder, a shitty little app on my phone that cost me nothing but eighteen seconds of download time. I had my questions, my wits, and my instincts at the ready, prepared to absorb every sound and syllable. Lucy was going to read me some poems—some perfect words cherry-picked in the perfect order. And it was a distorted, exorcized mess.

The most disastrously exquisite chunk of intimate chaos I'd sat through. I didn't feel like sitting, while I listened to the wrenching recount of Benjamin's turbulent death, painted with tar and flowers and blood and alcohol-infused bile. I wanted to scream along with Lucy, I wanted to share in her turmoil. She didn't monochromatically tell me about his passing—she dragged me kicking and screaming along with her. Slipping and sliding and reeling all the way. I remember how I felt, rotten and twisted. But that, too, was emotion worth noting. That was the pool of gritty-black-goop that she wanted me to sit in for a caesura's quick tick. I think I stayed a little longer than I anticipated and let some of it seep into bones of my own. And I loved it and loathed it for all the reasons I could, and my heart was sore.

"You can see the form of the poem is really scattered. When Ben died, it just felt like my life was disintegrating, and so the form was just natural to follow the story. Like how there's a lot of jaggedness in the lines and strange spacing," Lucy said, running her finger down the page of her poem. I nodded and followed with wide eyes.

"At the end here, when I say the month and that I'm not going insane—that's just an affirmation to myself that I'm here, now, and this is real and happening. To bring me back into reality," she went on, talking about all the worst pain with a low, sonorous tone.

Then Bill opened the door to the little attic hideaway and ran into air so thick it caused him to pause. He instantly knew the topic, knew the exact poem that Lucy was so graciously sharing with me. He lit up a little bit, probably hoping that hearing such vociferous language would help me learn how to get over myself. I mean, look at Lucy—she doesn't give a shit how she feels, she wrote the poem anyway. And she didn't just scribble it, leaving it hidden away—she's sharing it now.

We all stood there, three musketeers all looking for the perfect words to put in the perfect order. These were the big dogs, and I was running with them. The air weighed three tons, pounding us like nails into the creaky floorboards of the old English attic. And I was ferociously cozy and uncomfortable all in the same breath. The big dogs, the perfect prose-and-poem-terms. Bill suddenly showed his teeth through a big grin, masking his ultimate sorrow.

He gazed over toward Lucy and proudly exclaimed, "You know that he's going to be a prose writer, not a poem writer, right?" He chuckled as the perfect words spilled from his mouth in the perfect order, lips sparkling with elven pixie dust.

Lucy let out a cackle. She turned and matched Bill's sight-line, chiming back, "Nope! He's gonna be a poem-writer—he's practically overflowing with them!"

They both turned and stared at me now, expecting a verdict on the combating statements. As if I knew the answer, as if I had the answer. All I had were a million questions, a soupy brain filled with the paranoia and anticipation of a true-spring May. It was May outside the windows, outside the tree-top nook we were hiding away in. It was May and it was that time—not the end times, but the new ones. The time when the sun is yellow and lends you its warmth and you start sweating in the state of summer on the horizon. I was leaving, going away, ending the space between the phases, outsetting into a new one, and that scared the shit out of me. But that time was here, all the same. I wanted to live for it like they did. Breathe it and bleed it and sour my throat and heart and eyes on the moment, like they did. Maybe I juuuust needed permission.

Fuck you, Goldilocks.

PART TWO

Too Hot

Chapter 5

Intake Shit, Output Gold

I am just an adult
Out here
Trying not to lose
My Ability
To sit
Criss-Cross
Apple-Sauce

I wasn't insane—it was May and chummy and I was in Las Vegas, Nevada. I bounced out of bed earlier that morning with several tangles working their way though my guts. Today was outset day, when I would finally mate movement with desire. Apparently the baby they bred was taking shape in the twelve knots now tearing away at the walls of my stomach. I told myself I was just excited. I don't think I believed it. I'm just excited.

Nonetheless, I strapped my brand new kayak to the top of my golden rocket ship, loaded the last bags of food and ice into my astonishingly ancient cooler, and hoped against hope that I had not forgotten anything. But I probably had, and I wouldn't remember until I was far away.

At this point in the tale, I feel I should bring a new character into the picture—one that would remain with me every waking second for the duration of this trek. She turned out to be wildly important, talking back all the time, rebounding my ideas in perfect stares of her own, always staring, head tilting, big brown eyes like the last leaks of fall, when the world is soiled and deep. I haven't ever had a friend as loyal as her, and there are parts of me that doubt I ever will. She smiles and laughs and peels so deeply into my soul that I get lost just trying to figure out what she's pondering. There was never one word she didn't listen to, never one audible sound or slip that missed her perky ears. She's my very best friend, just like Lucy and Bill were best friends. Hell, we even shared an office, just like the Lucy-Bill-Experience-Room. But our living quarters were smaller, and we got to cuddle in the cold of night.

Her name is Mia. And when I whistled for her to get in the golden rocket ship set for the martian red-rock land of Las Vegas, she leapt all four legs into the front passenger seat, wagging her little docked-nub of a tail at three-hundred-and-forty-seven miles per hour, not one smidge of hesitation in her step. Boy, was she excited. She didn't tell herself, she didn't think about it, feel about it—she was just excited. I took note. I'm just excited.

I wasn't insane—it was May and brilliant and I was in Las Vegas, Nevada. It was dark when I rounded the top of the hill approaching Vegas, headlights stretching out across the rusty sand and sizzling asphalt of southern Nevada. It was after hours, and still so hot you could feel your yolk hardening beneath the shell. A midnight skillet of concrete, steel, neon lights, booze, and human flesh. Lots of human flesh—pounds and pounds of it rolling around the only city on Mars.

I'd been to this corner of Mars half-a-dozen times before. I always loved the first moment my eyes met the radiating light and musk that emanated from the city. One giant Mars bar ready to be devoured, digested, and regurgitated. Always with the regurgitating. I was just excited.

On any given night in Las Vegas you could find someone somewhere doing their fair share of regurgitating—after all, the city was built on that principle, and everyone needs to play their part. Running show after show for decades—every night the same little characters dancing across the same little stages. The same hotels bolted like fake, corporeal tits onto a boiling jungle of glitz and glamor. The same nascent strippers and corner workers, card flippers, hustle-seekers, business-end executives blowing their bulked-up cash, poker-playing, craps-shooting, blackjack-dick-jerking baboons reeling with their fifty-two-card decks upside down and ass-end-up. It was always the same oppressive musk of a thousand rotten taints, so sweaty and butt-buttered-up you could see the stenchy smell through your own red-veined, glazed-over eyes. Always the same red-veined, glazed-over, Mary-Jane-marveled eyes. And I was just excited.

Las Vegas is pretty gross, all things considered. When you really saturate in it, the vice wears off on you, blackens your bones a little. That's why everyone from every corner of the world knows the rhymes of Sin City—everyone's gotta smear some dirt-clods of their own on their pearly-white shirts. Here, where the clod-smearing was the business, the clod-smearing was a way of life rather than a few paint strokes across the canvas. Shirts weren't so white with dark streaks, as they were just dark shirts.

The drive to Vegas from the perfectly planned-out grid of Logan was about seven hours, and I don't remember a wink of it. I wasn't sleeping or driving drunk. I wasn't high on anything but anticipation. But boy, was I high on it—so much that I don't remember a wink of the drive south. Mia slept. I drove.

My first stop in the wild-west was a dingy shop on the outskirts of town, where the suburbs were named something other than Las Vegas. The vice of Vegas has concentrations all throughout the great state of Nevada. Starting at the Strip, pumping the promise of winning it big throughout a confused grid of their own. Out here on the fringes of sin, I found myself a little shop, peddling the most over-priced Mary-Jane I'd ever seen. That's right—my first stop wasn't a piss-break, wasn't to grab a three-dollar combo meal at McDonald's (although I would do plenty of that over the next few months), wasn't to gather groceries or tools for camping on Mars—it was to buy some damn weed. Overpriced or not, the Mary-Jane models they placed in the window displays were magnificent. It was all curves, huge asses, oversized boobs, wearing the skimpiest bikinis in the truest of Vegas fashion. Price tags didn't matter—I was here to secure a cache of goodies to last me the next month or so on the road. I was just excited and I was here now, ready to gather up my mind-reliever.

It was lightless and gloomy outside, and other than my golden rocket ship idling on the lot, there was only one other vehicle nearby, also idling. Their lights were off, windows tinted so black there was no telling who or what sat behind. A cloud of smoke rose from their driver-side window, filling the air with the pungent smell of skunk farts and burning plant fibers. All was set right and appropriate for this place. I aggressively turned the key in my ignition, killing the motor.

"I'll be right back." Mia looked over and nodded. I would always be right back.

There were several doors and gates I had to checkpoint through to get to the counter where I could admire and purchase my sex-filled Mary-Jane models. The man behind the counter played a smoked-out hood version of The Dude. His hat was angled forty-five degrees to the left and none of the words that tumbled from his mouth were coherent. It became painfully apparent that his first stop in the day was also this place, to secure his own bag of goodies. Only, he didn't have a seven hour drive to bide his time—he could start festivities thirty minutes after his head popped off his pillow in the morning. Part of me admired his dedication in testing his own product.

Another very salient part of me asked what he had just said over and over, and he never improved his tone or clarified his voice. Garbles, slurs—don't be so picky, it's all the good stuff. There was a lot of pointing at different Mary-Jane bunches, slanted audio, and three-quarters-closed eye exchanges. I couldn't even see the red veins in his eyes, so glazed over it was a miracle we were having discourse at all. I asked him what everyone asks when there are too many choices and all of them seem just fine. He pointed out his favorite flower bunch. I nodded. And just like that, I was right back with Mia in the front seat. The other car on the lot was still idling, still exhaling smoke from its cracked windows, skunking and swooning in the middle of the night in some suburb in Vegas. It was right, and I was just excited.

When I set out on my journey, I planned to use stealth as my biggest ally. Every night, the strategy was to disguise my rocket ship so it looked like it belonged there, allowing me to drift into a hopeful sleep in the backseat. I didn't have a tent, trailer, campsite, or hotel room—those things were all too nice and too expensive for me to worry about. Plus, rocket fuel is pricey enough, and my bank numbers would run down sooner or later. So I outfitted my glorious spacecraft with all the necessary measures to eat, sleep, lounge, and laze inside its cabin. The make was Volkswagen, model Jetta. I had a little mobile tent-on-wheels of my own, that usually looked like it belonged there. Wherever *there* happened to be.

I had my goodies and was now racing toward the red rocks of Mars at an alarming rate. Up there in the rising desert above Las Vegas, I was sure to find some spot of land where it would be safe to button up for the night. I must have driven up and down Blue Diamond Road, past Calico Basin, three or four times. Nothing felt right. The twelve knots in my stomach had multiplied into twenty-four, then forty-eight. My guts were roiling and toiling and I was drowning in my feelings amid an arid wasteland of grit and uncertainty; time now to live out here in the world, the wild-loving world where the roads run long and winding and aren't cornered at ninety degrees. My eyes weren't clear, my heart was empty, and I was losing fast. But I told myself that I was just excited. I don't think I believed it.

I suddenly pulled over, mounting my car on a gravel berm above the left shoulder of the road. This spot looked the exact same as any other along this stretch of yellow pinstriped asphalt. It would have to do. I scanned the horizon up. I scanned the horizon down. A Ford F-150 came rumbling by, listing up into the black silhouettes of the red rocks. Every vehicle that cruised past, headlights on, brights beaming, made my heart beat a little harder. I was anxious with the idea that each one of these individual travelers was actually a police officer, forest ranger, or wild-west sheriff, destined to pull over behind me, flip on their spinning red-white-and-blues, thump their fat knuckles on my window, and tell me to get the fuck outta' here.

Even worse, I painted pictures in my radiating skull of vice-ridden maggot-fiends, clangoring up through the gravel behind me, crawling out of their meth trailers, shattering my golden fortress windows, dragging me into the red-rock, stain-filled dirt on Mars and staining it some more. Beating me within an inch of life, cackling all the while. Their reasoning was nonexistent. They were just bloodthirsty and bored and wanted to enact an unconscious desire to hoist their pound of flesh high over their ape-like heads. They'd draw out pentagrams and put my broken bones in the middle and summon something evil and no one would ever know. My blood would spill and splatter all over the sand, and you wouldn't be able to tell my eyes apart from the round stones beneath my tires—rosy and warm rivers across the shoal, matching the crimson surface of this alien world. I would be dead. Mia would be dead.

I prayed real hard that my lever wouldn't be pulled tonight. I wanted to throw my guts up like Benjamin had, maybe that would disembody such a sinister thought. I didn't throw my guts up. I pulled out my little brown book, and I started scribbling.

What the fuck am I doing out here?

Why have I condemned myself to this empty hell, where life's greatest questions play over and over as if to dance like clowns before my eyes, screaming and shouting until I finally grab them by the ears, hold their faces, and scream back. But my screams are never ones that make sense or are even heard—they are silent, tears streaming down rosy cheeks, fists clenched so tight that my fingernails dig deep into the skin of my palms.

With this much alone-time, you would think I'm bound to come up with some profound wisdom, divinely gifted to me while soaking my toes in the sands of the red-rock barrens. You might see all the excitement that comes with graduating college, dreams finally coming to fruition as I left my hometown, speeding off into the sunset—just me and Mia. Years of hard work and dedication to the greater goal of being educated, wrapped up all nice and tight with a cute little bow on top. You might think that finishing the most challenging part of my life, up to now, would fill me with copious amounts of joy and exhilaration, throwing away old school hand-outs, exams, and notebooks, maybe even burning a few in a sacrificial ceremony of my own. You might think all these things, but you would be wrong.

I play moments through my head every day, reliving them in every way except physically. I see my friends, gathered around the pool table playing cards and laughing so hard one of them spills their beer and stains the emerald felt. I see the campus, with its lush sprouting trees peeking around every corner of every building in the spring, groups of students all adorned with backpacks, books, coffee cups, and earbuds, hustling to their next lab or lecture. I see all the moments where, for a split second, a lightbulb was prompted to shine brightly, as the lens through which I saw the world began to shift and change, growing one shade clearer with every class, every test, every failure, and every success.

All of these packaged moments are now wiped away, sent into a memory box of blurry remember-whens. How do you reconcile the immeasurable impact something or someone has had on your life? After its conclusion, how do you move forward, with only the airy image of those times when things were different, for better or worse? Where do you find the resilience to stand and push on?

I graduated and darted straight south for Las Vegas. It might seem like a great spot for a grand graduation party—all the alcohol, women, and cheers you could hope for. Only, those aren't the things I'm hoping for. And I'm supposed to be excited, I'm just excited. But I can't believe it.

I climbed into the back seat of my tent-on-wheels, hugged my knees so deep into my chest they almost popped out the back as lever-pulled angel wings, and lost count of the salt-filled tsunami flowing from my face.

I'm out here, I'm in my car. I made the choice and leapt, and I'm plummeting now and the bottom of the cliff looks closer than it ever did before. What are you going to do after you graduate? I'm going to be a dour hobo, asking questions all my life while I sit and spin both my thumbs around one another and convince myself that I'm excited about it.

"What the fuck am I doing out here?!" I wailed and broke my voice, cracking like thin bone shards and sheared wood chips up from my throat. I screamed it so loud into the deafening silence that Mia cupped her ears closed, timidly burying her snout into a pile of fuzzy blankets. She might have thought I was belting my voice at her, verbally thrashing her inaction, her adorable, comforting little spirit. She couldn't have been more wrong. She was the only thing in that dead and dry land that gave me any hope to begin with. She was the only living being with ears that could hear my wallow, listening intently to my stretched-out and pitiful soul being drawn into madness. Her eyes seeing my pain, her ears hearing my agony—that made it real, that was someone standing in the forest when the trees came crashing down.

She heard it and hated it, and I hated myself for it, too. But I still howled, and the tears that ran were hot and filled with emptiness and self-doubt.

She dug deeper into the comforting cloth, breathing the scents of home deep into her super-smeller nose. She was just as uncomfortable as I was, writhing and retching at the sight of her master drowning in wave after salty wave of snot bubbles and thick, sticky saliva. I was gonna fill this God-forsaken rocket ship to the roof, expelling an ocean of my own. And I wished I could just regurgitate the tearwater from my mouth all at once and be done with it. Regurgitate it up just like Benjamin had. Maybe once the car was full, I could suffocate myself in the sea foam, percolating the rancid liquid through my lungs, my chest, stomach and bowels until the windows would burst and my long-forgotten corpse would be thrust out onto the gravel, bloated and lifeless for the police to find in the morning. Maybe the meth-maggots would find me first, desecrating my lever-pulled carcass, leaving me raw and raped in the ditch. Leaving my sweet little girl to watch the process. Mia pulled her weeping head out from the blankets, panting hard in the humid, cabin-fever air of the car. Another F-150 rumbled up the road, passing just like the rest of them, and I reeled.

Living creatures do wild things when they're uncomfortable. They flourish, performing great and fantastical feats, saving lives, inventing new and unique ways to accomplish this or that. Or they freeze, burrowing deep into the sand to hide away from the endless eyes of the world. Baring teeth, growling, gnashing out at anything that steps too near. Ravenous venom flowing through their boiling veins as demon horns sprout from their skulls. And mine were sprouting, and I wasn't excited. I was free-falling and lamenting my choice right out of the gate. Dour hobos live off pity and I was getting high on that supply and loving the moments of hating too much. I was nine hours into freedom and already losing it. My carnal instinct yearned for the warmth of my bed back home. When everything was something of the future, goals to look forward to, stuff to just talk about. I wanted to go back to just talking about it, just thinking about it, sitting in my office chair, pressing hard against my ass, huge toothy grin on my face, floating back and forth, rocked to sleep like a baby in my sweet little caesura with my big and clear ocean-blue eyes.

Everything I've ever read says to make yourself uncomfortable. Leap into the pressure cooker willingly, with all the seasonings and sauces dripping from your limbs. Step so far out of your cozy element that the knots in your stomach threaten to tear themselves out. Only then will you see for yourself what lies on the other side of your sanity. I was insane—it might have been May but I didn't fucking care. I was somewhere on Mars swimming in the standing water of my own piss and tears.

The open pages of my little brown book looked just like the surface of the moon, wrinkly, rising craters dotting the page, running together, soaking into the fabric of my emotional expense. Black ink bled down into the spine, smearing letters together in a mix of confusion and torment. The little pinstriped lines broke their mold, no longer barring one prisoner from the next. Rows meshed together, swirling and soaking, swirling and soaking. My little brown book was crying too. Mia was crying too. We were all miserable, missing home, aimlessly wandering in a stupor that I was acutely aware of and loved to hate. But at least the three of us had each other and I screamed and shrieked and gasped at the stained air inside the car.

I slammed the little brown book shut, mashing my man-made moon craters together, creating my own little inkblot test. Rorschach was somewhere up in the midnight stratosphere cackling like a hyena at my results, pulling them apart and exclaiming to all my lever-pulled ancestors just how broken and ridiculous I really was. They would all be sitting cross-legged in an arena of ghosts and ghouls, listening to the madman himself pacing the stage, drawing out his attention-pointer, waving it left and right, stabbing this projective mishap, drawing grimy chalk-lines to that one. The audience would grumble under their breath, shaking their heads slowly as they so affably gave me the benefit of the doubt. Not Rorschach, though. He'd have my hide, linking together all the wishfully-bonded shapes that led me to this exact outset of wearisome hesitation. Nine hours in and I'm hesitating and I'm not excited. My eyes were soaked and pitiful, so full of shit they were shading over from their ocean-blue to brown.

My rocket ship's windows were foggy, steamed up from hours of hyperventilation and corpulent mourning. Could have been hours, maybe just minutes—I was wrung out. I composed a little smiley face in the condensation against the glass and quickly realized I had just the medicinal prescription for moments like this.

I drew out my vacuum-sealed bag of goodies and attempted to break the child-lock seal. It took more attempts than I'd like to admit, my shaky, booger-covered fingers fumbling with the Ziploc in the dark. I finally ripped open the cache and was greeted by an influx of Mary-Jane-musk so potent my eyes rolled back and caught a stark glimpse at the bathos bathing my brain. I drew out a little emerald flower, all bunched up and ready to whisk me away to mind-numbing familiarity. Familiarity—just what I needed when I was crawling in my own skin. A used-to feeling, please. Coming right up. The little buds cracked and snapped in my fingers, generating a crystalized glue. I compressed my thumb and forefinger and yanked them apart again, making a quaint, sappy little snapping noise.

Out came the five-dollar, twenty-first-century version of the age-old mortar and pestle. I like the name mortar and pestle—but in today's world, we call them grinders. I filled my plastic grinder, mulching my flowers until they were two turns from becoming powder. Out came a little pipe now, not extravagant or extra in its appearance—most weed-head-motherfuckers would have frowned in dismay. It wasn't colorful enough, wasn't curvy or sexy like the Mary-Jane-babe window displays back at the shop. It was something you'd probably find in the pocket of the meth-maggot-fiend from my dreams. Straight, narrow, and boring with a little round bowl at the end. A fleeting glass shard that I wouldn't be upset at parting with if circumstances required. Driving around the most weed-legal state in the union with the mentality of a true Utahan, ready to nix my paraphernalia at any moment. California was probably the most legal state, but we aren't to that part in the story yet.

I packed a tight little puck of green into the glass bowl, sparked the lighter that I had somehow managed not to forget, and inhaled a dense cloud of carcinogens and tetrahydrocannabinol. No coughs, no burps, no bleeding throats. A familiar feeling washed all the soot and soil off the inside of my head and hugged me real tight. I was clean and pure again, free from the agonizing uncertainty that was drowning me out. No tears, no snot bubbles, no ailing hearts.

Just warm, fuzzy blankets rocking my arms, legs, chest, and skull back into a beautiful, Keebler-cozy caesura. Another F-150 rumbled up the road, and I didn't give a damn if it passed or not.

Chapter 6

The Motherland

I won't torture you with all the excruciating details of all the times I pulled that little crackpipe out, crammed as much weed in it as I could, and snapped it all in one go. You'd probably get some twisted kind of high of your own off such decadence. What I will say is that there were a lot of these caesuras in between the living lines and leaves of my little brown book. These caesuras dried my eyes out and ballooned my cranium so often, I'm amazed that I had the fortitude to move an inch at all. It was a comical irony that I left home with the desire to start living, only to consistently blow hot smoke through my wind-caved lungs. I kneeled so close to the sand of Mars while begging to see the bigger picture, ingesting agents that only magnify consciousness further. Burying my head so deep in blistering grit, I thought it might pop out the other side of the world with a new-and-improved view. Just chill bro, feel the vibes. Don't be so picky, it's all the good stuff.

I can tell you all about Mary-Jane and all the ways you can sex her. She's a versatile one who'll take it in any position, anytime, anywhere. She's really quite the whore. And she's only getting more and more voluptuous as the years and decades pass. In the nineteen-seventies, she was petite and cute, standing there on the corner with her skimpy little red dress and leather side-purse. She was kind, she meant her best, and said her best—she was convincingly tempting and always worth a try. She would take you for a night on the town, wine-and-dine you, maybe even pitch a few bucks for the meal. She'd tell you a story while you were still awake, making you laugh and love and with a half-baked heart. She was welcome, she was reasonable—and then she was gone. Sometime in the middle of the night, while you drifted into a feathery sleep, she slipped out the back door, leaving you soberingly aware of the morning rays peeking through crusty motel curtains. You knew this was what you paid for, what you signed up for when you breathed her essence in. You knew that, and you were okay with fighting the morning with oversized sunglasses and ink-black coffee.

In twenty-nineteen, Mary-Jane stands on every corner from here to Timbuktu—big, protuberating, bolted-on tits, an ass that would suffocate you in seconds if it sat on you. She's lost her cute little side-purse and replaced it with kangaroo-boobs, storing four condoms, a bottle of water-based lube, her bejeweled iPhone, three-hundred-and-forty-seven dollars in ones and fives, and a bulky can of pepper-spray. She won't even think of going out to dinner with you, there ain't no time to wine-and-dine—her clientele list for that night is way too long. If you asked her to pitch a few of those ones on a meal, she would laugh you all the way to the bank and you'd still somehow end up giving her money anyways. She doesn't tell you stories, she doesn't know any. She probably doesn't know anything beyond what makes a man's phallus flood with blood. If she makes you laugh, you won't remember why—stuck so deep in sex-appeal, you're over-baked like a burnt loaf of bread.

She's invasive, she's crude, and she never leaves. When the morning light comes clipping through those crusted motel curtains, she rolls her fat-ass over and makes a gimme-motion with her tattooed fingers, expecting you to cover the cost of the three clients she blew off in order to blow you. You're not sober, not in the slightest—in fact you're so hung-over from a night with Mary-Jane, you start wondering if her essence has fused with your DNA. You didn't know this was what you signed up for, because you don't even remember signing up in the first place. And once you roll out of that cheap, squeaky motel bed, you see your own prone imprint stamped down into the box springs. You never moved a muscle.

Today's weed doesn't mess around. You're going to get so blow-your-brains-out blasted-to-the-great-beyond high that whatever little mental mogul was pit-stopping you before will fade so far from view, you won't recall why you were sobbing in the first place. You'll just look down at your pruney fingers and snot-glazed sleeves and wonder what in the hell happened to you, who gooed all over your favorite jacket? And I did.

I awoke the next morning, looked down and wondered who gooed all over my favorite jacket. Strands of dried-out, spider-webbed bogeys wrapped around my jacket sleeves like little yellow friendship bracelets. Gross. Not friends I wanted. I pulled off the soiled hoodie and shoved it into my dirty clothes duffle bag—the first contaminated casualty of the journey. This prompted the realization that all my laundry over the next several months would have to be done in laundromats, and I had forgotten the soap. I knew there was something.

Las Vegas. The first stop, after a seven-hour-speedway through all the southern Utah national parks. I hadn't thought of stopping at any of those, there weren't any Mary-Jane sex shops hidden in those sandstone hills, and I needed my fix. My medicinal prescription. My little crackpiped-lip-stick, ready to twist out delphic clown colors, painting my face outside the lines. After all, my jester-red smile isn't going to paint itself over this frowning soul.

I was different from the crusty, leather-backed skin-sliders that saunter around this kingdom of kill. A land of false idols—the awe-inspiring Luxor pyramid, plaster-pasted, fabricated castles at the Excalibur, crammed together, empty alleys at New York, New York, a giant golden-glinted penis shooting into the sky at the Trump hotel, fractionized Eiffel towers in a fake little Paris, sprawling Bellagio fountains blasting white sewage-water, streamed high into the pungent air, resting like death and failure up and down and left and right of the Strip. This was the land of the damned and you might not like this next part.

This shit-hole is filled with so many backwards-ass bimbos, it makes you lose a little faith in the whole deal we cut with our humanity. It's one giant decaying ashtray, sitting on a glass coffee table, neon lights blooming in a million unique ways, with a NO SMOKING sign sitting softly adjacent. No one heeds that sign. I don't even think they see it. They willfully choose not to see it, and when they finally acknowledge that ignorance, they paint themselves as VEGAS STRONG—black-sheep rebels going against the pearly-white grain. They all think they're so cool, vibing, nodding, talking to themselves so much they can't even hear their own voice anymore.

There's nowhere on Earth where people talk to themselves more than Las-motherfucking-Vegas. It's one giant river of blind consciousness, and none of these Walmart-spawned monkeys have an inner monologue, critiquing their every move. It's a dogged consciousness, animal-like, carnal to its very core. The demon-gods-among-men that birthed this sweltering hell treat the human spirit, the human condition, as if everyone were deficient. And I don't mean stupid. I mean actually mentally handicapped. It's a normal person that sees their natural, venereal tendency, weighs it against their values and morals, and makes decisions based in reality. Thanks, Freud. Thanks, Ego, for being realistic.

Here in this—quite literally—God-forsaken place, the Id has sadistically subdued the Superego, barring him down, wrapping loop after loop of a twine noose around his angelic neck. The Id has dragged the Super down Las Vegas Boulevard, his legs writhing, veins bulging at every joint juncture, a wondrous, celestial crown of thorns pressed so hard into his skull, it's not just blood running down his bashed-in face. It's brain matter, wormy cerebrum beans dripping out onto the one-hundred-and-seventy-five degree tarmac, cooking into dried, steamed-out shells. A hundred, a thousand maggots come running; they smell the sizzle of sanctified-gone-sour. The Ego died trying in this land of the damned.

We all like to fantasize about the inevitable zombie apocalypse. Spoiler alert: we're already living in one. In Vegas, the undead disease just bites a little harder. Everyone in this place has their lever half-pulled already, and they're doing everything in their power to pull it the rest of the way. Sitting their zombie-tush on shit-stained cushions, pounding thousands of zombie-farts and belches through their splitting-spandexed cheeks. Eyes so glazed over, gazing deep into the spinning wheels of slot machines, pulling real levers down here. Over and over and over again, telling themselves they are due the win and losing all the time. They smell machines ripe for the pullin', living out the gambler's fallacy in real-time. They stumble drunkenly stoned, eyes blown out, rose-colored, crying tears of blood and cum and not knowing why. They smell rotten brains, their favorite delicacy, rearing their heads and snarling with scowls and screams that chill a living bone. It's all levers—their guardian angels pulling theirs like Benjamin, or them pulling the machine arms down here. Pulling, pulling, losing, and dying.

They're slow to move and slower to think—they are zombies after all. And when they shamble to their undead feet or slide into their fat-tram-scooter-movers, they pull out their zombie-pixeled picture-producers, pouring through more neon-fueled, spin-salivating, vibrant mind-baking, coin-tingling, dollar-sniffing, candy-crushing, royale-clashing, pokemon-going garbage. And they really do.

Fueled by mainline IV's of Fat Tuesdays, watered-down Whiskey Sours, and over-priced AMFs (Adios, Motherfuckers), they got the zombie-jaunt down pat. You see their late-stage strip-zombie-stroll at two in the morning, seven days-a-week, three-hundred-sixty-five-days a year. Sometimes you hope for the undead to be wearing flip-flops—it accentuates the stumble a little more. *Clip-shuffle-shuffle-slide-slap. Clip-shuffle-shuffle-slide-slap.* There are little variations, the brilliance of dying unpredictability so splayed out both in view and in sound, it's a never-ending zombie flick playing out right before your eyes. They commit to their parts, and they wear their zombie costumes, zombie make-up, and eat their zombie meats with such consistency and devoir, it's almost beautiful. If you walk down zombie boulevard in mid-July, under the skillet-sun, or the oven of night, you'll never see a horde of souls so hell-bent on struggling to have fun.

They traveled all the way here, waded all day from LA through the parking lot of I-15, and are here now—would be a waste to not party my brains out, fuck whatever walks, pull every lever I can get my hands on till my wallet is a void and my brain leaks out my ears and I can't even remember which towering, bolted-on set of tits I'm supposed to be sleeping in. Another step. Another step.

Maybe there aren't any demon-gods-among-men seeking to enact their zombie-army master plan on the footsteps of Area 51. Maybe those demon-gods-among-men are just as functionally deficient as everyone else, Walmart branded with inadequate duo-processing.

Maybe they are just as lethally ironic as everyone else— going to zombie boulevard to live a little more, doing everything to make them live a whole lot less. Living through their phone screens, angling their picture-packers around the surrounding skyscrapers, filming everything they see, watching everything in their visual landscape through three inches of phone screen six inches from their decaying face. As if they are going to be alive long enough to ever watch the thirteen-minute video they just made of their parade down zombie boulevard. As if everyone else, all the other zombie-walkers, actually care to see the details of another zombie's rapidly depreciating existence. If there's one thing I've learned from zombies—they don't give three-and-a-half shits about what other zombies are doing. They just crawl over each other, piling up, endlessly trying to reach the top of whatever wall they want to spill over. The meat is always fresher and the brains always gooey-er on the other side.

And the regurgitation, let's not forget about that—a witting end to the zombie's night. Sometimes, they don't even make it to the witching hour, they vomit their stained guts up way before that point. So filled up on numb-numb juice that their roiling and toiling innards, although rotten and dead, still find the contents perverse enough to puke.

On one of my previous expeditions to Vegas, I entered a food court on zombie boulevard at five o'clock in the evening, a good seven or eight hours before the shamblers teeter at their finest. Five o'clock, the court was packed with the walking dead, fresh off feasting on pounds of flesh, some looking for more, waiting in winding lines for knock-off fast food. I chose some desecration called Pan Asian Express— such a poor copy-cat that the font for *Express* was in the same style as Panda Express—the clearly superior alternative. There's something Asians know about adding Express to the title of their restaurants. Americans love that shit. I don't think we know we love that shit, but we love that shit all the same. We are hungry and we want our glistening orange chicken, mountain of fried rice and chow mein, stinky-beef-and-broccoli, and an egg roll right now, dammit.

I got mine—a large platter of previously frozen nutrients, thawed out and tossed around a wok bowl until the sauces sank in and that tantalizing glaze covered the surface of every inch of meat. I got mine, not in express time, but I got it all the same. I made my way to a little table on the far side of the zombie court and found a spot unoccupied by other zombies. Sitting down, I looked up to see the most zombie-like character Vegas had ever shown me. She was hunched over a two-person table, imitating an undead machination that hadn't caught the whiff of sentience yet. She twitched a little, but remained largely in place. A six-foot-seven tower-of-a-man, apparently the zombie's caretaker, was approaching with a black garbage sack. Maybe he was going to suffocate the undead witch before she reanimated. He exhibited symptoms of ghost-watching, eyes wide and tired—he'd been caretaking all day by the looks of it. I put the first piece of orange chicken in my salivating mouth, previously covering it in rice and noodles. It wasn't the best, definitely wasn't the worst.

If that oversized garbage bag was to suffocate this zombie's brain, it was too late. She reanimated, rearing back in her cafeteria seat, and made a mid-toned gurgling moan as if she was experiencing the onset of birthing dilation. No concern for the two-hundred other neck-biters in the court, all feasting their eyes or mouths on something soft and meaty. My theory of zombies not giving three-and-a-half shits was immediately proven true, as everyone glanced over, saw the reanimation, heard the morbid sound, and plainly went back to shoveling pizza and Nathan-branded hotdogs down their gullets.

She moaned again, louder this time—was she birthing a zombie baby? The man with the garbage bag plan held out the sack, and all was made appropriate for this time and place. It was this fateful little she-zombie's turn to do some regurgitation of her own. Now, I was sitting enjoying a thoughtful meal, but my thoughts turned villainous, just as her stomach was preparing to eject maleficent bile all across the insides of that plastic-sack vomit-bin. My train-of-thoughtful-meal derailed. I immediately picked up my food tray, turned my back and speed walked to the other side of the court. I imagined the wave of hot-bubbling alcohol spewing from her throat in a slow-mo rendition of the opening scenes in Zombieland, and I felt sorry for Benjamin. It was a foul, evil, pungent smell that I had myself tasted before, albeit in the confines of my own home as a college undergrad, assisted through the personal disaster by all the free water I could chug and the almighty porcelain throne to catch my mess.

I imagined the bout of miserable regurgitation this girl was undergoing, and, perhaps unconsciously, knew that I might revisit that gaging affliction myself if I were to sit and see it all play out for her. Didn't want the smell, couldn't take the sound, most definitely didn't need to sit around and watch. I found a comfier seat far from that nightmare.

Another mouthful of orange chicken and broccoli and beef, coated in rice and noodles. I smiled to myself, enjoying the shit outta my meal. I was nearing the end of my platter, quite content. Glancing around, I noticed another table seating six or seven men, all eating meals of their own. A court-worker was approaching with another black garbage sack, and I noticed one of them was a little paler than the rest. His eyes were near-crossed, head bowed down to the table, aside from when particular wrenches forced him to adjust his midsection. He reeled, clutching the glass bottle of Michelob Ultra in his zombie-palm, white-knuckle tight. Ingredient number one, it's all the good stuff. I turned back toward my meal and started shoveling rice and noodles in my mouth, and I began to understand that escaping the zombie apocalypse was impossible. Regurgitation was in every corner of this wretched place, bile swallowed down, buried beneath even more beer and cocktails and any liquid other than the one that defines a living being—water.

I couldn't eat fast enough, forking all my American-Asian glistening chicken into my pie-hole. I was wearing shorts, and that undead brood of a man was sitting close enough that any miss from the black sack could result in puke-splatter flecking the backs of my calves. Can't have that. The thought alone was almost enough to pull a gag out of me. Infection wouldn't get me today—no bites, no snarls or snickers would emit from my lips. None of the other zombies cared. In fact, some were still just arriving at tables adjacent to the ailing he-zombie. They didn't care. Maybe they wanted to help slurp up the meaty, beer-basted bile malding in the man's belly. Didn't matter to me. I tapped out and was gone.

In the end, the lifeblood of the whole operation is the emerald bills in your pocket. That's the demon-god-among-men, not the zombies themselves. If you think you can get price estimates, accurate guesses at how much money you'll separate yourself from while you live on zombie boulevard, you really are on Mars. Rent a room for seventy-five bucks. Killer deal! You'll show up, check in, and suddenly be forking over a hundred-eighty-five. There's the facility amenity fee, the utility charge, the bill for the possibility of you ordering zombie whores to your room, the cost of considering room service, a stipend you pay for existing in their space in the first place, fees for the potential of Mary-Jane to be toked in your room, debts for parking the car you didn't drive—fees, fees, and more fees. It never ends, and it's all for the good stuff.

It doesn't matter what they're for. Somewhere up the chain of zombie command, the pit bosses found out that zombies will pay staggering stacks of emerald bills for nonsensical antes. Just to play, you gotta pay through your bloodied, rotting nose. But hey, you drove all the way here, waded through I-15, turning five hours into fifteen—so might as well suffer twice! Bunch of sunk-cost soaked bastards.

I opened the back passenger side door to my golden rocket ship and stepped out into the hottest seven-thirty-in-the-morning air I could remember. Back home in Utah, the temperature followed the light—a real belter during the day, sweater-weather at night. The heat follows light so much that you can lounge in some shade in Utah and actually start cooling off, drying the outermost layer of sweat in a salty, microbial paste across your forehead and cheeks.

In Vegas, and plenty of other more southern locals, you just never stop sweating—morning, afternoon, and night. It rarely has the chance to dry, leaving your body in a pillar-of-salt state of anatomical weeping. Everyone in Vegas is just like Lot's wife, breaking their necks to look behind them at big asses and glistening muscles, dancing pecs, shrink-wrapped peckers, and credit-carded thongs. They over-crank their brains like an owl, eyes wide like an owl. Sometimes they even hoot like owls. But all the same, they look back through their sweaty eyes, getting wetter all the time.

The scorching air of southern Nevada filled my lungs as I allowed mine and Mia's blended-up musk to ventilate from our tent-on-wheels. It was a new day, a new dawn, a new moment to claim a shiny new outset and set out into the world. I was refreshed from a good ole cryin' the night before, now soaking in some Vitamin D to heal my wounds. Mia pranced off into the desert weeds that were poking their little goat-heads through the sand and gravel. Even the shrubbery of this place was filled with sin and satanic symbols of vice and venom. Mia caught a couple of goat heads in her paws and came limping back to the side of the car, silently begging for their immediate removal. I quickly obliged.

For the first time in my life, there were no homework assignments I had to feel guilty about procrastinating. There was no class or schedule to adhere to—just the open road, my two feet, and Mia's four goat-head-free paws. Deep breath. I'm ready, Universe, tell me where to go. Pull these ten toes in whatever direction you need them. Crickets. Not a pip. The desert was dead quiet. Dead tumbleweeds rolled across the dead road. Not even an F-150 rumbled up the path into the dead-red-rock mountains. Silence. Devastating, directionless silence.

And why should I have been given some mystical God-sent inclination, arriving in a pretty little envelope with wings? Why should it ever have been that easy? With just as much desire as I had to be inspired by creative exploration, I was immediately disgusted with my feeble attempt at communion with God. I wanted a vibrant sign with neon lights to drop from the sky like a comic-killing anvil, overwhelming my senses, providing all the answers to a massive host of questions boiling in my prefrontal cortex. I wanted all the directions, the map, the gas, and the car all at once, spooning my cake down my ignorant throat while I looked at it. Give me a sign, paint me a yellow brick road to places and thoughts untold! Hey, God, or whoever sits up there in the midnight stratosphere, do all the work for me while I bask in a hundred-and-three degree caesura. I promise I'll thank you for it later.

There were a thousand things to do: hike the hills of Mars, stumble the Strip with a thousand other zombies, kayak the rippling waves of Lake Mead, find the most Keebler-cozy bar and pound several drinks. I could write in my little brown book, spewing lighting from my little silver pen. I could formulate my own scientific method on the best camp-drip-coffee known to man, sizzle up some fried eggs, over easy, with a side of over-cooked bacon. I could learn the harmonica, a boy-scout souvenir I had stuffed in my travel bin of things to occupy my time. It was packed tight with ten different books that I could read, pencils I could sketch with, cameras I could capture the preludes of Mars in. There were so many options. I set myself up so perfectly to battle caesura-riddled moments such as this. And I sighed and spun my thumbs around one another.

I climbed back into my tent-on-wheels and wrestled some more. Apparently, my spotty sleep hadn't erased the uncomfortable rancor that hid in my soul. I leaked the ink once again, one more time, let me see the refrain from last night in a new day's light. And it went:

What the fuck am I doing out here?

I occupied my time with none of those wondrous hobbies. I sat in the driver's seat, kneading my head with my sweaty palms, trying to withdraw the poison of idle uncertainty from my brain. There were no tears left to weep, and I didn't want them. I wanted the energy to do something, feel something, go somewhere. But I'm just here, on the side of the road in the middle of the barrens, and everything's dead and cooked. I turned the key, willing my rocket engine to life, spun out, shooting pebbles and dusty debris into the weeds behind. I realigned with the road and headed back toward the glorious decrepit aura of Vegas city-center. A zombie called home to the undead motherland.

Chapter 7

Fifty-Ticker

There's a smaller hotel on the southern end of zombie boulevard, across the street from the MGM Grand. It's not palatial by design, not attractive in any way other than the colossal orange letters that row the rooftop—HOOTERS. (In the current day and age, they've changed the name, now only housing a Hooters restaurant. No longer the primary establishment of women with triple Ds and men who've forgotten what it's like to receive personal attention from a blonde, glittery-golden angel. Maybe they haven't forgotten, maybe they were never introduced.)

I've never eaten at Hooters. I choose my restaurants based on convenience, flavor, and style—after all I can't eat with my penis. Some zombies seem like they can, though, filling themselves up on all the visual stimuli their pupils can absorb. I suppose Hooters has a very distinct style, so maybe one day I'll take the plunge and dine at the physically-feasted eatery. Not today, though. I'm eating with my mouth today. I've got bins filled with tortilla-mayo sandwiches to grub on.

The Hooters hotel became my favorite secret spot to submerge myself in vice. They sold one-dollar margaritas, hosted one-dollar blackjack, had penny slots as far as the eye could see, and peddled cheap Black 'n Mild cigars in the bustling side shop. They had an adjacent parking lot, twenty-five feet out the front door, where you could spark up and sex all the Mary-Jane you wanted, and no one cared. The whole structure was a perfect little bubble, free of nosy casino workers—juuuust the right amount of regulation for intoxicated brains to bump and stumble around. It was perfect. It always felt reasonably safe, always seemed like my fellow zombies were a little more animated here than everywhere else. I've played my fair share of one-dollar blackjack, too, getting sore throats off all the Whiskey Sour Margarita-flavoring and hearty earthen-burnt smoke.

It took several trips to Las Vegas before I discovered this little slice of Hell's heaven, but since then, I've always copped a visit, even though nowadays it goes by OYO. Whatever that means. At least Hooters committed to the Sin-City vibe, tits-and-all. Then again, OYO does look like a pair of boobs when it's scrawled in all caps. Well, ain't that subliminal.

I was approaching the Strip, single-mindedly anticipating a visit to my favorite carnal castle. It was hot, my windows were rolled down—all four of 'em—and Mia's tongue was wagging in the breeze, catching all the sweaty grime permeating the Vegas air. She kept her tongue out—all that human juice must have tasted salty and good.

The lot at Hooters was sparse, scattered cars parked every three or four slots. I found a stall, pulled in, and immediately realized this wasn't going to work. I had a dog—not an emotional support animal (although, in reality, that's exactly what Mia was for me). I couldn't just waltz through the front doors, zombie-shambling around with my zombie mutt, plop down at the nearest dollar-blackjack trough, and feed my pigged face while she... what, sat and got high off the nicotine-infused o-zone? Oyo? O-no. And now I'm hot and in the front seat, sweating idle.

Even then, with the lax casino-runners at Hooters, they wouldn't allow that. I punched my guts, damning my dumbness in driving all the way to this place with a creature that couldn't go inside anywhere. I started flaring up, my mind racing as I realized just how barred I was from any business in Las Vegas. Any business that sat in weather over seventy-two degrees.

The inside of my car was coated in black leather and it was almost a hundred outside. Damn. What a stupid choice— bringing this liability with me, her panting, grinning snout making all the noise in the world. What a dumb choice. I scowled at her, and she grinned back. I scowled harder, she grinned harder, leaned forward, and licked the anger-induced bead of sweat running down the side of my face. She grinned even harder, wide and wild and innocent beyond belief. That human juice must have tasted good.

I forced a copycat, big toothy grin myself, just as fake and loaded as the Hooters-boobs inside the tower to my left, and Sister Eubank would have been proud. The possibility of leaving Mia at a doggy day care briefly whiffed across my mind, and I stomped it out—not gonna happen. Not in this place. Can't have the zombies feasting on my sweet little girl. Even if there were signatures and contracts guaranteeing her safety. I imagined a Cruella-deville-esque witch-woman chain-smoking cigarettes through a telescopic Marlboro-holder, blowing clouds of tobacco leaf in Mia's adorable, beaming face. She wouldn't be smiling anymore, gagging and retching in a cold-steel cage, broken and tormented and abandoned. And where have I gone? Away. Gone to gamble my pennies and dollars to the big man upstairs.

My grin grew into one of true emotion. A grateful part of me began to realize the crucial role Mia would play in all this—making my undead ass try new things instead of reverting to old ones. I knew the draw of the Hooters casino, the cheap drinks and long nights. I'd lived 'em, drank 'em up, soured myself on a hundred losing blackjack hands, losing a couple hundred bucks and partying all the way on the good stuff. They were great times, memorable and marvelous, through and through. Not this time though, this was going to have to be something entirely different. New times, not end ones.

I cracked the windows and sprinted for the lobby door. I breezed past the one-dollar gambling table, a semi-circle of cackling hyenas tossing in chips, betting five dollars even though it was a one-buck minimum. Vegas was working on those glaze-eyed schmucks tonight. I smiled, wished a little I could join them, knew I could another day, week, month, or year down the line, and continued my sprint-turned-jog. I passed the one-buck margarita counter, flying by a group of tantalizing women, all dressed their best. Skimpy gowns that piled their chests high and up over their low-cuts, golden and shining in the mellow lights like a foaming mug of sappy beer. They swayed and bent their knees a little and leaned on the counter and winked at all the old men. They were more than prepared for a night of town-living and owl-neck-jerking. Another step, another step.

Finally arriving at my destination, I unzipped, propelled against the porcelain urinal, zipped up, washed up, splashed my face with a cooling film of water, and repeated my dogtrot back to the panting mutt in the front seat. Three-minutes, fifty-four seconds. I like timing myself. That was quick—back as always in record time. I pulled a manilla sheet of torn-out paper off the dash of my car. Scribbled down pinstriped lines, in a very clear and emboldened composition, it read:

Have to pee, will be back in 5 minutes or less.

My cell phone number followed, along with a little squiggly smiley face. Zombies are zombies, but when animals get involved, they become God's-holy-army, ready to go to war to protect the unbroken sanctity of an innocent animal. It's both ironic and beautiful. They might not give three-and-a-half-shits for each other, but they sure won't hesitate to shatter car windows for the sake of animal cruelty. I knew I'd be fast, but I didn't feel like risking a smashed window and the ensuing brawl of fists and slurs. So I covered my ass, ripped a leaf from my little brown book, and penned my promise to prying eyes. Luckily, no eyes were prying. And I liked timing myself, so here's my evidence, you pig-nosed judge.

When I was sixteen years old, a nefarious little seed was planted in my awareness—one that would play itself out over the course of an entire decade. My parents like to claim guilty credit for the planting, but they just drove the car. We spent an extended stay on the north end of zombie boulevard in a jet-black pyramid, spot-lighting a pearly-white hell-beam far up into the midnight stratosphere. I'm sure the lever-pullers up there get tired of us shining our brights at them and bragging about it. It was the Luxor and it was magnificent and had skin everywhere on all the fantasy posters and I had drool and foam spilling over my lips the whole time.

We packed up the entire family—my younger brother and sister, older sister, Mom, Dad, and we even brought an equally-teened friend of mine along for the ride. We had the third-from-the-top suite at the jaw-dropping architectural masterpiece of Egyptian wonder and the elevators went diagonal and I was smitten.

Why we chose to go to the city of tits-and-wine as a family get-away is beyond me. No one in my family drank, no one smoked, no one gambled. It must have been the shows. I didn't care, I was brimmed and sixteen, and farcical brain-plays of me scoring some kind of sexual contact with a female body danced in my head. All I wanted to see were those sugar plums; touching them was another story. Those little theatrical performances danced in every sixteen-year-olds head. They were dancing in my head, dancing in my friend's head, all while my older sister tried to cover my younger brother's wide and pearly-white eyes in hopes they would never dance in his. There would be no dirt-clods for that budding boy. But I painted and smeared and foamed at the mouth like a rabid dog.

All the same, we chose Vegas for the family vacation that year. Maybe that choice is where my parents blame themselves for my inevitable corruption. But the thing about inevitability—it's gonna happen, all the same. And it did.

A little here, a little there—the bites and snarls of the zombie apocalypse dirty up your pearly-white clothes; just you try and get through without a few racing stripes down your shorts. A little black in your bones. Even the undead slugs that slouch around zombie boulevard aren't all bad—they have their charm, their moments of glimmering hope, even if you don't outwardly see it. Their potential isn't wholly negated due to specific drunken circumstance. If wind rackets through their wheezy lungs, undead or not, their potential remains.

So the nefarious seed was planted, a city of vice, fiending for another fix, another hit, another buck, another fuck. Another step, another step. And that's just it—that seed was to be planted all the same. If not then, when? And if your primary mode of operation, your life's sole directive, is to saunter about in a half-cocked zombie-walk, then you haven't been listening. You really are on Mars. And I was, there in the spring-soak of May. Have a little faith, it'll all come together. It's the good stuff.

The most egregious sin of them all was perpetrated long after that funny little family trip. I recounted our expedition through zombie-land to my mother years later while she shook her head and frowned at her supposed failure. Apparently, at some unknown point in time, years after our vacation, I claimed that teenage soiree in Las Vegas was, and I self-quote, "My favorite family vacation we had been on." I was offended at myself and my own gall to drop such deceitful language, especially to my parents, whom I know still rue their decision to speed walk their kids through a teenage boy's wet dream.

I was stumped at the anti-truth of the phrase. It wasn't just a lie, it was the complete opposite of the truth. Something I was convincing myself of because, you know, vice is cool, broads are sexy, winning money is badass, and promiscuity is a man's badge of honor. Zombie beliefs spouting from my snarling, foamy lips. I'm here to live, really live with circulating guts of gin and jello shots and M&Ms.

I skirted around the curb, exiting the lot of the Hooters Hotel and rejoined the red-and-white blood-celled brake lights that pump north and south down the Strip. If our bodies pumped blood this slow, we'd have died a long time ago.

In a fit of vengeful anger, the lever-pullers above upped the heat-ante and the Clark County sizzle-skillet hit blistering new heights. My car's air-conditioning battled for superiority, hardly coming out on top. Mia and I wheeled south, out toward a freely managed land called Lovell Canyon. I hoped we might find a secluded little square of gravel to park again for the night, away from the neon buzz-glow pollution broadcasting from the city. The road to Lovell was tight, a slot canyon for cars, all thanks to a never-ending orange stream of hard hats and construction signs. There couldn't have been three inches between my drivers-side mirror and the oncoming traffic. No mistakes now. Hopefully these trucks, sedans, and semis aren't being controlled by zombies yet, hopefully they have a little awareness, a little life still left in 'em. My life depends on it.

In moments that require acute vehicular attention, I tend to let my mind drift slightly, if not for the right reasons. My knuckles turned white, but not out of fear—defensive driving was my strong-suit. My hovering thought process always leads me to every time I've ever heard anyone talk about all their drinking and driving and how they are just so good at it—or at least, always juuuust good enough. I hate stories like that.

It takes a high level of ignorance to man your motor-roller while under the influence of alcohol. Driving is already the most dangerous thing any of us do, we just complete the actions so often that we never think twice. We barely even think once. And when we're undead-drunk, we don't think at all. It's not a victimless crime, and the worst part is that for some reason, the lever-pullers in the midnight stratosphere think it's another sick and twisted joke to pull the levers of the family of five, or worse yet, maybe just three-out-of-five. Meanwhile, the inebriated bitch who just slurred head-on, upending a mini-van engine through the family's front dash somehow gets out unscathed and they're drunk and ragdoll against the airbag like it's nothing.

If you're too single-minded to understand your intoxicated machine-wielding impact on others, at least understand it on yourself. You might get home, crawling into your zombie lair, sliding under the sheets into a bubbling drunken slumber. You've done it. The third time this week, eighth time this month. You've lost count how many times this year. Maybe you are just aware enough to put a glass of ice-chilled water on your nightstand, prepped for the dry-mouth, gaping-stomach feeling you'll wrestle with briefly when you wake up in the middle of the night to relieve your beer-filled bladder. You've done it—holding fast to your Déjà Vu-inducing routine, yet again. You've done it—gotten through the good stuff and made it to your blankets and pillows, where the sheep bounce over your bricked head.

But what are you telling yourself? Not with your lips, but with your movements, the horribly successful apex of a night out, ran by you, drunk by you, drove by you. What are you signaling to the hard-wired synapses sparking around your cerebellum?

I'm a man that can make it home, not a brain-washed billy-goat, day-drunk on the world. I'm a man that's different, I know how to stay in the dotted yellow line, disasters and devil-plays don't befall me. A ten-thousand-dollar fine won't conjugate my crime. I'll make it home, simply because I've made it home every other time. I always make it home.

If that ain't the Vegas mentality, I don't know what is. Dripping in gambler's fallacy, believing that every roll of the dice, every flip of the cards, every spin of the roulette wheel can be dictated off the history of every previous attempt. Casinos make money hand-over-fist off this one simple ideology. Police departments and city governments make money hand-over-fist off the fines and fees of the same one. And the victim is always the same—you and me. But we smile often enough and join the game like it's one worth playing. It is the good stuff, after all.

I made money hand-over-fist one night in Vegas, circulating a giant virtual wheel-of-fortune, believing I had found the key to success in this predictable little game. My money multiplied rapidly, and my mouth couldn't vomit words fast enough to explain my inspiring strategy. My fellow zombie friends, eyes veiny-red and glazed over in weed and cocktails, shook their heads, still shoving hundred dollar bills in the almighty wheel and we all started winning and my strategy was working. And I couldn't talk fast enough about it.

The catch with the wheel was to analyze the history, look back through the previous twenty spins so nicely displayed on the oil-smudged screen. Whatever number wasn't getting hit, that was the one to invest in. I even used the word "invest." There were two special tickers on the wheel, each paying fifty times what you originally bet. Ante with one dollar, win fifty. Only if the wheel landed on the marker, of course. And it would.

I began by putting one dollar on the fifty-ticker. The wheel would spin, miss by a mile, and I'd put another dollar out there, adding a little tally to the notepad app on my phone. I was using my phone to count bets. I was smart, I was winning, I was a brilliant little investor. Little did I know, Vegas was investing in me. Biting my arms and legs up and down, leaving me with all the zombie-venom I could handle, and then some. And I promise, Vegas had a lot more fiat to invest in me, than I had to invest in it. So I put more bills on the ticker and clenched my fists while the wheel spun round and round and dinging music rang through the speakers.

I won big on that trip, I was convinced of my strategy. Betting one dollar on the fifty ticker forty-eight times, and then hitting it on the forty-ninth would still bring me a net profit of another dollar, just to start the process over again. That trip never saw me go over thirty bets, thirty magnificent wheel-spins, without landing on my coveted fifty-ticker. I even started betting two bucks, three bucks, and I hit those once or twice, too. I was the king of the wheel, smile so shit-eating big and toothy that it touched both my earlobes. My whole zombie group started winning, mirroring my bets, using the same strategy, believing that a technological machine owed us a fifty-ticker every now and again. We all believed it. It was playing out before our very eyes, and it was the strongest stuff, the good stuff. It beat the hell out of the watered-down vodka-cranberry glasses I kept ordering. Chaining back and forth between my Mary-Jane vape-pen, Black 'n Mild cigars, and sipping on the drinks delivered by big-busted Mexican ladies with scarlet lipstick and browned teeth behind fake smiles. I tipped them a buck for every dram, and I was still making my dough while the wheel spun, ticker after ticker, landing on the fifty too many times. Look at the history—it's the good stuff.

Beyond our purview, escapading before us in the money-grubbing world was the goblin-gold-hoarding game that Vegas was investing in us. They parted with juuuust enough money, the perfect ratio in the perfect order, to have us believing that rolls of the dice, rolls of the wheel, rolls of the roulette ball, weren't all that independent of the last. The zombie venom now coursing through our veins later turned us all undead, when all that money we gained was lost on subsequent trips to zombie boulevard in the coming years. Always lost—but that one winning trip sticks out like a golden thumb among the rest.

But I'm tunneling down a car-slot canyon, passing hardhats, making for the secluded western waves of sand and dirt. I wouldn't part with a single cent on this staycation. Vegas could pull my pennies from my cold, died-trying hands.

The turn-off for Lovell Canyon slid into view, posted on a brown reflective sign on the right side of the road. I slowed my rocket ship, veering off into clouds of kicked-up dust and gravel. The government-managed macadam path was smoother than I anticipated, with only a few pot-holes here and there. My sight-line angled up from the dirt road, meeting the rusting horizon and majesty of colossal stone giants rising high into the baking atmosphere. The left side of the canyon was filled with these squatting, mountainous behemoths, and on the right side—open air. I wondered out loud how a canyon could be called a canyon with only one definitive wall.

Little camping spots dotted the sides of the road every fifty yards, with pullouts big enough for midsized trailers. There were a few previously occupied firepits, scarred dark from a thousand fires of the past. The only thing missing were some trees—but this was the desert, that would have been asking too much.

I found an appropriately sized pullout, positioned up against a gravel wash that rose twice the height of my car. I slowly drove-reverse-drove until I landed my ship at a well-leveled halt. I opened the door, and Mia burst out over my lap, slipping a little on pebbles, and skipped off into the sagebrush. She stopped, looked back at me, squatted down in she-doggy fashion, and propelled her own piss down an unfortunate moles-hole. He must have thought it was raining, except for the smell. And except that it never rained here.

The sun was starting to bleed out, leaking bright-red rays down the backs of the squatting stone giants. I prepared my tent-on-wheels for the night, unfolding my sleeping bag and camp pad, blowing some air into the manually-inflated, bright-green mat. Every breath I pushed left me feeling a little more compressed than usual. As if there was someone sinister watching me from atop the gravel berm. As if there were a hundred important things to do, but I couldn't quite remember any of them. More air into the pad. I felt an anxious trickle tickle down my neck, through my arms, and into my fingers. Another forced breath. I dug my nails into my palm, trying my hardest to leak out a bright-red drop of my own blood to match the sun's ailing demise. Another angry shoot of belly-air. My face was maroon, veins bulging out the sides of my head—my hands were shaky, mouth dry and sweltered from a day of aimless wander. One last blast of oxygen. I screamed a hoarse shrill, rekindling my previous night's bout with fury. My head ballooned, compressed so tight it might explode and blow my brains all over the windshield. I screamed again, and salt started rimming my eyelids.

Again, gurgling blood in my throat, ripping the insides of my voice box to shreds. I think I like screaming, and I'm solving my own problems with it. I'm howling out in the burnt descent of the sun, and maybe if I ruin my voice box, I'll have solved all my problems. This was the good stuff, my hoarse vibrations. Compressed so tight, veins bulging out from my neck and sweating forehead and I'm uncomfortable and this is day two. Only day two. Night number two and how am I gonna make this work. This was Lovell, the open air and freedom from school and the duties of home and when I suck it deep into my belly, I'm just knotted and lost. Enough air and time and space out here that every day should hit like a fifty-ticker, wide and western like the old movies. Just like the old movies and books when the beat ones rode the railways out west and fell in love with the world and all its chaos. But I'm wrung out and my voice is gone.

Twilight was resting on the desert, a shade of amethyst so deep and satisfying, it was hard to keep my tears framed in anguish. I laid on my makeshift bed, staring up into the midnight stratosphere, unsure if the droplets on my back windshield were puddled from my eyes or the gathering purple and velvet clouds beyond. I wiped my lids clear, squinting at the glass barrier between me and the outside world where there was more desert air and vacant space than I knew what to do with. It was dead and rolling like tumbleweeds at dusk, everything dehydrated and hollowed out from an onslaught of sun in the wraps of May. It started raining.

Chapter 8

Off-Brand Control

I cracked open the faded-blue lid of my mobile fridge—a cooler manufactured in the late nineteen-eighties. For some reason, I had deemed it suitable for road-tripping through hell-on-earth in the year twenty-nineteen. Every piece of ice I had previously dumped in there was now wholly melted, bathing my sandwich meat, jam jar, and other fridge-required items in a lukewarm liquid that wasn't all that clear. Parts of egg carton had peeled off and congealed in the water, creating a papier-mache-like substance, gray and curious in its appearance and stench. Most of the items in the cooler were sealed, so I wasn't overly worried about cross-contamination. More so considering just how often I would need to refill the case with a fresh bag of frozen water. I had left home from Logan, Utah only two mornings ago, and this was what I was working with. Bags of ice hadn't been a factor when I did my pre-trip budget planning. Neither were laundromat visits or washing detergent. That's more money out, another chore to lower my bank numbers. Add that to my growing list oh-shit-I-forgots.

I lifted a pack of Western Family-branded bacon out of the cooler, eyeing it meticulously, searching for any ounce of gray-mache blubber within its vacuum-sealed contents. None that I could see. I sliced open the bag with my oversized pocket knife, withdrew four strips, and realized I wouldn't be able to just toss the other sixteen back into the cooler, bag now gutted wide. Raw bacon-water, bacon-milk, bacon-jam, bacon-ice, bacon-mayo, bacon-eggs. That last one sounded good—I pulled out three eggs, setting them delicately on the notched edge of my Coleman travel stove. The sun was warm and rising up into the sky and the reaches of Lovell stretched far and lay quiet under a deep ocean of teal and wonder.

Next came the loaf of bread, thankfully not stored in my catastrophe of a fridge. I had a special bin for dry goods, filled with tortillas, trail mix, ramen noodles, crackers, peanut butter, and all my cooking utensils. Carbs for days, and it really was the stuff to get fat and happy on. I pulled out two slices of wheat, and balanced them on the edge of my cooking stove, too.

Everything you do every day always takes a few extra steps once you're on the road. Cooking isn't just pulling things out of a double-wide fridge in your kitchen, throwing them into a pan, waiting for that succulent sizzle, and then plating the mess for pleasure. Food-prep, and not the kind involving a hundred little containers for a hundred little meals throughout the week, isn't just gently slicing veggies, buttering bread, sterilizing knives from chicken-cutting under a faucet of hot water. Pissing isn't just shouldering the bathroom door, tossing up the lid, propelling a yellow stream into the toilet water—or for you ladies, sitting and enjoying a brief moment away from the world while you tinkle. Cleaning isn't just lobbing a scrambled egg-crusted pan into the sink to soak for an hour, only to come back two days later to thirteen other dishes that aren't even yours. Relaxing isn't just hurling your worn-out frame onto a cool leather couch that's sucked up the A/C, flipping on the pixel-box and letting your mind go zombie-like-numb for the remainder of the night. Everything takes extra steps, extra effort, and suddenly, you realize how you've always taken everything for granted. And I had. But this morning was bacon and eggs, and that was fine with me.

One of my buttered-up bread slices slid off the top of the other, landing face down at my feet in the powdery loam. The dust was so fine, it even made a little poof of debris swirl up around it. In an effort to attempt a heroic save, I lunged forward, bonking my knee into the side of the stove, sending one of my perfectly balanced eggs to the same dusty fate. The shell busted open, oozing broken yolk and viscous egg-white across the earth. The grimy substance picked up flecks of finely-ground gravel as it rivered toward the fallen slice of bread. They met, and for a moment I considered making an earthen flavored wedge of french toast. I'll bet Mia would eat that delicacy right up. Before I knew it, she already was.

Not wanting her to Zamboni up the raw egg seeping into the dirt, I tossed the desecrated piece of bread off to the side, now looking like its face was coated in grainy-brown peanut butter. It was dirt butter and she loved it. It got her attention, and she inhaled the wheat piece in seconds. I pressed my boot into the raw-egg-moot-soup, mushing it into the ground and whirling it in counter-clockwise circles. Earth-flavored scramblers, comin' right up.

I pulled out a replacement egg, buttered up another slice of bread. The whole ordeal made me chuckle to myself, which surprised me. Here I was, in the middle of Mars, things going wrong left and right, parts being forgotten, head blown all over the rear window of my car the night before and the night before that, and I had a de facto smile creeping across my face. There were still eight eggs soaking in my gray papier-mache cooler, my water jugs were mostly full, rocket ship three-quarters filled with fuel, most of a loaf of bread, plenty of butter, and not one of my four bacon slices was covered in dust. There was darkness and confusion surrounding me, sure—but there were also some shreds of light. Dear ole Sister Eubank would have been so proud.

I leaned back in my black-and-blue backpacking chair, the kind you can buy off Amazon nowadays for a quick twenty bucks. My butt hovered six inches off the ground, forcing my knees to rise up higher than my hips. Probably how my knee slammed into the camp stove in the first place. I loved this chair, my juuuust right chair, a tiny hammock that supported my back, legs, and core in all the right places. I did it all in this scoop—I cooked, read, wrote, harmonica-ed, sang, swayed, drank, bled, cried, sweat, and screamed in that chair. I still do.

So I leaned back in it, arching my back, stretching out my twisted-up muscles, and let out a cacophony of tension-induced clatter loud enough to be heard from the highway. Or so I thought. I wasn't trying to be heard that far out, and there was no one out here to do the hearing anyways. Belting goblin screams while you stretch is magical—I implore you to try it some time. Muscles store a lot of wound-up pressure as the world smashes you over the head with a club every day. Sometimes a good stretch-'n-shout is the best release valve. And it was.

My head felt a little lighter, an ounce of me blown into the wind, forced out by my stretch, forced out by a humble chuckle at my own mishap. My eyes and veins weren't bulging from my skull anymore, a moment's respite from the seriousness of solving the great and wavering problem of life.

Suppose that's why I'm out here. I had poked a little hole in my brain, and let out a little air, and I started to feel just a little better. But things still weren't perfect—and I think I was starting to realize they probably never would be while I lived out of a car, wheeling in a hundred-degree heat, under a blistering sun, separated from everyone and everything I had ever known. No more ninety-degree corners on a grid back home, just wide open wilds and giants that crouch and hide the sun away before dawn. None of this was perfect, and my expecting it to be would only make a clown out of me. None of this was perfect, and in that moment, that was perfectly okay. I had bacon and eggs and toast and all the good stuff to ponder about. And I did.

The sun was a little higher in the sky, closing in on ten-thirty or eleven in the morning. I still sat planted in my black-and-blue everything chair. I was scribbling in my little brown book, displaying the strange idea of decompression that came at the cost of a broken egg and a slice of bread. A hearty steam rose from my stainless-steel tumbler. While I wrote, I was concocting the best camp coffee you can imagine. The brand might have been Western Family, but that's not important— brand didn't matter. The setting was what made it taste so divine.

In doing a bit of quick Google-ing on my phone, before I was abandoned by cell service, I discovered a handy little Wiki-How article on making coffee in the great outdoors, when you have no electricity, no k-cups, no Mr. Coffee-pot to steam-roll your grounds into that fictile liquid-lightning that runs the world. The article was complete with awful picture examples, in true Wiki-How fashion. Comic-book characters with flat faces, bending their arms and legs in ways that would never be possible elsewhere. But it was Wiki-How and it was awful.

One of the popular methods was to dump coffee grounds directly into the tumbler, pour boiling water in with it, and stir it like chocolate milk. They called it cowboy coffee. I was in the wild-west, I had my steed and noble sidekick, hell I even had a gun and boots. I could very well have called myself a cowboy. But there was no way I was gonna sift granules of coffee bean through my teeth every morning. Cowboys are more innovative than that. The final step to cowboy coffee, if you're impatient, is to stand up straight, hold your mug from the top, and spin your arm around, generating enough centrifugal force that no liquid leaks out, but all the grounds shoot to the bottom, leaving you to enjoy your hot-cuppa-joe over a bedrock of ground black beans. The idea seemed hilariously impossible, not one I wanted to try. One big ruse.

Wiki-How letting me down once again. My way was much more intelligent, and with a delicate hand, would leave no grounds in the muddy water. I took a coffee filter, placed it in the mouth of my tumbler, folded the paper fringe up over the rim of the cup, and rubber-banded it all together. Next came the grounds, poured into the filter, not quite to the top. Then, the boiling water. The remainder of the operation must be done with a steady hand, or you risk overflowing the filter, spilling grounds and ripping-hot water everywhere. It also takes time—it's a drip-drip process, similar to the standard coffee maker in your kitchen. But like I said, this way was better. It could have been Motel 6 coffee that normally tastes like the underside of an hourly-rented-room's springboard in the seediest places of Las Vegas. But out here, where the air was fresh, and stone giants sat happily basking in the sun, coffee was coffee. Brewed with love before the eyes of God and all. And I was drip-dripping it gently, foaming at the mouth for my electric drink.

As I sat cradled in my everything chair, I noticed a majestic, auburn hawk soaring high in the cloudless sky. It was flying in a flat line, then it dipped, gained speed, and rose leagues higher than its original altitude. It repeated the actions, climbing and climbing until it was a little brown spec amid a blanket of baby-blue nothingness. I wondered what the desert, the cactus, the stone giants, zombie boulevard, the red rocks, my rocket ship, little Mia—I wondered what all of that looked like from up there. With eyes so pinpoint accurate I was sure the hawk was preying on homeless vermin that even I couldn't spot when hiking around down here. It was in control, so able to dial in on whatever speed, distance, and height it needed to be at, the master of its body and pea-sized brain, unified into a single force. I was a little jealous of the hawk. Here I am, mentally lost in a dust bowl, stumbling and bumping into everything by accident like a toddler. I felt like I was four years old, staring up at true wisdom with wide and youthful eyes, marveling at a creature who had achieved perfect harmony. I started scribbling in my little brown book, documenting the hawk in all his enchanted beauty.

Control. Perfect, <u>complete</u> control.

I underlined *complete*, darkening the original pen-stroke several times so my eyes would catch it someday in the future. I gazed back up into the atmosphere, seeing the hawk spearhead toward the earth now. It looked like it had a change of heart, deciding that suicide by dive-bomb was better than the scorching heat of the southern Nevada sand-wash. Just as it was closing in on the ground, prepared to be crushed into oblivion, it re-angled its wings, leveling out inches off the rocky surface, and snatched a small rat-tailed rodent that never saw it coming. Hawk claws embedded in its tiny, furry body, eyes wide and youthful, marveling at his growing altitude from the dusty barrens he was accustomed to. He was getting that all-encompassing view that I had wondered about. I don't think he was enjoying it all that much. The little rat's lever got pulled, and he was being flown straight to heaven, first class.

That night, I backtracked slightly, making it to a little town named Boulder City. It was the closest inhabited place to Hoover Dam, which I was hoping to visit the following morning. As nine o'clock rolled around, I started searching for a good spot to park and button-up for the night. Everything and everyone in Boulder City looked like it had always been there. The buildings and back-alleys were sun-fried into the rocks and dirt, edges and corners caked in dried-out gum and an unknown inky-black residue that gathered up all the dust it could muster, just like my runny-raw mud-egg-scramble. It had a little bit of charm, but was still rank with the Vegas aura—all the musk and none of the shiny-bright neon beams and glitter that so characterize zombie boulevard.

I scouted out several spots, none of them giving my gut the okay-to-go feeling I looked for before killing the engine for the night. The sun had set, and my search got slightly more frantic. I saw a glowing red sign on the corner of a darkened intersection that read HOSPITAL, with an arrow pointing back to a building with a vast parking lot, scattered cars slumped in random stalls. That would have to do. Hospitals never close, and logic went that if I were to get mugged or drawn out of my rocket ship and slugged half-to-death by some maggot-fiends, I'd be just a short, grueling crawl from the one place that could save me. That would have to do.

I found my own landing pad, subdued my motor, and fixed up my sleeping pad and bag. Mia nestled into her own little bed, directly to the right of my head. I always made sure she would fall asleep with her ass pointing away from me since she was all too prone to fart away the night in her snoring slumber. I also cracked the windows an inch, allowing for some air circulation—but not enough that a nosy-bugger could fit his hand inside. We learned that the hard way on night number one. The air-circulation shit-smelling lesson, not the nosy-bugger one.

I didn't need to learn the nosy-bugger lesson the hard way. It was stammering, half-drunk zombies that I was overly aware of in the first place, sleeping with my four-inch bladed pocket knife under my pillow every night. Just you go ahead and poke some dusted-knuckle sausages in here, and you'll lose 'em. Just you see. Don't try me, I'll shriek at the top of my lungs, crazy-up my icicle eyes so wide you'll see the blood they're sitting in. I'll match your lunacy and then some, you butt-crusted, nosy sons-of-bitches. Just you see. I'll dice those prying fingers off so fast and eat 'em just to show you how wild and willing and awake I am. And I am, and you'll lose every time, just you see. I don't need to be afraid of the bad guy in the night when I am the bad guy in shrouds of black when the sun's slipped away. I am the bad guy, and you don't wanna go poking just to find out. Just you see.

This wasn't the way the calm and collected version of myself viewed an intoxicated homeless man, but it was when someone came-a-nosing. It had to be. This was my rocket ship, bought and paid for by me, debted for seven years for this little golden zoomer. This was my body, filled, healed, and disrespected by me, cursed into an existence of solving the problem of life. This was my sweet little girl, fed, walked, and loved deeply by me, debted into years of wondrous adventures and a lot of dog hair. This was my life, and ain't no motherfucker is gonna strip that from me, especially not some opportunistic zombie-shrew looking to score a fast twenty on his way to the local meth dealer. Just you see. Just you give me a reason to be the bad guy. I could be the bad guy, and I told myself those letters over and over and stared at the canvas car ceiling.

It all played out in my head, probably more times than you'd care to hear. I'd slice the nosy-bugger's fingers, easy-as-pie. They say the pinky finger snaps like a carrot. I'd jump out of my rocket ship, channeling my high-pitched laugh-scream, shrilling like a foaming hyena, one-upping every part of this invader's insanity. You think you're crazy? You don't know crazy. I'll show you deranged. I've got shit to lose. I'm awake, I'll be missed. You know what that's like? Course not. Don't matter to me, you're done. I'll prowl up the steps into the midnight stratosphere myself and see to it personally that your lever gets pulled so damn hard you go straight to hell for messing with me in the first place. If you really wanna get things going, I've got a sweet little nine-millimeter loaded to go, and I'll fill your knees with metal if I have to. It's waiting gingerly in the glove box and that trigger isn't going to pull itself. But don't worry—we're just outside a hospital. I'll drag you inside after we're done dancing.

Did I actually believe I could do any of that? Maybe. No? Definitely. I landed back on maybe. After all, creatures do wild things when they are uncomfortable, and when I watched myself scream at myself in the mirror, it looked pretty deranged to me. I could see the blood around my eyes, the blood my eyes were sitting and soaking in. Maybe I'd even rip my shirt and pants off, just to add shock value. No one wants to tussle with a naked maniac, especially over a fast twenty. It wouldn't be fast, it'd be bloody and slow and taste metallic and salty.

My eyes blinked open. The windows to my car were letting in a gloomy light, similar in shade to the papier-mache that was growing in my cooler. It must have been just past six o'clock in the morning, and the first thought I had was that I needed more ice for the nineteen-eighties abomination sitting in the front passenger seat. I spurred my rocket ship to life and drove off the nearly empty hospital parking lot. I thought more cars would show up in the morning, but who knows, it might have been the weekend. I had lost track of the days of the week. Who cared anyways—it was warm and overcast and the days grew long in May.

I drove at a slow pace down the main street of Boulder City. It didn't look like a main street should. There were hardly any businesses or diners lining the sidewalks, instead being swapped for a whole bunch of those old houses our grandmas grew up in—square and plump, with front porches decorated with putting-green astroturf, hanging pots of flowers that were dried out and near-death, and lawns that were starting to look a little overgrown. Weeds poked up higher than the grass and it was untended and wild like Nevada. All the same, there was a little charm to this fringe village, forgotten and lost to its older, more interesting brother—Las Vegas.

I found a gas station, parked, and went in to score a new bag of chunked ice. It was one of those dingy little stops where twelve vacant slot machines sit, advertisements on every stickable surface telling you how mind-blowingly certain it was for you to win the lottery, even if it was only enough to cover the cost of a boot-bottom cup of gas station coffee. The setting here wasn't right for any old cuppa-joe to taste great. Nature was the third element needed, and this place was dank and tainted and dark grime ran down the cracks where an aisle shelf met the tile.

But they had ice, and ice is usually ice wherever you go, and that's all I needed. I snagged a ten-pound bag, paid the worse-for-wear station attendant, who grinned a big toothless grin, and made my way back onto the might-be-should-be main street of Boulder City.

Hoover Dam was just up the highway northeast from here, so joining the rest of some early risers on the gray and gloomy road, I listed up towards the arch-gravity dam that held the Colorado River in check. The second my wheels hit the open freeway, a wave of yellow fury struck my bowels. Remember how I said that everything gets a little harder, has a few extra steps when you're livin' on the road? Well, I wasn't kidding when I mentioned pissing and all its difficulty out here where bathrooms don't exist. I figured I could make it to the dam, get through the gate checkpoint, and find a federal restroom to relieve myself in time, so I stepped on the gas, flaming my rocket ship a little faster.

Every quarter mile sign I passed turned my eyes a darker shade of dehydrated yellow. If I started crying, it wouldn't be salt, but piss streaming down my cheeks. I started feeling my guts turn over, wanting to form a new urethra from my bladder circulating into the rest of my body. It felt like I had a little alien chest-burster squirming around inside me, stretching out my innards, wailing for sweet release. In my adult life, I've accidentally shit my pants before, but I can't say I've ever accidentally pissed myself. When you've got the flu, you can't trust a fart.

So I was wheelin' fifteen or twenty over the speed limit, livin' on a prayer, literally pinching the tip of my piss-propeller closed so tight nothing spilled into my underwear—this pair still needed to last me another twenty-four hours. Up ahead, there was a gigantic sign with bright beaming arrows pointing to it like God's finger, saying stop here, for the love of your pecker. I have no idea if the light-bulbed arrows were actually there or not, but my eyes met the message and I swerved off the interstate. The sign read: HOOVER DAM LODGE AND CASINO in massive sans-serif font.

My tires squealed to a stop. I told Mia I'd be right back, cracked the windows, and sprinted into the red rock rusty-colored hotel. It was a ghost town inside, silent to the bustling steps and slides of any human or zombie-look-alike. There was a low buzz of arcade noises, various machines prompting you to put another quarter in, zipping lights rimming the edges of every slot lever. No one was gambling, not one lost soul flaying away their day's paycheck. I surveyed every wall for a bathroom sign, still clutching my privates tight. There was a little ice cream shop planted right in the middle of the casino. I ran up, spitting out my words with a crack in my voice, begging for information on the nearest toilet, bush, tree, corner, garbage can—anything that was legal for me to put my piss into. I let go of myself for a moment so as not to give the wrong impression to the small Asian woman behind the counter, and that cost me a couple drips.

She pointed off into a nook I had already passed but somehow missed the sign, probably blurred through my pee-stained, watery eyes. I jaunted to the restroom, and finally was able to dump my liquified guts into the urinal. It actually hurt a bit more before it felt all better. Everything is harder when you're living on the road, and the bathroom problem was one that plagued me for the entire trip. I never seemed to solve it, almost growing a six-pack from the bladder control I exercised daily.

It was a humbling moment, stumbling through that empty casino, trying to perform the most basic and common human function. I found myself keeling over in laughter, making fun of my own donkey-ass once I rejoined Mia in the car, reeling at the sheer comedy of the whole thing. Why not just pull over off the side of the freeway and leak myself there? Why didn't I relieve myself at the gas station I got my ice chunks from? I had an empty plastic water bottle and a hundred places I could have stopped between here and there. None of that crossed my mind as I envisioned the golden throne for me to propel into. One option. One way. One perfect little spot where everything would be juuuust right for my private time. Where I'd perfectly wash my perfect little hands with a puddle of perfect soap-jelly in my perfect little palm. And I did.

So far from being in perfect control, I sat and cackled like a witch at my own comeuppance. Nothing on Mars was perfect, and in that slice of time, always back in my front seat, I was a lip-sticked clown, high on laughter at the expense of my own sanity. A rat-tailed-rodent, waddling around with my tail pinched between my legs, having thought that everything would be as magical as it looked from the hawk-elevator windows of heaven. This whole thing's a drip-drip process. Some drips just end up being a little better, a little tastier, than others. Nothing on Mars was perfect, and in that moment-between-moments, that laughable little caesura, that was perfectly okay.

Chapter 9

Live For It

I was back on the highway, bladder spick'n-span clean from my emergency stop. Clouds were still looming overhead, flooding the canyon rise with a bleak, ghostly light. Reflective emerald-green road signs started passing me on the right. Two miles till Hoover Dam, one-and-a-half miles, one mile—the turnoff was up ahead. I veered my rocket ship off the road, falling in behind a growing line of cars, campers, trailers, and trucks, all trying to fill their eyes and minds with historical wonder. Hoover Dam, the arch-gravity wizard that's wedged between the red rocks, beige and concrete and peering through the dark Colorado River-water—you shall not pass. It all looks small when you see it from a plane. Must have been small from the windows of heaven. I've seen it at plane height once, and it was so small. But not down here.

It wasn't hard to tell I was from out-of-state. Other than the obvious fact that my license plate was decorated with the Zions Arch—UTAH plastered front and back—it wasn't hard to see I was either road-tripping in this ship, living out of it, or both at the same time. It was both at the same time. Scanning up the line of cars, it became apparent that the guards maintaining the gate into Hoover Dam took their job seriously. They would aggressively motion for drivers to roll their windows down and then bombard them with a litmus sheet of questions—none of which I could hear clearly, I was still too far down the row of idling vehicles.

Most transports would pass the verbal test, then be subjected to the physical one. Big men, and some big women too, would circle around, stooping to their knees to survey the undersides, poking their hands and fingers up into the privates of each and every car, copping a very informal and uninvited feel. They would cup their black-gloved hands around their eyes, pushing their faces up against the front and back windows, taking stock of the contents. One motorhome was motioned over to the sideline, forming a new waiting queue where the big men and big women in their big bullet-proof hoodies tossed open the back door and marched inside, scanning the innards in a more intimate way. And back out again and onto the next one.

It seemed like a lot, just for some folks to see a big slab of concrete. All the same, it had to be done. I suppose that big slab of concrete held back billions of gallons of water, generating billions of hours of electricity for millions of Nevada inhabitants. Not to mention the sheer amount of energy needed to pump black sludge-blood through the veins of every shambling zombie that limped down the Strip. Trillions of neon bulbs, buzzing to their own blue-light tune weren't gonna ignite themselves. All the same, all that power to fuel all that vice had to come from somewhere. Compromise that, and you've compromised the entire state's ability to generate billions of bills off tourism—the place Nevada gets most of its income. The place where wallets go to die and everything is spectrum-ended and untamed.

The line was shortening, my turn was coming up. The only thought side-scrolling through my head was that I had a generously sized bag of Mary-Jane stuffed and sealed in my pantry bin. Would they turn me away for having the audacity to bring drugs into a federal facility? Would they smell it? Would they bring out the hounds, have them sniff their super-smellers all around my rocket ship, searching for one little bud to condemn my attempt? Worse yet, would they yank open my door, grapple me to the ground, and arrest me for such negligence? Those guys and gals were big and muscley and that was obvious, even under their black and metal-proof hoodies. What would happen to my sweet little girl, my sweet little Mia? Would the drug dogs take her out too, put a little set of paw-cuffs on her just for associating with such tomfoolery? Were we gonna spend the rest of our trip in a sweat-filled cell in some federal dungeon locked deep beneath the concrete slab with a mountain of Colorado River-water hovering above us?

My mind was racing now as one stupid scenario bled into another. Stress slipped back into paranoia, my eyes darting from one guard to another. Everything was falling and it was all slipping and going from one thing to another. Part of me wanted to duck out of line, turn around and wheel back toward Vegas, the land of uninhibited, unfiltered, unmitigated splendor. Where everything was allowed, and no one gave a shit what you did, how you did it, or which imaginary friend you talked to while you did whatever you were doing. I was out of my comfort zone again as I replayed my run-ins with the law back in little gridded Logan, Utah. They hate Mary-Jane there, and they hate alcohol too. They hate it so much they'll arrest you, ticket you, gas-light your youthful eyes and call you stupid for doing the things that every kid meddles in eventually. Things they meddled in when they were kids in nineteen-seventy and everything was musk and psychedelic.

They hate all that in little Logan, Utah. It's all degenerate, all leads to the same things, all signifies the same type of person. And it doesn't matter if the cop is family or strange or fresh off a romance or beating with their overweight wife, they'll pack you up in their cruisers and drive you to jail, all the same. And those images were the cinema, recalled now for me in the idling line before Hoover Dam and my heart was slamming hard.

I shook my head, trying to flick off the mental sabotage soup I was concocting in my skull. This wasn't little right-angle Logan. It was my turn to undergo the comprehensive exam, get my car all nice and whored up for the groping it was about to endure. I tried to make my eyes look a little less wide, darting a little less frantically. That type of behavior was probably exactly what they were looking for. I got the animated motion to roll my window down from the big man outside and prayed to God that a wave of skunk scent didn't reach out and slap him across the face. Hopefully the rank odor emanating from my armpits would cover it up enough. The questions began.

"Sir, do you have any firearms in the car?"

Oh, you have got to be fucking kidding me. I didn't even think of that. Not only was I toting my goodie stash of Mary-Jane, I had a nine-millimeter pistol sitting heavy in the glove box with a trigger that never pulled itself.

"Uhhhh…." It was probably the longest mental fart I've ever floated through. I replayed the four or five times I had conversations with my parents about how to answer such a question. One of them saying to tell the truth, the other saying to just not lie. One of them said to go out of my way to fill in police officers with the details of my little pistol, where it was, and that it wasn't on my person. The other said to only answer if directly asked. Either way, the objective was not to lie. But then, if I did lie, would the officers really know? Would they actually strip search the car? There were twenty cars behind me, a lot to digest for them. It was hot, and they were impatient and covered in black clothes, sweating angry beads of human-juice from the sides of their necks and temples and I was sweating too.

Most of my conversations with my parents about my little nine-millimeter were in the context of California—a place filled with insane things happening to insane people every crazed day. And here I was, insanely playing out mindless performances in all the wrong contexts, focusing on all the wrong things. A gun in my glove box. I was insane, it was backwards and reminiscent May, and I hadn't been to this part of Mars before. What to do about a gun in my glove box. Never tied with the fact of having an ounce of weed in here, too. These rules were different and I was insane and the question was hovering over me like all the Colorado River-water sitting still and dark and it wasn't so small.

"Uhhhmmm… yeah, I have a nine-millimeter pistol in my glove box. I'm on a road trip, so it's just for my own safety, and I have a license to own it." I started puking words out my car window, trying to tell the story of how my gun got there, why I had a gun with me. Before I got too far down the self-incrimination road, the big man outside interjected.

"You're gonna have to turn around. No firearms are allowed inside the Hoover Dam premises. Sorry man. Rules are rules." He pointed his massive black-gloved finger to an oversized sign that read: NO FIREARMS ALLOWED in bright red blocky letters. I immediately retorted back, claiming that was just fine, and that I hadn't seen the sign and apologized for wasting his time. I turned my car around in defeat, heading back up toward the highway. At least I could read the stop sign anchored in gravel before turning onto the road again.

Nice job. I was holding out my hands and watching them shake so bad and counted down from ten. The cinema was still rolling but no cuffs were wrapped around my wrists and I wondered if this was what post-traumatic stress disorder feels like and hit myself because that's ridiculous. You think they really give three-and-a-half shits if you have a little bag-o-weed on you? This place is a stoner's throw from the most vice-ridden, dank-smelling, skunk-stenching city in America. You think you're the first one to bring a joint through a checkpoint? I'm just leaning back laughing now. I'm keeled over like a hunchback in the front seat, pounding the wheel as if I should have seen this coming. And I should have. But I didn't. C'mon then, scuttle back to the city of sin, so disastrously safe that you can do and be whatever you want, with no rules, no guidelines, and not one other zombie-blasted mind-sucker will care. Go on then, give a shit about how you feel, run your very own litmus rulebook off that one damning factor. How I feel now, while my hands shake and I laugh and hate it all as it goes from one thing into another. Maybe tomorrow I'll feel like taking that peashooter out and pointing it into the pink beef-meat between my ears. That trigger isn't going to pull itself. Maybe I can follow that wretched thought-train, cause hey, all the same, that's how I feel, isn't it? Is it? My hands shook and I was sweating.

As the morning drew on, the clouds broke apart, revealing an aquamarine sky. The temperature was climbing and the gray doom-and-gloom of early daybreak faded away. I felt the need to do something physical, get out of my rocket ship and move my legs a little. The driver seat to my ship provided solid support, but not in the most substantial way, like my everything chair did. It was incredibly easy to go long hours without realizing the C-shape formed in my spine, only called to attention when a radiating soreness set in. I was wheeling up the road away from the dam, and I saw a sign signaling a hiking trail at a turn-off up ahead.

The parking lot looked like it had just been dug out the day before, with one extension of road looping around and disappearing down underneath the interstate. Another fork of dirt road rose up the canyon side, angling off to the right out of view. I love breathtaking scenes where I can see for miles around, so I chose the uphill path, rather than the moderate downhill one that sank into the red rock depths under the highway. It must have been nearing a hundred degrees, humidity following suit. Everything was red rocks and cyan skies and immense.

I'm a real shirt-soaker. Put me in the sun, spur me into exercise, and I get dripping wet pretty quick. I like to think that part of it is condensation caking my forehead, especially when the micro-beaded droplets start forming. I like to think that, and that theory may hold some water itself, but really I just sweat like a damn pig. Always have, always will. Back home in Utah, where the mid-summer temperatures top one-o-five, I could fill you a glass with my own human-juice just off a three-mile run. I'm not a large man either, quite the opposite, really. The perspiration gene must run in my DNA because my dad is the exact same way. But my brother isn't. Guess he got skipped. Must be nice.

I think my brother got the good hair genes, too. I was in my early twenties when I started seeing my hair thin out, its frontline receding back further than my ears. It made a little widow's peak in the middle, and, when styled right, didn't look too awful. But the thing about too awful is that it still has the flavor of awful. And who wants to walk around dealing with that. Just like my profuse sweating, I'm not interested in trying to make things stay on me that are actively trying to leave. I like to think I'm good company, but my swampy ass and diminishing hairline didn't think so. They could kick rocks for all I care, I've got better things to do. This path is uphill and the temperatures are trying to top the Logan summer beats. I've got better things to do than engage in negotiations with the strands of hair that once were.

So I smeared a thick layer of sunscreen on my blissfully bald head and threw back on some shorts and a shirt that I had already steamed through. This would have to be the final casting call for the undies I was wearing. No way could I sit in a restaurant with these bad-boys on after this adventure and feel good about it. My biggest and brightest grin at a waitress wouldn't make up for that soiled fume. It was all of Vegas right in my trousers.

I hiked on, all the same. Mia was leashed, with the excess cord wrapped tightly around my hand. She often got curious on hikes, super-sniffing all around at every little scent that caught her awareness. But this trail was turning treacherous, steep banks that shot off down the slope and under the interstate on the left and jagged rocks rising high to the right.

She would attempt to leap from one boulder to another, believing herself infinitely more agile than she actually was. It was only one year prior that Mia and I were traveling through Yosemite National Park, and we stopped to do a little bouldering and catch a few fantastic views before rocketing out of the park on the final night. Bouldering alone is already a dumb enough idea, but toss a leashless dog into the mix and you're just asking for it. And it almost got us.

There was a steep rock face, and I wasn't even sure if I wanted to make the leap for it, but before I could decide, Mia lunged and landed and immediately experienced little doggy regret. Staring down the rock face, her paws were grippy but not on this much of an incline. She started sliding, and the drop was at least ten feet into more unleveled boulders and sharp cobblestones. I had two feet to consider when landing, she had four. She was sliding fast and my eyes were wide and I had a clarifying break in calling myself a God-damned idiot.

In a moment I don't think I'll ever forget, crystallized in time and memory, I screamed her name in true fear. I howled it like a Yellowstone wolf shrieking into the valleys and ravines of pine and moon-shine. I heard the nightmare in my own voice. I matched my terror with action, jumping over to the sheared boulder, gripping her collar in my dominant hand, while using my other hand to anchor myself to the ledge like an action hero. I didn't feel heroic. I felt like a careless moron. Then I hoisted her up the boulder face, sternly telling her to stay while I threw my legs up and crested the rock myself.

I don't think she would have died if she fell, and I know I wouldn't have. But she would have broken her legs, and there's a seven-in-ten chance I would have too. Those stones below were angled all wrong for landing in. We agree that a leash is the best remedy for her curiosity when we walk through dangerous places. We also agree that better decision making on my part is an even better one—remedies for my own stupidity, for the things I know I'm lacking. Be grateful. Say it. Always. Grateful was a leash in the wild-west Nevada rockland.

We reached a little nook, where three or four boulders had fallen on top of each other, forming a cave-like point of interest on the ridgeline. This was the only place forward or backward that would offer any respite from the high-noon sun, by the looks of it. We both crawled up into the space, and I pulled out a collapsible silicone water bowl, pouring a third of my bottle out for Mia to hydrate. We both gulped and gulped, her shlop-shlop-shlopping and me bobbing my Adam's apple up and down until my canteen was empty.

The view wasn't all that stunning, truth be told. The sky was clearing more and more, clouds dissipating, reevaporating higher into the atmosphere. It was a scene full of Mars rock, dirt, sand, and right through the middle cut the interstate. Cars, trucks, and trailers caterpillar-ed their way along, far enough away that their speed appeared to have dropped from eighty to twenty-five. The occasional yellow-green shrub dotted the scene, a marvel that something could grow out here at all amid the pebbles and stones that chipped and crunched underfoot. Power lines ran down the ridgeline, further detracting from the natural essence of this desert escape.

I didn't feel like I had escaped anything. Mia's beating hot breath was wrapping me in the face, her tongue dripping white bubbles of water and saliva onto the tops of my sneakers. I drank all my water, sweat caked all over my pounding head, dripping down my chest, soaking into my tank top. Zombie-boulevard ran down the front of my underwear, looped up and out the back. I was rank as hell. My head felt a bit burned, despite my best efforts at creaming it with sunblock. Anytime any part of my pale and perspired skin brushed the crimson stone, it stuck to me like glue, little red dust particles clinging to me like germs searching for a host. Savage Nevada was trying to get inside me. The weight of one-too-many tangles with Mary-Jane hooked my eyelids, dragging them halfway across my eyeballs. I'm sure the whites of my eyes were about as red as the dirt plastered to the palms of my hands.

I sat there, breathing in an empty sea, listening to the hum of echoing engines bounce off the canyon walls. Not much of an escape, not sure where to go next, not believing in my ability to figure any of that out. And I sat discontent and watched mechanical worms etch up the road. They were going somewhere, all of them going somewhere. And I wasn't.

I like to scream, I like to cry, I like opening my little brown book and scribbling every venomous, confusing, enlightening thought that's bouncy-balling around my brain. That practice turned my bouncy-ball into a Tetris block, aligning it nicely, compartmentalizing each little hour, day, month, and year of my cerebral trash can into something that sort of made sense. If it was aligned in my little brown book, on little pinstriped rows, it didn't have to cause me any more grief in toiling up in my head. Once it was on the page, it wasn't mine anymore, just like Bill said. It was the world's baggage to carry. A thought wasn't reality, an idea wasn't the actualization of truth. Thoughts and ideas are nothing. They don't inhabit the same world we do, Mia dripping drool everywhere, me sweating bullets. I can wipe my forefinger through her congealing spit and leave a trailed smudge. I can wipe that same finger through the puddles of human-juice gathering in the crotches of my elbows, and I'll feel it, I'll see it, I'll smell it. And sometimes I might even taste it for good measure. It's all real and physical.

But when I sit atop a dehydrated mountain, with my dusty-ass planted like roots into the bedrock, thinking about my existence, pondering the infinitesimal paths I could take, trolling my prefrontal cortex with my inability to read a NO FIREARMS ALLOWED sign, wishing I could be just as perfectly controlled as a rodent-devouring hawk, breaking my addicted brain on the desire for more with Mary-Jane—I'm not doing anything. None of that is real, it's nothing—simple little pink-meat-cocktails, and when you tip them upside down, nothing spills out. All empty glasses, their insides covered in dead flecks of dust from how long they've been idle. And they were idle, and I sat and watched in thought.

So I like screaming, I love crying, and I fucking live to open that little brown book and scribble every bleeding drop of venomous, confusing, enlightening goop that's oozing around inside my brain. Screams are real—they're heard, they're felt, they leave scars on your lungs and steal your voice away, and when you go to order a burger from McDonald's, you'll open your mouth and a squeaky, hoarse sound will eke out and you'll remember what it was like to hate, to love, to do something with the boiling broth inside your head. Tears are real, too—embodying emotive reactions, their salt content is the extracted poison of your soul, manifested in rivers running down your cheeks. Tears are real and they let you know that when they slide through raw cuts and sting a little.

But when you put real black ink in order down little pinstriped lines, you make sense of the complete chaos of nothingness in your head. You're willing to life something far greater than you. You're living for the unlived, unknown, uncertain substance jam-packed into the shrink-wrapped dome that rests atop your neck. You're looking your ancestors dead in the eye as you bring into being everything they ever died for. You're moving, you're acting, you're scraping your knees, scabbing your elbows like a bright-eyed little boy playing in the dirt with swords and axes. You're writing in your own blood that maybe you have what it takes to leap.

I opened my day-hiking backpack, digging around past an empty water canteen and Mia's roll of scat bags. It wasn't there. Of course it wasn't there. I left my little brown book back down in my rocket ship. A lot of good it was doing me down there, pages cooking in the hundred-and-fifty degree black-leather sauna the car was turning into. I imagined the ink in my little silver pen reaching a boiling point, ejecting out the tip in a dark, seedy mess, staining the rest of my clean clothes midnight. The crimson gore in my skull felt just about the same, bubbling and boiling until it, too, would escape out my ears. And I had no water left to counteract the attack. And I hadn't escaped. I was just talking to myself.

I rose to my feet, gathering my bag and dusting off the little red martian cling-ons stuck to my elbows and palms. Time to start the descent back to the car, a hundred degrees and all. I've never known what all the fuss of going uphill was about. Downhill always seemed a lot more dangerous. When you walk downhill, your momentum is moving that way, carrying you bottomward. At some juncture, it becomes less about muscle exertion and more about foot aim. That must be the catch with moving down—it takes little to nothing to start and a whole lot less to keep going. But are the shin-splints worth it? One slip, one micro-mess-up and you're cascading with all that built-up momentum rushing in behind you. That, and anything else you knocked loose on your careless tumble. And these sandstone slabs aren't all that sturdy.

Uphill is a much more calculated struggle—and it is that, a struggle. Especially in a hundred-degree desert heat. But it's one you can rely on your calf and thigh muscles for, taken at your own dedicated pace, with something awe-inspiring as the reward. Even if it's just the ability to rest those exerted, brawny tendons and tissues at the tippy-top. But more often than not, the treasure trove you get to keep once you mount an uphill war far outweighs the tip-toe game you play when you bounce downhill. If hiking has taught me one thing, it's that little physical lesson. But I'm going downhill now, and I'm cooking and slipping onto my butt and my feet are sloshing around in my soaking wet socks. I'm sweating, really sweating now. Mia's tongue was dripping and panting hard, and I wondered if life would be better in a constant state of hyperventilation or to be cursed with a weeping, salty body. She panted and I sweated and we both went downhill.

I slumped into the flaming hot front seat of my car. It felt like my rocket engines had turned on me, barreling in swathes of molten lava-air. As I pulled back out of my parking spot, I rolled down my windows, a futile gesture in an attempt to cool down mine and Mia's bodies. Everything was hot, everywhere was hot, and there was scarcely anything I could do about it. I thought about stopping by a local library, stepping inside for an hour or two to soak up some chilled air. But what about Mia? She couldn't join me inside, and she sure as hell couldn't sit in the drinkable humid heat that pressurized inside my tent-on-wheels. I smacked myself for not getting her registered as an emotional support animal again. What a complete hindrance that neglect was turning out to be. I toyed with the idea of buying a cute little doggy vest, sewing together a little badge of my own that claimed she was as much an emotional supporter as any other already-enlisted pet. No one would doubt her, she was well behaved—listening to my commands, never barking, ears always perked and methodical in her movements. Well, for the most part. There was that time in Yosemite.

Instead of augmenting her to fit in my box of needs, I unconsciously chose to augment me to fit in hers. Libraries, mid-day visits to grocery stores, or indoor coffee shops—they would have to be sacrificed on this wandering expedition. Everything except in-car and outside activity would have to be given up whenever the temperature was above seventy-five. Below that? I could do whatever I wanted, go where I pleased and Mia would happily relax in the cozy, moderate car cabin, windows cracked, watching the movie of the world. May in southern Nevada doesn't dip below that temperature grade all that often, so a majority of the day would be consigned to parks and recreation, or idle lounging in my ship, begging for the A/C to work its magic. Always begging and never getting what I wanted. And it was just hot.

As I wheeled onto the freeway, Hell's winds rushing past my face, I began to understand what it must have been like to live in the old days, trudging across the plains as a pioneer. I mean, I had a third-of-a-tank of gas, toting over a hundred pounds of gear, easy access to food and water, and a fair bit of technology at my fingertips. Not to mention I was zipping at seventy and had asphalt roads to follow. So maybe I didn't understand it to a very high degree, but the heat—that aspect I caught a glimpse of.

When something in the outside world prompts a physiological response, especially one with a lot of oomph, it tends to take up a disproportionate percentage of brain space and awareness. When you're blistering hot, sweating endless bullets—well, that's the only thing on your mind. You aren't playing with new hypotheses on what makes Rorschach's ink-blots such bullshit, you aren't stress-testing the Pythagorean theorem, you aren't applying the third law of thermodynamics in new and unique ways. You're just hot, your brain's hot, and your brain's telling you you're hot. And it was.

It's a small wonder how singularity can only be hit once humanity stops worrying about being comfortable, being physically safe, not fretting over being eaten by lions and bears. Once we are able to sit, cross our legs in a moderate climate, free from our fight-or-flight instinct, we get to really think. We start writing, we start producing, building, crafting, acting, painting. We start changing the world around us, melding it into something new and different. Damn if that can't happen in a hundred-and-four degree scorcher.

I opened Google Maps on my phone, scrolling around the barrens of Vegas and beyond, searching for something to occupy my time for the remainder of the day. I had already been out west on Blue Diamond Road past Calico Basin and stayed in Lovell Canyon, already driven in from the north when I arrived on my first evening. I had already tried south, sleeping in Boulder City. The only option left was to try my luck east. I swiped over to the right side of Clark County, scanning the map in the palm of my hand with careful eyes. They met Lake Mead, and I instantly felt inspired to try that place out. After all, I needed a bath and it wasn't that far from where I was. And water is cool. It better be cool.

There was a little shack up ahead, the only building for miles, designed in a desert-stucco theme. Adjacent to the structure was a mechanical arm that kept cars from blowing right past the gate attendant into Lake Mead National Park. I pulled up, now attempting to read every word on the sign before me. Everything seemed clear, aside from the inflated price figure slapped on in little red stickers. A ransom to pay in order to raise that mechanical arm and let me in. But hey, I drove all the way out here, I was here anyways. It was a one-lane ride into the park, so turning around wasn't much of an option. I might as well fold and fork over the dough. I looked around for zombies. I didn't see any. There might have been one or two down by the lakeside.

The park entrance attendant sat in her little booth, getting the shit beat out of her by the heat, just like I was. She still smiled, all the same, and greeted me with an I-love-my-job-I-promise tone of voice. She didn't have to tell me. We exchanged information, me asking a few questions about what there was to do down by the water, her answering everything in far more detail than I needed. More detail than I needed, but the perfect amount of information that I wanted. God sent us people like her on purpose—they take care of us, they employ their ethic in everything they do. They live for it. And out here, in the middle of an igneous skillet, this woman was still livin'. I got a little ASMR (autonomous sensory meridian response) tingle on the back of my neck and spine as she went out of her way to make my day just a hair better. I smiled a lot and she smiled a lot and she reminded me of Cassady and the other treetop elves back home.

Those ASMR videos on YouTube work, but not like this. I have never gotten the strength of response from a YouTube view than I get when I see, hear, and feel someone genuinely going out of their way to help me or improve a few moments of my life. If you haven't felt that sensation, and you're cruising through every early-twenties chick on the internet looking for something that works, stop. You won't find the meal of meridian there. Just a snack is all. Instead, pause and really—truly—watch someone next time they do something for you. But they gotta want to do it, and you gotta want to see it. And we did.

She mentioned a National Parks pass that went for eighty bucks, which seemed insanely steep. I was running on semi-meager funds, trying to save every penny I could for my restaurant visits and gas station bills. And my bank numbers were only going one way, just like this federal road—down. Then she told me that it would get me into any National Park in the country. The whole of these United States of America. I immediately sling-shot forward in time, running through ten vignettes of all the parks I would be passing on my road trip. And every one charged twenty bucks to enter—visit four parks, or the same park four times, and that's a pass that's paid for. I handed over the eighty, and she handed me the card and front mirror holder for it in my rocket ship, signifying my high status of National Park Explorer. I thought that was pretty damn cool.

The drive down to the lakefront was well maintained, routed through switchbacks descending to water level. I parked my car, hopping out into a far less harsh sun. It was early evening, and the temperature was in a steady decline, now tipping back into the low nineties. I started loosening the straps that secure my kayak to the top of my car, elated with excitement since this was the first time I'd ever used it. My rocket ship was breaking through the atmosphere, and I was about to drop the dead weight, blasting off in a whole new kind of adventure-craft.

I slid the boat across the rack atop my car, bearing the weight on my arms and bent-over upper back. I attempted to keep a solid posture, lifting with my legs. It wasn't overly heavy, mostly just awkward to handle alone. This was one element I had stress-tested already, lifting the kayak on and off my car at home before setting sail on the open road. It would have been outrageous to get all the way out here and find myself incapable of maneuvering the thing off my rocket ship's roof. Jeez, what a massive oversight that would have been. At least I saw that sign. NO WEAK BITCHES ALLOWED. Get me a bumper sticker with those letters on it and I'll plaster it to the inside of my balding fivehead. I grunted the words out loud, toting the kayak like Jesus with the cross on his way to do the deed of sacrifice. And I was on my way.

As I oared the smooth waters of Lake Mead, breaking for the middle, I took some deep breaths, leaning back into my cushy little kayak seat. Mia was perched on the bow, standing stout with her front two paws on the gunwale. As far as I knew, this was her first boat adventure. I had tied a bright orange life jacket to her collar—the kind you find in an emergency under your seat on ferries—and wrapped the excess strap in a secure belt around her belly and backside. I committed to myself that one day I would spend the right money in the right place to get her the right kind of life jacket that would fit her perfectly. But this U-shaped eyesore would have to do for now. All the same, it would keep her afloat if she slipped in, and it was less than ten bucks, and she was bit-chomping to test it out.

Mia's little padded paws slipped off the front end, blown overboard by the forward momentum of my paddling, sending her plummeting into the dark waters of Lake Mead. She didn't bark or yelp, didn't make a sound. Just a hilarious little splash that I immediately started cackling at. So calculated and careful sometimes, and at others, downright clumsy. This dog. In her shock of being engulfed by water, she turned, saw the shore a half a mile away, and started doggy-paddling in a dead-straight line for the beach.

For all the folks overly concerned with my carelessness, or Mia's likelihood of drowning, I'll put your anxiety at ease. She wasn't gonna sink, and I sure wasn't gonna let her swim the half-mile back. That being said, I was choking on my own spit, har-de-haring so hard at her slight misfortune that I let out a snort or two. All while I reamed a bit quicker against the water, pulling up beside her while she desperately attempted to reach the shore. I snuck my fingers beneath her life jacket, yanking her out of the water and back into the boat. She stood, soaked in a refreshing coat of liquid, and shook herself out all over me. We were both laughing now. The water was cool and we breathed out the desert and took in oasis.

She immediately remounted the front of the kayak in true Kate Winslet fashion, placing both of her front paws right back where they were when she accidentally slipped and fell in. Her chest was puffed up and out, a confident young pupper commanding the slice of our ship through glassy waters. I was surprised by her willingness to assume the exact position that had originally caused her plummet—but then again, dogs usually take a few tries to get something adequately in one ear, in hopes it doesn't fly out the other. But then again, so do I. Sitting there, leaning back in my little beige boat, I stared deep into the back of Mia's skull, understanding that both of us just liked learning things the hard way. Slick against the plastic edge, her little legs slipped again and she dunked herself over the rim and back into the water. This dog.

It occurred to me in Mia's little plunge and second subsequent dart for the shore, that she really liked doing things the hard way. Now probably closer to three-quarters of a mile away from the shore, there was no way she would have the energy for such a swim. And I, of course, wasn't going to let her try. It seemed counterintuitive that she should point her nose toward some far-off place, beyond her capable reach, and burn out her muscles in a forlorn attempt to escape the engulfing lake. Meanwhile, I was floating right beside her, beckoning her to the boat side, shouting my presence, laughing at her ignorance. She was gonna go for land, or she was gonna die trying. Don't you know you'll drown out here?

Once again, I laced my fingers under her life jacket and lobbed her back into the safety of the kayak. Once again, she shook her water-logged fur out all across my face and body, splattering my sunglasses with little liquid droplets. We both rolled around in the boat, laughing and cackling like a pair of hyenas, soaking each other in the waters of Lake Mead. It was warm and cool and wonderful and her eyes were deep brown like the mountains back home and she smiled and wagged her tongue everywhere. And I was grateful to have a friend.

We were nearing the shoreline, so instead of gently brushing against the sand, I grabbed the starboard and port gunwales and in one sloppy throw, flipped the kayak, sending both Mia and myself upside down into the five-foot deep waters. I rose, swinging my head back like an Instagram model, flinging all the hair I didn't have. By the time I had surfaced and wiped my eyes, Mia was already panting with a huge grin, legs half-covered by four inches of lake water. She had raced up-shore in no time at all. Her head suddenly turned as an angry voice bellowed out across the lakefront.

My own massive grin flatlined, as I immediately started scanning several other vehicles scattered in various alignments, about twenty-five yards back from the shoreline. Off to the left, there was a Toyota Tacoma parked, with one renegade-looking dude shouting at an unseen person still residing in the truck. The man had a dark goatee, spearing out to a point several inches below his chin. He wore a pair of wrap-around sunglasses, black hat backwards, shorts hanging a bit too low down his butt. My gut judgment told me a man yelling at someone in public would probably look just like this. Judgment or not, he kept shouting at the anonymous person sitting in the front seat.

I couldn't clearly make out full sentences, but I could hear the anger, and Mia's perked-up ears could too. One phrase I could hear was his liberal use of the fuck word in between every chunk of inaudible blabber. The front door to the truck opened, and a slender young woman stepped out onto the gravel-sand mixture that paved the lot. She had long coffee-colored hair framing her face, along with a pair of pink wayfarer-style sunglasses. Once she got out of the truck, bombarded by insult and cuss, she hung her head in embarrassment. I glanced around the beach, taking note of another family or two scattered down the sand, now folding up their camping chairs and repacking coolers. The man kept on with the verbal battery, the woman hung her head a little lower. I grimaced.

Far be it from me to get involved, I started dragging my kayak up the sand toward my car. I quickened my pace slightly, unnerved by the man's complete disregard for the woman's public experience and right to privacy. And his infringement on mine. The sun was setting behind the rows of switchbacks up the hill, temperature now hovering in the mid-eighties. Aside from the unwelcome malice the renegade brought with him, all was calm and still. It bothered me that he felt so entitled to stain that purity with a sheet of lingual diarrhea.

He reminded me of a little boy, toddler-aged, stamping around, throwing a massive fit. His diaper-shorts hanging low, filled with piss and shit that his mommy never cleaned out. He screamed and cried and didn't get his way, and he wanted everyone to know it and be miserable with him. He balled up his little fists and maddeningly punched them at his hips, trouncing around like it was mommy's job to make it alright. Much more of this and he'd fall into the gravel and start kicking his furious little feet back and forth, wailing like a sad little prick, ruining everyone's national park escape. I had escaped. And now he was messing it all up.

The renegade's display of anger was pretty weak, truth be told. More of a fit, less of a freak. All the same, pissing and shitting your diaper in public is despicable. It's despicable in private, too, but at least everyone doesn't have to sit and smell it. Someone get this dude one of those weak-bitch bumper stickers, paste it to his wrap-around sunnies.

More than anything, I felt bad for the woman. She was embarrassed beyond belief, probably lamenting the day she said yes to this high school sweetheart and got hitched to him at eighteen. He was still yelling, and I still wasn't listening, and I don't think she was either. The words didn't matter—he may well have been beating his flat, muscle-less chest, grunting out monkey calls like the ass-ape he was. Clearly, it hadn't occurred to him that no one wanted in on his degeneracy, and treating someone like shit in public earns you no sympathy, no company in your misery. I had escaped and he was ruining it. His piss and shit-filled jean-short-diaper was starting to smell, green comic scent-trails eking out, crawling across the pebbles and dirt and into my nostrils. I scoffed at the fitting boy who didn't care for control, ruinous and belligerent. I had escaped and he was ruining it.

I reassembled my rocket ship, strapping down my kayak to the roof, doing everything a little louder than normal. Maybe he would hear me, notice me, and shut his dumb, dense mouth. Save it for later. In fact, save it for never. All the same, if this was Mr. Renegade in public, I wouldn't care one bit to see him in private. That poor woman. Those poor jean-shorts. I was mad and contempt pushed a bead of sweat out my temple. I rolled down my window and broke the zombie rules, caring too much about what the other shamblers were doing.

"Hey, buddy!" I yelled in a low, growly tone. "Why don't you try shutting the fuck up, yeah?" His head spun around and our sun-glassed eyes locked and he whipped out his middle finger and I shook my head and chuckled and gave him two middles back. Mia and I headed up the switchbacks.

The sun was setting, prompting my nightly ritual of searching for an adequate spot to park and sleep for the night. Adequate wasn't even half of it. The shoulder of most roads can be labeled as adequate. But adequate doesn't mean safe, legal, or logical. I didn't want adequate sleep, I wanted good sleep, deep sleep—and how I felt about where I parked was completely indicative of the quality of sleep I'd get. I wanted to fall asleep with visions of sugar-plums dancing in my head, not nightmares of maggot-fiends beating me, or police officers banging on my window with their batons. It didn't matter the likelihood of those horrors occurring, it all was tied to the vibe and possibility of the place. Reality be damned.

Before I knew it, I was back on zombie boulevard put-put-putting my way down the Strip, tearing open a wound that was a few stitches from being sealed. How many times would I dangle this undead place in front of my eyes, tempting myself with a night of solo gambling, solo drinking, solo smoking, solo strip-club hunting? It was clear I wasn't on this trip to engage with any of that, but for some habitual reason, I couldn't understand that. I knew it, wrote it, slammed it into my skull a hundred times, but it was just a fact I thought about, not words I believed or individualized. I threw myself into the quicksand, pointed my nose to the place where the lights buzz and neon streaks your eyes and everyone is mushed and blurry. The motherland of accepted foibles and rotting flesh and sex and skin everywhere. Swimming for a shore, swimming hard and slicing wide for the place I was familiar with. Don't you know you'll drown out here?

Mars is scary. Everything uncertain, everything a foreign amalgamation. You try stomping around like it's the Earth you know and you'll get yourself killed. But don't let that turn you back, because it's either another step while you die trying, or it's nothing.

Chapter 10

Just Powerade

South Point Hotel and Casino was up ahead, and I was convinced they had free parking. I was also convinced it was far enough down the Strip that I wouldn't be bothered by local homeless schmucks or dead-drunk zombie bleeders stumbling and screaming all night. Plus, it seemed like a solid launching pad for my exit from Clark County in the morning. It was golden and glowing while the sun peeked between the pastel clouds, half sunk under the horizon already. Hopeful and teetering May. One more night in the land of the dead, and my bones were feeling a little black and I had scarcely played any of the Vegas games.

I stayed at South Point once before, years prior, when some friends and I came here for our first no-holds-barred, all-or-nothing, parentless undertaking in the city of sin. There were six of us, all cramming into one hotel room with two queen beds. Two of us slept on the floor, the other four cuddled in the queens. I was a floor sleeper on that trip, thinking that small comforts didn't matter. I was there to get fucked up, drink enough that the position I passed out into wouldn't matter once I zombie-shambled my way back to the hotel room. If I was sore in the morning, I'd chug an iced coffee, top-up my Just Powerade and start all over. My liver didn't get a say in the matter, and neither did my lungs, as we smoked so many Black 'n Milds and vaped so much Juul with no consequences that we all thought we were invincible. And we were. It was wild and reckless and we salivated at everything. It was all the good stuff. We hooped and hollered in our hotel room and went out on the town dressed in black collared shirts, acting like the big man upstairs with oversized, flamboyant watches on our wrists.

Our favorite was Just Powerade. A simple little concoction that cost next to nothing to produce on the round mini-table in our hotel room. One of our bags would typically be crammed with various flavors of Powerade, stocked up on a buy-two-for-three-bucks deal at Walgreens. We'd crack the cap, breaking those little plastic bridges that seal the lid together with the lip, and swallow five or six gargantuan gulps of alcohol-free energizer. Next came the Vodka. Or rum. Or whatever liquor we could get for under twenty bucks a handle. We'd fill the vacated space within the bottle, tainting it with the nose-singing scent of cheap booze. Lid went back on, screwed tight, and we'd shake and shake the bottle till it was mixed juuuust right. Lid came back off, more gulps followed as we pre-gamed our way around the hotel room. Once we'd passed a bottle around, drank it down a third the way, we'd fill it right back up with more firewater, shake it like it was a blender-bottle, rinse and repeat. I have no idea what the record for refills was, but eventually, it started tasting like the ratio had flipped in favor of the liquor.

We were damned brilliant. Each of us with our Powerade flavor of choice in hand, collared shirts and ironed slacks donned, we'd exit the hotel room and join the rest of the zombies breaking their clumsy way up and down zombie boulevard. No one questioned us and our secret cocktails, and if they did—hey man, it's Just Powerade.

I'm sure the card dealers at South Point could smell the satanic mix of high fructose corn syrup and plastic-bottle-vodka permeating our breath. Those belches could light a match, that is, until we covered the scent up with more cigars and vape. Too bad we couldn't whore ourselves out on Mary-Jane back then (Nevada wasn't a legal state yet). But if a substance left us a little more numb, a little more jaded on reality, and a little clumsier, we were sucking it down, gallon upon gallon. We may have been young, dumb, and broke, but we weren't naive enough to follow a beckoning drug dealer behind the local CVS. Young, dumb, broke, with shreds of rationality poking through here and there. Dear ole Sister Eubank would have been so proud at the Powerade surrounded by all that vodka.

I pulled into the South Point lot now, slowly pouring down row after row of cars. The lot stretched far around the golden structure, leaving those who parked on the outskirts to a lengthy luggage-ridden stumble to get inside. Even the spaces on the fringes of the lot were taken, so filled up with gamblers and slot-spinners it took several rounds down each and every row of this mechanical paradise to find its g-spot. So many folks come down from the hills and out of the woodland somewhere to rent a room and go nowhere. Just to the hotel lobby, where the games happen and everything is dimmed and clicking and wallets grow thin and weary. I swung wide into my home-sweet-home slot for the night, flipping my keys for the last time till morning.

As I sat in my back seat, lounged out, legs resting up front on the middle console, I caught a glimpse of a hotel security car making the same rounds I had, up and down the rows, one after another. Except, he wasn't searching for a spot to shut his engine off. He was on an endless prowl, looking for naughty little moochers like me. Or so I had convinced myself. I quickly embraced the stealth aspect of my journey, moving around a little slower so the car wouldn't wiggle. I hardly peeked my head up above the back window dash, and when I did, it was only my eyes that were revealed as I spied on patrols and speed-walking newcomers, dragging their plastic suitcase wheels against the pavement.

Every time the security cop drove past my tent-on-wheels, he seemed to slow, peering out through his tinted windows at me, or beyond—I couldn't tell. Eventually, after several passes, I shoved my sunshades in the back window, as I did every night before bed, blocking any view from the outside in. I was banking on the guard not remembering that these back windows were clear on his previous drive-bys. After all, there were hundreds of cars out here, and a Volkswagen is a common enough vehicle to see anywhere you go.

It was dark and humid, the sky encased in a velvet sheet of stratified clouds. Rain started falling, sounding off in little pits and pats on the roof of my car, bouncing off my kayak, splashing down the windshields and windows. I had never seen so much rain on so many consecutive days in the desert. It didn't rain here, it was dead and dry and tumbleweeds paraded down mainstreet like July 4th. But it started raining again. Maybe the midnight stratosphere was weeping for me, wracked at my inability to rip the bandaid off and move along to somewhere with a little more substance, a little more meaning. A little less blackening of the bones. Maybe up above they were frowning in disbelief, unapproving of my chosen destination. Maybe they wanted me to know it, see their tears dribbling down the glass of my mobile home. And they were. And I saw them and smoked the night away.

As each drop carved its way through the desert dust and grime plastered to my windows, they picked up sediment, leaving a shiny new trail while infecting the droplet with weight. Many of the early beads never made it down the full span of glass, stopping three-quarters of the way through their streak, laden with a mucky vice of their own. Crystal tears turned clumps of dirt, separating from the soaked glass membrane of my car, plummeting down onto the asphalt. It was all the same, inevitable that each pure heaven-sent tear should be polluted, leaving in their wake a new path for more tears to follow.

As the mire encasing my rocket ship began to wash away, more tears trail-blazed downward, forming more streams for new tears to take. Tributaries of water and mud became one shimmering ocean pulled across my windows, wiping my chassis clean. The pits and pats of the sobbing God intensified, wave after wave, baptizing my home, washing away all the sin, all the worry, all the anxiety pressurized within.

It didn't make sense to me that a place so dry as southern Nevada could produce so much water, let alone withstand the coming torrent. The ground never soaked up the tears, filled with rock and sand and dead-root. There was evidence everywhere you looked that the soil of this place rejected stratospheric tears. Leaving them to flash-flood the low places of the land, until they eventually—inevitably—washed away into the deep and dark Colorado River and Lake Mead. Collected and stored behind the Hoover slab, used once again to power the meat and mean of a million little neon bulbs shining oh-so-bright up and down zombie boulevard.

How perverse that the weeping angels of heaven were so inadvertently fueling shamblers who gaze upward, fulminating our God-given, self-driven agony. We shine our Luxor-pyramid-born brights at the skies and make the lever-pullers wince, and when they cry we use that for power, too. Cursing our ailing bodies, chomping and gnashing our rotten teeth through maggot-ridden beef and lamb, begging for a penny, a dime, and nickel, anything to augment our current state of mind. Anything to escape from our dehydrated lives, anything to make us feel like we're livin'. Anything to smear our pearly-white clothes with so many clods of corrupted dirt, swimming in shit and wondering why we stink. Less and less shirts that are white with some dirt on them, more and more just black shirts. And black bones.

I sat there, dawdling in a long caesura, blowing out smoke rings from my Mary-Jane-filled crackpipe. Eyebrows raised halfway up my fivehead, eyelids dragged halfway down my eyeballs. I was far away, escaped to a land of pennies, nickels, and dimes, augmenting my mind so much I forgot I had pee.

Shit. Another wondrous adventure of pinching my pecker till I could find the perfect place to piss. I told you I never figured out how to solve the potty problem. And here it was again, knocking at the door. The endless function.

I peered through my weeping windows, peeking around the sunshade still wedged in my back windshield—the patrolling guard was nowhere in sight. I opened the back passenger door, hopping out while chiming over my shoulder to Mia that I would be right back. I'd always be right back.

I shambled my way across the lot, dragging a bladder-luggage of my own. Luckily, if one or two drops leaked out this time, it was raining outside, so a little drip stain could be mistaken as a bout with inclement weather. Not that any fellow zombies inside South Point would take half a second's notice. They were clinking and roaring and leaning back and forward and hooting all at the same time. It was raining out here, in the West where rain never fell. Raining and humid and no one inside South Point would ever know. And they didn't.

The inside of South Point was scarlet-gold and low-lit, decorated with brilliant chandeliers and ornate carpets, deep-oak poker tables and scantily dressed bartenders. Always dressed in too-too skirts with low-cut tops that showed off all the cleavage in the world. They barely smiled and wore their work uniforms and balanced oversized trays teeming with whiskey, gin, and rum-tummy drinks. The casino was clicking away, semi-circles of gamblers and onlookers cheering and commiserating together. The ringing of a thousand slot machines echoed off the paisley-painted walls. It was the west and southern place they all wanted to go, and they were here now, throwing away their wallets to the big man upstairs.

I speed-walked past the first table I ever played blackjack at, years ago. The dealer still looked the same, and the skeletons fielding his cards and betting their chips still looked the same. No one had moved in the years since my time there, Just Powerade in one hand, robot-penis vape-stick in the other. Time passed differently here, where mirrors lined the front and back walls, giving the illusion of infinite opportunity—juuuust one of those games would give it to you big, surely. And no one at the slot-troughs ever shrieked and gathered up their gold like a goblin hoarding treasure as you see in the movies. They just sat and watched and pushed the buttons and lost and lost, and won a dime once, then lost three more times. They chain-smoked Lucky Strikes and waited for their not-so-free drinks, giving over their reward cards to the hotel and comped free rooms for next time, when they'd be back out west and south to do it all over again. And they always were.

No windows here, no possible way of telling night from day within this shining castle. It was raining outside and none of them would ever even know. Even the inch-thick glass doors of entry were sheathed in a dark tint to prevent too much sunlight from getting inside. No visible clocks, no way to tell time aside from pulling out your phone or glancing at your watch. But no one cared about those things here—time, night, day, heaven's tears, bank accounts, mirror mind-tricks—just a laundry list of barriers that control people. And dammit, this was the land of the free, home of the undead. And the big man looked down from upstairs and grinned.

I stopped at the semicircle of onlookers riveted by a game of blackjack at that table I once tried to beat. I hadn't intended to stop, but my feet braked, and I was rooted, watching some dumbass with two eights trying to explain to the dealer that he didn't want to split 'em. If you know anything about blackjack, you know that when you get two eights, you split those suckers without a second thought, even on your last dime. This guy had all his priorities wrong, believing that sticking with his dealt-out sixteen was better than giving things a second go, and perhaps doubling the payout. I was shaking my head in disbelief. Everyone in the inner semicircle playing, and everyone on the outer semicircle watching, were all shaking their heads, too. We all knew how to play, knew the rules. This guy was gonna ruin the game for everyone by not hitting for the cards he was supposed to, hiding behind his dumpster-tier sixteen. Sixteen ain't gonna beat the dealer's inevitable nineteen plus. He stayed. The dealer landed a twenty. They all lost.

Everyone groaned, and the dealer moved to the next hand. I shook my head again, this time at myself. I had forgotten my quest for the toilet, sucked back into zombie mind games, if only for a moment. I didn't even notice the gut pain of having to piss while I stood there in disbelief at this unsplitting goon. I broke back into a speed walk, scanning another wall for any signage designating a toilet. In all their mental trickery, they even make it hard to find the bathroom you've been to several times before. Toilet time was just time spent away from gambling, away from slot machines, away from slimming your wallet. Can't have that.

I saw the signs, finally able to relieve myself against the porcelain urinal. Now donning my usual strut, I paced my way back down the rows of betting tables, my eyes always shooting first to the minimum bet amount. Most of them were ten bucks, twenty-five, or even fifty per hand. Too much for me. It was raining outside in the cool evening air, and Mia was fine.

There was only one time I had ever dared a twenty-five-dollar game, years prior, and not at this casino. It was the MGM Grand on a hot summer weekend when the tables were filled and the money-losing was running heavy. But not for me and not for my friends. The only reason we took the risk was because we were already up several hundred, so we thought to increase those gains some more. Miraculously, we did. That specific Vegas expedition still remains the only time I've ever walked away from Mars with more money in my wallet than I arrived with. I call it a lucky fluke. But it was a hot and sticky summer and the tables invested enough.

South Point had just a couple five dollar tables, which were more to my liking. Always better to lose money slower than quicker. Praise be to the one-dollar table at OYO or Hooters or whatever boob-synonym people call it these days.

I stopped again, peeking in on a different five-dollar table than the one with the unsplitter. There were a few empty chairs, ripe for the taking, and no outer circle of waiting zombies to have their turn at gnawing. This was it. My last chance to get in on some action, maybe make back some money I had spent on this little road trip and have a bit of fun in the process. I'd win—I bet I'd win. Get a couple free drinks, relive the glory days, only this time I was flying solo and it was raining outside, cool and calm and Mia would be just fine. I could escape into a night of chip-flipping and play basic strategy blackjack like it gave me better odds than fifty percent.

This was it, now or never. The six-deck stack was about to be reshuffled, the perfect time to join in. The zombies gnawing at this table were older, and juuuust drunk enough that sparking up conversation would be easy and hilarious. They seemed to be winning, each with a big flesh-filled grin on their face and smoke in their eyes. One of them pulled out a Black 'n Mild, flipping his lighter open and brazing the end to a cherry-red tip, puffing out a hearty cloud of sweet-smelling smoke. Another held a cigarette between her middle and forefinger, and in the same hand, swirled around a half-glass of Whiskey Sour, red maraschino cherry bathing in the ice. The dealer made some remark I couldn't hear, and the pair of zombies cackled like hyenas at the unknown joke. That was my favorite—dealers who were animated jokesters. They made everyone's night, and they made more tips for it. The pair of bettors flipped a few one-buck chips onto the tip line and the dealer dealt the hand and this was it.

The stars were aligned for a night of nothing but wins, nothing but free drinks, five-dollar hands, and facetious conversations with a whole bunch of friendly folks. It was perfect. It was the right packaging, the sweet fruity scent of Powerade mixed with four shots of Malibu rum and ready to gorge. The night was right, it felt right, and I was high on it and withering. I'm here anyways, here and now. I waded through all these strange Martian days, escaping foolhardy and thick, ready to enjoy the cool air, ready to do what I wanted when I wanted to. Mia was fine, it was nice outside and raining and the movie of the world was wonderful for her.

I opened the back passenger side door to my car and climbed back in, giving Mia a little scratch behind the ears. I was right back. Alone with my sweet little girl, in a sea of increasing darkness. But tonight, it was one that I chose to bask in. Hidden from view of the patrolman, listening to the pits and pats of stratospheric tears bouncing off my rocket ship. And they bounced and beat with forte. Maybe they were crying happy tears now, proud of my decision to be right back. Proud that, regardless of the situation, I made a decision—and that choice started to stitch back up a wound that I loved to tear open. I walked through that casino, I saw the signs, and they were pointing me right back into the paisley-padded chair I always found myself in, looking for life in all the wrong places. Looking for feel-goods, easy-outs, quick-wins, fast-fixes. Make it all happen now so I can go back to vibing in my weed-induced caesura, twiddling my thumbs, building up all my expectations, thinking up a hundred lucky futures, living none of them.

I stood on the ornate carpet of South Point, and for reasons I still don't know, my shoulders turned, my legs followed, and my feet started walking out of that casino. It wasn't until I had pushed through the weighty tinted doors that my head owl-spun back around and reoriented atop my neck, looking forward into the elongated parking lot. An endless field of machined cows all grazing on soaking wet asphalt. The tears of all those angels ricocheted off my bald head, leaving little wet puddles in their place, draining down across my brow, around my eyes, and down my cheeks. Their tears were mine, I could feel their marrow soak into my skull and down into my bones that were trying to whiten up a little. And they were. A pep in my step, I arrived at my rocket ship, high off a confused and south-western outset I just staked for myself. For once, I felt in control. Maybe not perfect, maybe not complete. But controlling, all the same.

Later that night, I climbed into my sleeping bag and slept like a rock, not stirring or shaking once in the darkness. And I think I made ole Sister Eubank pretty damn proud.

It felt like home.

Chapter 11

Hell's Vents

The morning air blanketed Las Vegas in a stuffy sheet of smog. There wasn't one cloud in the sky, allowing the sun full reign and dominion over a quickening sand-griddle, pan-frying every walk of life into a red-shaded, sweat-seasoned heap of meat. I had a beaded line of perspiration crowning my head. I always did in the daytime languish of this place. I leaned forward, twisted my keys into the ignition, and sparked up my rocket ship. At this point, I didn't care if a patrolman found me out. The worst he'd do was kick me off the lot, and I would be on my way south and west out of Clark County long before that happened.

As I joined stop-and-go traffic on the short stretch of road leading toward the interstate entrance, I flipped open my retro cooler and took a peek inside at how my science project was coming along. There were still visible chunks of ice, but most had melted down, joining the gray papier-mache water, ebbing back and forth with the turns and bumps of the car. The new ice brick additions lightened up the shaded liquid, making it appear a little more clear than the previous morning's cold-brew. I knew I was heading into the open desert today, so another ice pit-stop would be necessary to tie me over for a couple days until I rejoined civilization.

Myself and a thousand other zombie boulevard sunbakers were listing down the freeway, using the main vein that shuttles people from Las Vegas to Los Angeles and back again. From one smoggy stain to another. Like finds like. Like always finds like. And it did, all the cars stopped on the Strip with their little cursive California's painted on the ass-end of their bumpers.

I was deep in the throes of the first Game of Thrones audiobook, having found the perfect cache of literature to entertain myself on all the long drives, all the six-hour plus connector expeditions between one wandering destination and another. Just the first book itself was slated at over thirty hours, so I figured I had plenty of time to get involved.

Everyone always told me to give in to the George R. R. Martin fantasy, claiming it was so much better than the widely praised show. It wasn't hard to believe their opinions, as the visual medium rarely surpasses that of the written word. Plus, anything—and I mean just about anything—would beat the shit-show that was the final three seasons of that HBO exclusive. As my brother-in-law always says, Game of Thrones only had five seasons. I nod my head in agreement and try to forget about the worst television travesty in history.

Apparently, in all my anguish watching the finale of season eight, I still yearned for more narrative from the land of Westeros, and thirty hours for just one book would be nothing short of an overdose. Thank God the narrator had a captivating voice, donning different accents and voice inflections for many of the main characters. Thirty hours of the same, monotone bleating would make that peashooter in my glove box look real nice. That trigger wasn't gonna pull itself.

The further south I drove, the fewer cars there were. I couldn't figure out where they were disappearing to. There's an entire span of nothing between Vegas and the southwestern cities of California. As traffic thinned out, the number of lanes followed suit. I had passed a tiny checkpoint named Primm, the last stop before savage Nevada transformed into the Golden State. The mysterious line where taxes went from next-to-nothing to give-me-your-first-born-child, an arm, and a leg. Filling my gas tank suddenly became a serious financial decision, and everyone walked around thinking their government officials were doing all the right things with all that extra dough. I blew over the border and didn't look back toward zombie-land. I was entering a new one. Gold was on the horizon and it was chipper, wide and intrepid May.

The side of the freeway started getting a little more colorful than just swathes of sand and tanned boulders as far as the eye could see. There were little arrangements decorating the sides of the road, spelling out words, slogans, and ideological phrases in a rainbow of spray-painted rocks. I wheeled past them, reading each one, and mentally congratulated the sweaty buggers who trekked all the way out here to the middle of nowhere to plaster billboards of their own into the landscape. Their vibrant colors were a whole lot more welcoming and inspirational than the usual garbage pinned up on steel poles to distract drivers in every other place on earth. I'd take an *Eye for an Eye Leaves the Whole World Blind* rock display over the *You Only Live Once. Get the Lips.* plastic-city billboard any day of the week.

I drove on and on, gripping the steering wheel and shaking my face in a feeble attempt to stay awake. The heat was magnifying through my front windshield and my air conditioning could hardly keep up as wavers of exhaustion crept in. The narrator of Game of Thrones droned on as I barely put sentient thought to the story he was telling, even with his voice augmentations. It was all droning, all speaker-tones and words I couldn't grasp. Stopping out here in the weeds and grit would only eliminate the hope for an A/C victory, only amp up the pulsating heat resonating inside my black leather seats. My pits, creases, and cracks were flooded with sweat, as torrid beams bent me into a hunchback of vacated energy. The C-shape took form and my back was sore and begged for movement and I swayed left and right to stretch.

I had already veered off the freeway, making my way out into the middle of the Mojave. There was no one, there was nothing. Wave after wave of sand and gravel, broken up by the occasional jutting stone. I had a couple of frying eggs sizzling between my ears, tricking me in sound and smell. I was cooking myself alive and only getting hotter. Out on the horizon were dancing shimmers of baking light, flushing and squiggling back and forth. It looked just like stratospheric angel tears leaking down my windshield in veils of blurry water. Only, these must have been Hell's oven vents, broaching from down under, spewing calescent steam out into the mortal world. They wiggled hard and I was in them and broiling.

A dangerous trick nature likes to play on the dehydrated—glancing shrouds of light off the road's surface, making it appear that up ahead, there's water—a little oasis to wet your beak, break your miserable existence with a quick swim-and-soak. Just when you think you've made it, you gaze ahead, and the same pot of gold at the end of the rainbow-road awaits. Just a little further, and surely you'll make it to whatever sheen produces such beauty. A target that never sits still so long as you chase it. And I was chasing it and swaying in the Golden State, dry and hacked to pieces. Another step. Another step.

There were used fire pits scattered off the road—I had made it to the land of free camping. I wasn't interested in any of these spots so far, as most of the pits were way too close to the dusty path I was driving down. I may have been alone now, but that could change any time, and the last thing I wanted was a fresh coat of dirt powder kicked up onto my sweaty skin. There were no laundromats, no lakes, no ways of deep-cleaning my tainted buns out here where the plants and granules of sand had no word for water in their silent conversations. I'd have to rely on the old red-neck whore bath to fend off my encroaching stink. I had a pack of wipes stashed away somewhere. I smoked and steamed like an ant under a magnifying glass.

I spun my wheel left, angling my rocket ship off the track and down a side path that cut through some dying sagebrush and rubble. Twenty-five yards down, the little road widened into a cul de sac, and sitting in the middle was a quaint fire pit with one or two of its rock-teeth missing. I had been roving for hours, body so bent out of shape—this would do nicely. I parked, jumped from my front seat, and Mia lunged out behind me. We both scurried off into different corners of the circle and propelled our own pee-streams down two separate mole holes. They knew it wasn't raining. It was dark yellow and this was the Mojave, the driest desert in these United States. And it was, as the water in my bones was stolen away.

After we finished marking our territory, I snagged up two extra sediment-teeth, and marched over to the incomplete fire-mouth, lodging the stones in place, crowning the wowing circle that would cook my meal tonight. I put my hands on my hips and took a deep breath. The sun was lower, the heat was briskly retreating, and I seemed to have found the perfect spot. I breathed and found my space between moments where it was cool and the time in my cockpit when I cooked alive seemed so far away. I drank the desert in. Everything was so far away. I had escaped, was escaping into the wastes of the world.

As distant as my vision could take me, there was nothing but dunes of sand. Rise after rise of piled up particles, sent here to live out endless days under the scorching sun. Rolling tumbleweeds and bereft sagebrush scattered the lower spots, sprinkled like pepper across mounds of mashed potatoes. The clouds felt like the closest thing, billowing up in monstrous plumes, mixing with the dunes in a steamy gravy. Everything felt a million times bigger than I was—the clouds, the stretching sand, the rolling hills—all dwarfed my little body by comparison. There weren't any man-made structures to compare with the stratospheric creations painted before me. Look, God, you make a pretty good artist, sure, but give man his due—we built a glass pyramid with diagonal elevators, just in spite of you.

I was completely insignificant in this place. I was starting to love that. I didn't feel like I was drowning out in nothingness, but instead, slicing, streaming fast with freestyle strokes. I wasn't drowning at all. I was turning into a sand-breathing fish. The air was open and circulated clean and deep, flooding my lungs with the distinct purity captured by this place. So pure and wild and open and moles ran rampant and hawks flew above, and it was all just as it should be. And I loved that. Every intake was accompanied by a stark reminder that my beating heart, my measured breath, and Mia's panting—that was it, the only sound for miles around. Light thumps and wagging tongues and the great open expanse of the west.

I was sitting in my black and blue everything chair, its legs sinking low into the sand. Scribbling back and forth in my little brown book down little pinstriped lines, I was filling the page with my bewilderment and visions of the place the sun is always going.

I can scream and it will be stolen to the wind before it reaches another's ears.

I kept writing, bleeding ink into the manilla parchment, line after line. I couldn't believe a place like this existed—free camping, free parking, not another soul in sight, no sound, no man-made light. No neon bulbs buzzing in bar windows, no mustard-air fouling up my nose, no smog of a thousand farts and churning factories—just wide open air. And as much as anything could be wide and open and sublime, this was.

I read what I wrote, playing it out in my brain. I wasn't aware of how scared I was to break the natural silence. I arrived back at the line again and stumped myself on it.

I can scream and it will be stolen to the wind before it reaches another's ears.

I closed my little brown book, banded my little silver pen to the spine, and stood up, tossing the writer's combo back into the seat. I took a few steps, sand filling my sandals, covering my toes in a warm blanket of creamy mashed potatoes. I looked left, up the road where I hadn't yet been. I looked right, down the path where I had come from. Nothing. No one. Thumps and tongue-wagging and it was clear, and I was a part of it.

I took in more air, expanding my ribs out wide, and screamed so motherfucking loud that I might have ripped a vocal cord in half. My blood-curdling expense transformed into confused laughter as I grinned, veins bulging from my head. I screamed again, loosening some gathered-up gunk that was stuck somewhere in my heart, caked to my amygdala like dryer lint. This time I howled like a wolf swooning at the moon, in love with the wilderness, the gone away places of the world, loud and magnificent. Mia was staring intently at me, working through her own bewilderment. I smiled at her, using my body language to show that I wasn't angry, wasn't mad, wasn't ripe in agony or anguish. I didn't know what day it was, and I had lost my mind. I was insane and loving every second of it and the desert was inside of me and I swam and swayed and hollered at the animals beyond and told them I was one of them.

I felt lighter, as if I had rid myself of some unknown baggage in my fanfare of shrieks and shouts. The world around me had been wholly unaffected by my cacophony, resuming its silent, stone-giant sized demeanor. No one came running, wondering what was wrong. No one had any idea how raw I had just wracked my throat. And I didn't want them to. I had proven my little brown-book theory correct, screaming in spite of my previous suffering. Howling out to the nooks beyond and watching the vibrations steal away, wiped clear by the desert breeze.

I was splitting open my voice box and spilling its gel across the sand. Driving all day through the driest places, sight-seeing the world's raisin, sucked free of any moisture.

Wheeling up forgotten roads into places unknown, with just enough water, just enough food to tie the nights over. My food could rot, my water spill, I'd do it all again. And I would. This time eating piss-soaked moles and drinking salty sand-grains and smiling and laughing, all the same. This was my own space, wide and open and watchful, my own Sydney Opera House-of-Horror. Out here, where my smoked-out, dried and decaying guts could cook in the sun, baked into Mojave-flavored jerky for the rodents and hawks alike. And they could have a bite—I'd let them—it was all the cycle of life and I'm one of them and I was yowling and telling them that.

The silence of the hills was deafening. Crunching gravel adjusted under my sandals. My car door slammed. Mia's metal dog tags jingled lightly. I farted. I swallowed. A cricket started serenading his tune in search of a mate. A brush of wind shifted dead sage leaves against one another. Slammed another car door. My Adam's Apple bobbed up and down as I hydrated. My piss hit the dirt, bubbling around in a crater of yellowish liquid. I threw a rock, it hit another, clicking in muted tones. My pen scratched across paper. Every intricate blip of sound deafened my ears, impossible not to hear the thoughts of every meditating grasshopper. This place was ticking and alive and I was in it, a part of it, and it was hushed and still.

I was knighted the guardian of noise, as every worldly utterance failed to slip past my ears, instead being subjected to search and seizure by my audio-obsessed attention. I had big black gloves and a hoodie of my own, and the sounds of earth were lining up for miles, ready to be felt up by my inquiring hands. I even had a super-sniffer dog to examine each and every audio infraction. It was surreal. It was intoxicating. Having just spent a couple of days in zombie-land, where my senses were raped beyond recognition, this new place was trying to realign the blocks, bring my harassed and broken senses back down to reality. Back to a place where their essence could be grounded, captured in nature's grasp. It was marvelous and I let it take me.

I dug around in my trunk, rifling through bins and bags searching for my bluetooth speaker. The quiet was nice, but just like with Game of Thrones, I was near an overdose and needed to switch things up. I found the wire-mesh tube, flipped it on, and connected my phone. It always made a little "duh-ding" noise once it successfully acquired my phone's bluetooth signal, ready to play whatever tunes I had available in offline mode. I scrolled through my playlists, landing on my favorite compilation—*The Road Home*. It was filled with the type of music that radiated road-trip. Modern folk, old-folk, a touch of light alternative, indie, and all the best easy-to-sing-along, four-chorded beats that were my favorite. We like folks. They make the best music, too. The kind of songs that spill from their hearts and out their fingertips like the purple mountains on an autumn morning when the coffee steams and the frost still clings to the brown blades of grass outside. It's Cassady music, where they sing that way and it's intimate and native.

Pouring through my treasured playlist, I swiped up over and over, scrolling for an unknown song, just something that would fit juuuust right. And there it was—*Angela* by the Lumineers. I probably had three hundred listens to this song, and by the end of this trip, I'd have three hundred more. Volume turned up to maximum, I jammed my thumb with purpose into my phone, and the flittering guitar strings started bouncing back and forth.

I catapulted out of my everything chair. My shoulders were trading off, jutting forward and backward, arms following suit. My knees were bending, lifting and falling as I hopped from one foot to another, sandals hanging onto my toes for dear life. The melodic voice serenaded about the wilderness of the world inside the soul, and I was living it all out.

The song picked up, my voice joined in the chorus, and I started dancing my ass off, flipping up sand and dirt, spinning in circles, belting refrains at the top of my shattered lungs. Pebbles rolled into my foot-thongs and I didn't care. One sandal did an accidental backflip off my big toe, so I kicked the other one off too, now galloping around atop my bare-soled feet. I didn't care and it was lovely and I felt like a Keebler elf under the open skies.

I was cackling, singing my best and loudest, circling my rocket ship before the grace of God in the biggest batch of nothing I'd ever been in. It was melting into something wild and unashamed, and I felt like a little boy tuning in with mother nature again. I laughed through the lyrics, mixing them in a garble that I tried to align with the lead singer. I was standing outside my body, down the road, watching myself twirl and frolic in movements of pure bliss. It looked hilarious, like some drugged-out maniac performing an Indian rain-dance in the dead-center of the driest desert in North America. I saw myself, and I thought I didn't care what I looked like—no one was there to criticize my freedom. Mia was grinning, rolling around, and laughing with me. She gazelled around our rocket ship, too. She loved this song, just like I did. We high-fived and I held her two front paws and she hopped and skipped in beat. The thumps in my chest were loud and her tongue wagged and waved at me and all the space beyond.

The song bled on and on, verses etching across my bones and seeping into my marrow and I was listening, really hearing the words at last. I was home at last, finally able to understand and string it all up and shake it down into what the artists were really plotting. I felt it and was with my best friend in the wild, gone away out into the wild. It was a long time coming and my mind did the same flips my sandals had, rebirthing me on the sands of the Mojave.

A salty tear cut its way down my cheek, parting the sea of dust that had gathered on my face. As more tears came, my smile got bigger, my singing got louder. Every pass around the rocket ship left me feeling lighter, left me feeling more myself. A little boy exchanging with creation where the dead things of the world go to rest. I was dropping facades, letting loose an inner me that had been stifled for so long, I scarcely knew he existed. I danced and danced, proving a new kind of expression in confidence, rewiring some part of my brain that hadn't seen electrical flutterings since I was that little, bright-eyed boy. It was dormant, slumbering away behind all the adult questions, all the good stuff, all the lint of life that had built up. He was peeking now, spying in on what I'd been up to for all these years. He peeked and we danced, and fear and death stood by watching and Bill would have been with ole Sister Eubank being proud.

I wouldn't have romped around like I was if there had been people watching. Even throughout the charade I was projecting another version of myself out across the expanse, peering into my little isolated desert snow-globe with twinges of self-judgment and social anxiety. Social anxiety in the most unsocial place I could possibly be. Those malevolent ideologies were still stalking me, vignetting the image of my physical expression. I wouldn't be dancing if there were people around, people around watching. Would I keep dancing if there were people around watching? I kept asking myself the adult questions.

Over and over I tried to crack the glass of my snow globe. Tried to convince myself that I'd do my dances over again if a cavalry of trailers and campers arrived for the night, posting up down the road. I couldn't believe I would, so stuck in the quicksand of everyone else's judgment. My tears fell a little harder, cut a little deeper. I wanted to be me. I wanted to believe that I didn't care what everyone thought, that I would dance all night if I had to, just to prove it. I wanted the little boy to stop peeking and stand out, chest full, side-by-side with me. I wanted to open the front door to my vulnerable, teenage past, where I lost my confidence and replaced it with narcissistic anger and anxiety. I wanted to kick that pseudo-steel piece of shit in, walk up to the slow-globe pedestal deep in the corner of my mind, baseball bat in hand, and crush the entire veneer. Splatter the contents all across the walls. Murder the little anxious devil-adolescent toying with my cortex, shaking my globe over and over, clouding up my vision with the snow-flurries of everyone else's predicted opinions.

I kept dancing as another song began chiming out of my little tube speaker. I was past being a pillar of salt as my tears dried to my cheeks and stained across the shoulders of my shirt. I spun around, and saw a truck—a real, rumbling F-150 trudging down the road, almost in line with where I had turned off to find my little cul de sac dance circle. I had no doubt the driver could see me, probably had seen me for a minute or two from a distance. He drove past the turn off, continuing down the road where I hadn't yet been. I stopped dancing, surprised at the advent of another human being existing out here. Instinctively, I lifted my right hand and waved at the truck as it rushed by, huge toothy grin pasted across my face. A hand inside the front cab waved back, and again, instinctively, I resumed my desert boogie. And I really did.

I felt absurd as the snow-flurries started to shake and cloud my mind. I kept dancing, kept frolicking around my camp, and with every tear, every cackle, every movement in bodily truth, the flurry subsided a slight bit more. I was at war in my mind, bashing the little fucker who was shaking my snow-globe. I bashed him into pieces. I was his maggot-fiend, dragging him out of his little corner of control, blowing his brains out all across the stage of my mind. My mind. Not his. Not some self-subjected Truman show for me to be laughed at, gawked at, made fun of, pitied, or bullied into submission. I was wild inside, ravenous with a desire to pull this little bastard's lever so damn hard, he'd fly right through the heavens of the midnight stratosphere and land right down in Hell where he belonged. That's where he belonged, gone away. Leave me and my little-boy self alone. I kept dancing. And the peashooter trigger was pulling in all the right ways.

The stage was bloodied up, my baseball bat clotted with chunks of teenage me. My feet were adequately dusted with thin lines of brown soot jammed up under all ten of my toenails. There may not have been a shower for a hundred miles, might not have been a laundromat for another hundred after that, but it didn't matter. I'd roll around in the mud just for a glimpse at the spiritual freedom that came with massacring the little anxious, little angry, little all-too-self-aware me. I'd sift my hands through mounds of dirt, smearing as many clods across my traveler's jersey as I could manage if it meant I could be rid of my own toxic influence. So I kept on dancing, every step providing one more data point, one more citation of truth to counter-argue my own self-destructive, adolescent critic. Evidence. I danced. Mia pranced. Another step. Another step. And we were living for it now, skipping and howling at the rising moon.

It was dusk, as twilight rested upon the endless dunes of sand and sage. Blueish-purple streaks stretched like ribbons across the sky, wrapping the desert in a mystical contrast—a dusty, dry shell mirrored into a deep-sea of the coming night. Tiny dots of twinkling light started revealing themselves. A million little stars winking and cheering on my evening of ceremonial spins and shimmies. Exhausted, I powered down my music-tube, rejoining the esoteric silence of the world around me.

I had gathered a small stockpile of wood—broken limbs and sticks fallen from the pepper-flecked bushes in the vicinity of my camp spot. The wood was intensely dry, with many of the thicker branches forming hollowed husks, filled with sand and beetles. They cracked and snapped with ease, as I twisted dead grass, twigs, and wood-fibers into bundles with my bare hands. I set up a small teepee in the center of my fire-mouth, drew out my Bic lighter, and set flame to the overly combustible structure. In mere moments, I had a four-foot tower of blazing light, shimmering and dancing its own jig across the ground and backs of nearby bushes.

I moved over my everything chair, wedging its legs back into the soft earth, and plopped down, once again sinking low into the sand. I pulled an unopened bag of hot dogs from my papier-mache filled cooler. Using a livelier switch of wood as my roaster, I shaved long strips off the end, narrowing it to a point for wiener-stabbing. As I went to close my cooler, I noticed a clamped bag of bacon and once again smiled that big shit-eating grin. It's gotta be pig-wrapped-pig tonight.

I salivated and got a little excited for my grin to eat some shit. They say pork hot dogs are made from all parts of the pig—their flanks, their tummies, their assholes. Show me the documentary footage of that, I'll watch while I eat one. Hot dogs have a special place in my heart, and an even special-er place in my stomach, pig assholes and all.

I wrapped my first hot dog in a spiral of raw bacon and stabbed my poker through one wiener-end and out the other, stapling the bacon to the dog on each end. I leaned forward in my sunken seat, jutting my meat-spear into the edge of the flames.

Before long, sizzling pork juices were bubbling out of the bacon, seeping down around the hot dog, showering it in a succulent grease-covered mess. Both ends of the sausage produced their own leaking sauces, boiling out and dripping down into the coals of the fire. Every drop made a fizzling sound, echoed out into the vast reaches of darkness.

My perfectly brazened pig-in-a-blanket-of-pig was done—and I was more than ready to snarf it down. I placed it in a bun, drew a line of ketchup down the middle, and within forty-five seconds, I was pulling another hot dog out of the bag, wrapping it in more bacon, sticking the end with my poker, and serving myself seconds. Then thirds. And fourths.

It's impossible for me to eat a hot dog while camping without getting ketchup everywhere. I wish I knew how it happened, when the ketchup leaps off the bun into my lap or onto my knees. The strangest part is that the red goo always ends up on my elbows. My only hypothesis is that I prepare my delicious meal of meat in my lap, and at some point in the darkness, I overshoot the tomato paste without seeing what I've done. Then, after my belly is packed, my taste buds satiated, I lean forward, planting my elbows atop my knees, cupping my chin in my hands, while I stare into the fire for hours. This is the only way I can guess that the ketchup finds its way onto the backsides of my arm joints. Even worse is when I fail to notice, and crawl into my sleeping bag for the night, painting streaks of tomato-blood down my bag liner. Maybe I just want a little snack to lick like a tomato popsicle in the middle of the night. I should start cramming tater-tots in my pocket when I go to bed.

I lifted my arms, double-checking my elbows for remnants of my dinner. Sure enough, one little red splotch sat menacingly a quarter the way down the backside of my forearm. Of course, I had to spill red sauce on my favorite mustard-colored hoodie. I scraped the bead of ketchup off with my forefinger and sucked it clean. I may not have been wrapped in bacon, but I slow-cooked like a sausage all day in the car, I was bunned up in my steamy clothes, salted and seasoned, colored with mustard, and now the desert was putting on the final touches—a last bit of ketchup on the me-meat—before being devoured for the night. Gobble me up then, you dried out bastard. I'm a part of all this open space, I'm an animal, too. And I was.

The flames of the fire were lowering, waltzing around the pit in beautiful, arcing wreaths of orange and yellow. My eyes watered as they dried out from staring too long at the flickering bosom. Smoldering and crackling chunks of wood broke in half and melted into a bed of glimmering coals. I pulled out my little brown book, wielded my little silver pen, and started scribbling down the little pinstriped lines.

O brilliant blazen glow!
How you shimmer and dance
A volatile measure of slippery
Flame
Slithering like a writhing snake
Whipping this way and that
Ripping hot life from the air
Around you
A deadly transfer of scorching ash
Crumbled and decayed as you leave
A wispy pile of soot in reminder
O your burning power!
Unleased to absorb the matter
Suited to your fiery tastes
Frozen eyes, I catch a band
Probing its enchanting core
Enthralled—lost, and then
Found

I repacked my writer's combo, securing my little silver pen to the spine of my little brown book. My fire prayer scrolled like end credits down my glassy eyes, mirroring the subsiding ribbons of flame still wavering in the pit before me. Mia was trotting guard circles around the camp, each rotation a little further out than the last. There were no lights from late-night arrivals on the horizon, no rumbling F-150s, no noisy families unpacking their oversized trailers. All was velvet and muted, aside from the occasional flame-split branch breaking away into embers.

Tonight, there was no anxiety about where to sleep, no concern with fat police knuckles wrapping against my windows, no chance of methed-out maggot-fiends pulling me out of my car for a fast twenty. My writhing mind and its worries were stolen away, blown into the wind, scattered and left idle among the grains of sediment. I was opened as wide as this forgotten place, dry and cracked and revealed and I was a part of it. I succumbed to it, let it inside and it washed my bones and I felt free and wild, and I cradled in the womb of mother nature.

Years of conversations, a thousand voices and vibes all intermingled with my own, scaffolding my brain in all the best and worst ways. Years and years of breathing in everyone else's ideas, everyone else's conceptions of the world—the bleating horns and buzzing neon lights of zombie boulevard. The drugs, the sex, the rock 'n roll rigmarole of too many friends crammed too heavily in too small a college apartment. Too small a hotel room. The convictions of too many college professors all professing to know what's juuuust right. A religious culture of too much judging, surmising, guiding every move, warping into infinite ironies sprawled out across my graphing paper back home. Where everything was ninety-degree angles and the songs of death were the ones you sang idly while the world passed you by. Years and years of beautifully foolish Aprils. Of me hating and loving it all, screaming tears of joy and laughing at my agony. Years of taking everyone's good with everyone's bad and sucking it all up into my veins and living off it like manna from heaven. I'm alone out here now, and I love that. I'm an animal—opened wide, entranced and frothing.

Years and years, step after step, shaking my snow globe, winding my story, muffling my screams and shimmies, trodding a path uphill, across the desert, up a dusty byway, into a cul de sac of dizzy dancing, now lost into a mouth of fire. Now found having silent conversations with sand and plants. All the same, woven like ribbons, paved like asphalt, to this very point—my gory, marvelous, horrendous road home. Wherever home was or would someday be. It was brazen and lonely and I peeled apart my mind in the warm breaks of May.

Chapter 12

Silent Conversations

My eyes cracked open somewhere in the middle of the Mojave desert. I climbed out of my tent-on-wheels, stretching my arms out wide, still basking in solitude. My retina's were assaulted by the vibrance of the sun, shining so brightly, reflecting off a trillion tiny specks of sand. Morning dew didn't exist out here, where water is foreign and fleeting and sent back up as soon as it's sent down. I assumed the normal morning position while camping in isolation, filling another mole hole with piss. I smirked—always surprised at my body's uncanny ability to know when there's a toilet available or not. Not for peeing, but for pooping. My bladder had no conception of when and where a urinal would be on the scene next. See images of me pinching my pecker closed while sprinting through South Point and Hoover Dam Lodge. Always sprinting, always addressing the potty problem head-on with no solutions.

I had four hot dogs, four slices of bacon, and a slew of other random snacks and grease sliming their way through me—and no desire to crap whatsoever. My pee might have an I'm-coming-now-dammit mentality, but when I camped, my biology knew to make some room, get ready to pack shit in tight, because the toilet bowl from home is missing and I'm not long for the public seat. I patted myself on the back. Thanks, asshole, I appreciate that.

My eyes adjusted to the vivid hills and undead sage still surrounding me. As I scanned the horizon, I heard the booming thunderous noise of a jet engine passing overhead. Not one cloud in the sky, not one airstream or plane to be seen. It was clear and crystal and the cyan void was deep and empty. The sonorous boom sounded again, accompanied by a hearty gust of wind, kicking up loose grains into little dust-nados. Looking back and forth, there was nothing that could produce such a bombastic noise anywhere—just endless dunes of golden sand. I thumped and Mia wagged and the world was still and sounding off somewhere.

Freshly hopped up on an earthen pot of drip coffee, I started packing away my effects. My plan for the day wasn't solidified, but some map-scouring led me to believe there was a hiking trail not far from where I spent the night. As I finished binding up my everything chair, I noticed several vehicles arriving, pulling down different offshoots into little camp-cul de sacs of their own. Maybe I had gotten lucky, having this vast landscape all to myself the night before. Maybe this was the weekend now, I didn't know. Didn't care. It was May and booming again and I was an animal and beasts under the sun don't keep track of things like that. Trailers, trucks, and minivans were finding their resting spots for the day, producing little figures from their cabins, leaping from their seats and skipping around in circles in search of their own mole holes.

I manned the cockpit of my rocket ship, Mia in the passenger seat, and crawled back out to the main dirt path, turning left up the trail I hadn't yet been down. A couple of jagged turns later, we were parked again, staring up a mountainous pile of sand, all shaded the same creamy color of soft, buttered potatoes. I leashed Mia, tossing a few necessary items into my little red hiking backpack. My little brown book was the first article to go in the bag this time. Another boom sounded off against the hills. There were no planes. I furrowed my brow and scratched my head.

If I liked uphill climbs, my work was cut out for me. I cursed aloud, trudging my sandaled feet up the sheer. On an outcropping, there was an information board with various facts about this dead-scape's local flora and fauna. I paused my journey upwards to learn a bit about the silent sand and plants I had been having conversations with all night. It was probably time they had someone speak for them amidst my endless jabber. Another boom reverberated.

The panel had a particular paragraph, backgrounded by a gorgeous picture of a pyramid of sand, baby-blue sky bathed behind it. It began with, "Do you hear that booming jet engine sound?" I was sucked in immediately. Please, O wise panel of fiberglass, please, tell me the secrets of these invisible jets. The booms were sounding still, and I was lost under the roars of the ocean in the desert and thought I'd gone mad. My eardrums are broken and chiming strange noises deep into my skull and no one else seems to notice or hear the tones. But I haven't slipped into insanity yet, this sign hears booms and has confidential knowledge. I kept reading.

The paragraph explained the cannonade that had blared all morning. Still blaring every few minutes out across the brittle and boney environment. When the wind gets strong, it races up the sides of the dunes, carrying with it the outer layer of sand, wisping the grains up to the peak. Once they arrive at their highest destination, there is nowhere else for them to go but back down the other side. Trillions of sand atoms launch from the sand caps, tumbling down, still charged by the momentum of the wind. Down and down, and as the sediment shifts and sheers the backside, it creates its own Sydney Opera House-of-Horror. All this friction—sand grist hopping, bumping, and rubbing against itself—generates a low, rumbling boom that echoes out beyond the world of dead and dying, shaking your bones and vibrating inside your skull. And it was. It was booming again and again and it was colossal and godly.

The fiberglass wizard, with all its ancient command, filled me in on the scripture of the sands. The drones were loud and louder all the time and they moaned out Gregorian and long, filled with time untold. The reverberations were full-chested and cried for the dead, wept for the dying, sang in their honor in the glassy morning, wrapped in sunlight and the blue tints of space. The hills sounded off, and I felt it deep in my living bones and I shuddered under the power of the stratospheric God. I sat, chair legs sunk in the sand the previous night, yammering to the silence of sand and plants—and here they are, singing back to me in a mourning chorus of howling beauty. And they have much to say.

I paced around the fiberglass sign, beginning again at my upward climb. The trail I followed weaved up the biggest sand dune, following the ridgeline high into the sky. I should have knocked on wood, if only I could have found some back on my hike above Hoover Dam. If I like uphill so much, how about I try it in three feet of shifting sand in ninety-degree heat with a pair of sandals that try to dive off my feet after every stride. The sand was getting hot—Hell's ovens must be particularly enraged today, radiating the scorching souls of the lever-pulled damned. Sand probably makes a great insulator for those fiery soul-roasters. Maybe all that wind-blown sandy friction is actually just the monotone groan of burning anima, swirling around hundreds of feet below, shrieking with screams that vibrate up through the bedrock until they find a way out onto the surface, signaling to us mortals of their torturous permanence.

Pits stained with sweat, neckline soaked a darker shade than the rest of my light gray shirt, I finally mounted the summit of the penultimate dune. There were no trees providing shade, no benches to plant my ass on. Just waves of silky smooth-sand. Every spot just about the same, I hiked my shorts halfway up my back and plopped down into the moaning sediment. My back pockets filled full, but my butt-crack remained grain-free. I pulled out a microfiber towel from my backpack, draping it over my head, creating a little tent as I half-tucked my knees toward my chest. Now basking in my man-made shade, I filled Mia's silicon bowl with water and beckoned her to drink. We both gorged—her shlop-shlop-shlopping and me bobbing my Adam's apple up and down, this time leaving a healthy portion of the liquid for the return journey. I was a speck on the side of eminence, microscopic and experiencing it all at once.

And now...
I'm out
here

I stopped scribbling, stretched out my hand, and dunked it under the surface of the embering sand. It rose back out, sifting a billion little grains through the spaces between my fingers. It was the softest sand I had ever felt, draping like velvet puddy streams back into its original resting place. This feathery substance couldn't be captured or built into castles, drawn in with sticks leaving little love-the-world sayings for future passers. Brushing the surface, breaking the waves only separated the granules for a moment before they seeped back inward, resuming their endless rest in a graveyard of dust. The cycle had them steady, only shifting in power when necessary, to blow upward and downward, emitting answers to isolated guests.

As I watched the silk drain from my palm, I wondered if any of these specific grains had been to the bottom of the slope or had they always clung to the peak, enjoying their view. Maybe they'd been further still, perhaps as far as the red rock mountains barely visible on the horizon line. They were broken down to their smallest component, even smaller than a usual sand-spec found on any coastal Californian beach. These bits weren't new to the world, each one having been somewhere, resting infinitely since the beginning of time. Ground down and eroded century after century into smooth, buttery bluffs that glimmered in the early light. What had they seen? Who else's palms had they been sifted through? Maybe one out of these trillion had been cemented in the structure of a hotel on zombie boulevard. A chunk of stone hoisting up one of the two towers before nine-eleven. A brick that helped bear weight in the Roman coliseum. Now all these bits—little fibers of sand, blown across the world to their final resting place. Now they joined together, singing songs on windy mornings. Shaking my brain against my skull in a natural massage of harmonious droning. And droning. Not so silent, with much to say.

The cycle of life continues.

I closed my little brown book, satisfied with the answer the sand had given me. Back home in Utah, where everything was planned out on a perfect sheet of graphing paper, we always wrestled with drought. Every year, announcements scrawled across newspaper headlines telling the community just how much water we didn't have. Sprinkler schedules would narrow to an hour every other day. People were encouraged to turn the faucet off while they brushed their teeth or soaped up in the shower. The mountains would transform from their vibrant shade of verdant green in foolish April to a dusty dead-pan brown over summer. Everyone would repeat the same refrain—pray for rain! And they prayed and prayed and it never fell.

But as every morning rolled around, right in the roast and husks of August, you could sit on the front porch, listening to choruses—cht-cht-cht-cht. Millions of little sprinkler heads spouting millions of gallons of water we didn't have out onto the greenest lawns you'd ever seen. Those golf-green squares were perfect. Perfectly out of place. Striving against the environment, a trillion little emerald grass blades raising their grassy heads to the beating sun, jutting out their little grassy middle fingers and screaming, "Fuck you!" in unison. Soaking up the liquid gold, the west's ailment, the west's neverending strife of perpetual dehydration. But they keep praying and watering and kneeling and watering, all the same. And the newspaper headlines never change.

Those lawns had to be juuuust right, like the graphing paper was. One block by one block, charted and built in the most predictable way possible. You couldn't get carsick on those roads if you tried. Everything was ninety-degree angles, painted in shades of the same while the mountains grow dead and the reservoirs dry up cracked and withered and everything is boring and perfect.

Out here and now, where I sat—this place didn't try to be anything other than what it was. Mountains of drought and velvet sand. Fields of dead sage. Rolling tumbleweeds and scampering critters. Soaring hawks clawing into the furry flesh of baby mice. Empty air, piss-filled mole holes, sand that actually spoke back to you when you spoke to it. Solo desert dance parties, screams and shrieks, and brown book theories. This place was so authentic it would kill you to prove it. I could see the cycle of life turning and circulating warm before my very eyes and I was a part of it. And I loved the idea of it killing me, of it trying to.

Nothing about this place tried to be perfect. There were no ninety-degree angles, just ninety-degree beams of sunlight cooking everything above and below. It was raw, unfettered, X-rated—it would string you up just to cut you down, and it wouldn't give three-and-a-half shits for your opinion about it. It let me alone, let me dance, let me scream till my throat groaned hoarse. It didn't ask my permission, I never gave my consent. It was sly like that; my body suddenly bent over in the middle of a big spacious nowhere, echoes and thumps and wags rippling like water across golden waves of the softest sand I'd ever felt.

It was midday as I dusted out Mia's dog bed and swept the encroaching sand out of my car. It was impossible to get every hiding particle as they dove down into every crack and crevice between my seats and under my bags and bins. I conceded that some of these grains would stay with me for the entire trip, if not for lack of trying.

I wheeled out onto the dusty main road that originally channeled me deep into the dead center of Mojave. Heading southwest, the road gradually became less rocky, more smooth. Game of Thrones was ragging on, and all my prior accompanying buddies started setting in again. My eyes drooped, the air conditioning failed to gain the upper hand, sweat beads streaked my forehead and neck. My left arm was a dark shade of maroon from resting on the windowsill. My right-hand knuckles were light pink as they hung at twelve o'clock on my steering wheel—pinned up like pork links for snacking on later. And my bestest buddy came flooding back in, too. It was time to find a mole hole to fill—only, as the rocky road became asphalt, trucks towing campers and family-filled SUVs were racing by at twenty-five-second intervals. No road shoulders or berms, no chest-high bushes nearby for cover. And I wasn't all that interested in accidentally showing a very different pork link to the prying eyes of a passing family if I could help it. No eyes should have to snack on that. I drove on, kicking my everlasting pee problem down the road.

Up ahead, there were a few ratty buildings—more like sheds, with the sun peeking in between rotted wooden slats. It appeared to be a junction of several roads, the main one linking up with a few other dirt tributaries feeding in from various parts of the Mojave. In the middle of this forsaken town, there was a little visitor's center—a structure that had time-traveled half a century into the future when compared to the shacks scattered along the sides of the road. Kelso, California, and I was in it now.

There were several cars in the visitor's center parking lot, and the odd truck-'n-trailer duo rumbled past, heading either out of the desert or deeper inside. My bladder was starting to expand a bit more than was comfortable, spurring a sharp pain as I worked out my holding muscles. This place had to have a bathroom, and if not, the backside of one of these ghosted sheds would do just fine.

I jumped from my front seat. Mia leapt out behind me, already leashed up. We jogged toward a long concrete building that wasn't so forlorn, cemented immediately off the curb of the baking asphalt lot. I could see the sign for the men's room, thanked my lucky stars, tied Mia to a pole outside, and practically kicked the door in. That pinch—then sweet relief.

Mia's leash in hand, her following on my heels, we circled the sandy courtyard in the center of town. Usually, town squares have statues of magnificent people, or historical figures that remind us of those who trailblazed a half-century ago. Usually, there are little placards that give you a glance at the impact the effigy had when there was blood pumping through their veins, not iron. They are usually standing forthright, chest puffed out, dressed in their metal Sunday-best. Frozen forever with stoic looks, thousand-yard stares, built for us to remember the times that came before the one we're in now.

There was a figure of iron in this town square, here in the middle of Kelso, California. But it didn't have a face, or eyes, or a puffed out chest, or any human features. It dared to be a little different, detailed a contrasting picture against the wide-open desert-ghost, dead-panned, dust scape of Mojave. The iron in the middle square was woven over and under itself, forming a thousand little windows threaded in checkerboard bars. It was a cage. It was actually two cages, smashed side-by-side, strap-welded at every point where metal brushed metal. They weren't large—two rectangles enclosing a five-foot by ten-foot plot of iron-bottomed space. The little square windows were rusted a shade of dark orange, then painted over in beige to match the sand. Rust still poked through, though, emphasizing to onlookers just how old this relic really was.

According to the signs scattered around the visitor's center and courtyard, Kelso used to be a railroad depot, the perfect pit stop on the journey between Los Angeles and Utah. At one point, it even boasted a population of roughly two-thousand residents in the nineteen-forties. There was a restaurant in the depot (now turned into a visitor's center), where rail yard workers, residents, and drunks all gathered for meals. Trains would shuttle minerals, ores, food, and other goods, and they'd stop here for a moment's respite before the long, slow climb up toward Las Vegas. John H. Kelso was a railroad worker, and when he got to this little spit of land, he and a couple other men tossed their autographs in a hat, drew one out, and that's how this place gained a name. In twenty-nineteen, this place looked like it was entirely built, governed, and ran off that same hat-drawing principle. It wouldn't have surprised me one bit to see a pair of men wrestling around in the dirt to settle their differences out here where the snakes and scorpions ruled.

In fact, that very aspect is why these iron bars were brought in the first place. Lots of men coming through town, lots of nothing to do out in the middle of nowhere—so the bottle started looking real nice, gave them some real hobbies to escape into. When the beatings got a little too rough, or the howling cries grew a little too loud, it was in the cage with your not-so-sorry ass. If you can't handle all this empty air, all this free space and untamed wild sand that sings on crisp mornings? Well, you could spend the night in the center of town, behind slap-ironed cells, waiting till the sun cooks you like a fried egg for breakfast. It really must have been an Opera House-of-Horror back then—when there was no

Google, no fiberglass wizards or all-telling talking heads to fill everyone in on what those sounding booms were. Morning ghouls soaring above the plains like cowboy-wraiths, rounding up hungover railroad men, stricken with fear and wonder and addiction all at the same time.

I stared at the cage for a long stretch. I found a bench on the courtyard's edge, planted down, and stared until my eyes were bloodshot and sunburned. The tops of my knees and head were rosy and I was thumping. I understood what the cage was there for, the purpose it served all those decades ago. I understood everything about its metal doors and iron windows, the rust and paint, the metal flooring. I felt every inch of it up with my scathing pupils.

The history of these little bars was chalked up to one sentence, one little blip on a modern-day fiberglass wizard sign in the middle of nowhere. This was a cage meant to trap zombies who were too far gone. A simple little structure, self-governed in a time and place that no one remembers. As I sat and stared through the little iron windows, I found myself staring back out. Take all this free air, all this wild-inside space—just to wind up in a five-by-ten-foot prison because I can't handle my own agency.

I stood up off the bench and walked toward the cage. The doors were left open, and the locks didn't work, so no one in today's time could accidentally incarcerate themselves. I stepped inside the space with a ceiling lower than six feet. I peered back out, weaving my fingers through some of the iron windows. The metal blistered hot and I held my grip. I stared at the bench I had been sitting on, but I couldn't see myself sitting, staring back.

I had always been inside this cage, always pressing my face up to the burning metal, so close I couldn't see the bars holding me back. But they were there, all the same. I could taste the open air, feel a little breeze as it grated in between the bands of steel. I could see the endless ocean of sand, and far out and away, across the limit-line in shades of dark blue and purple, I could see red rock mountains rising to meet the sun. But no matter how hard I tried and wanted, I couldn't get any closer. I couldn't reach the oasis that lay beyond the wavering heat strokes from Hell's ovens. I pushed and thrashed and stomped my feet, never noticing the metallic sound that rang back when my sandals slapped the iron floor. I told myself I could do it. I convinced myself every day I would make a big step. But every morning, as I sat and baked myself like a fried egg, seasoned heavy with green Mary-Jane flakes, I was still in the same place. The mountains, the sky, the sun, the sand, the open air—it was no closer, no nearer to my heart than it had been the morning before or the morning before that. Welcome to every morning of my adult life and I'm really thumping now. It wasn't enough to want it. To want out.

Even in little moments, when I'd catch a slice of sober awareness, stumbling to the side and glimpsing the iron bars, I'd return to my pressing position. I'd convince myself of dull platitudes, of how someday the cage would be juuuust right for me to make my steps. Someday I'd grate myself like cheese right through these little iron windows and somehow, someway, come out on the other side whole.

My jail, my slap-ironed cage, my entrapped, infinite caesura. My whored-up, Mary-Jane-motherfucked mind—there I was, there I had been. Every morning, afternoon, and night of my adult life. Stuck in a stockade of weaving iron. Me looking out looking back on me.

The history of these little bars was chalked up to one sentence, one little truth that reached to my core. This box was for those who sang their idle songs of death a little too loud. When I was outside the cell, I wanted nothing more than to party and play my way in. And once I was in, I just wanted out. The other side of the iron windows always looked a little more fun than the one I was on. But it was never about wanting steps, never about wanting outsets. Those were just cart-before-the-horse quips I repeated to myself as I pressed my body harder against the cage walls. And it wasn't enough to want. And the cage was there and I felt it branding into my skin and I committed to leave and move my hands and feet and my sandals slapped the metallic floor. I was leaping and landing and leaping and landing all in the same spot.

I wanted to escape. That's who I am, that's what I was, as I'm out here, looking through the bars, looking back on me. But the world was beyond and the western folds and the groans of the dunes droned on and on and they sang for my sins, sang for me and my identity—the song of death, the song of escaping. And I was silent and knew that tune well.

Chapter 13

Shamrocks and Stars

A warm evening light cast long, creeping shadows across the roads and up the sides of buildings. I picked my way down main street in Palm Springs, California, maintaining a twenty-five-mile-per-hour gait as I swung my head left and right, bumping in tune with the radio. Crowds of tourists and locals mixed on the sidewalks, bustling through side shops, toting oversized shopping bags filled with new clothes, new iPhones, and styrofoam boxes of left-over dinner scraps. Everyone's sunglasses were oversized, too. It was communal and happening on both sides of the street and everyone was here for it.

Everything about this place was friendly and welcoming and palms drooped down and reached their arms out trying to hug the city tight. There weren't any skyscrapers or towering hotels, no neon lights to burn out your eyes—just row after row of sandy trees, wood-slat mom-and-pop shops, kitschy little dinner restaurants, and the sweet smells of cinnamon rolls and gelato. Everyone wore tank tops and short-shorts, foot-thongs, had tans that were several shades short of skin cancer, and teeth stained dark brown from countless mornings of cigarettes and coffee. My rocket ship windows were rolled down, my seat leaned back a bit more than usual as I putted down the main avenue, easing into the vibe of this place I'd heard everything about, but never been to before. Palm Springs, California and it was all cursive and smiles and spring in thriving May. I grinned and fell in love a little.

I made several laps along the length of the balmy main street, absorbing the little city and all its beach-infused western character. I was also searching for a cheap parking lot, not too far off the avenue. Each pass up and down the street, my hopes dwindled a little more. I clicked my heels and started realizing that I wasn't in Las Vegas anymore. This was California—where milk and gas were five bucks a gallon and taxes were so high, they left me questioning if I was buying a product with a little tax added or paying tax with a little product added. It was somewhere in the middle and the ratio tasted strange and scraped at my wallet and I wasn't in Vegas, but I wasn't far from it.

Every lot I stumbled upon had a little robot-box planted off the edge, beckoning to be fed oversized fees for an hour of parking. I reiterated to myself that I was stealth camping, so in reality, I could choose any old road, free of NO OVERNIGHT PARKING signs, and hunker down there for the night. But my drives clashed as I painted my expectations of getting the perfect spot, just off main street, for just the right amount of money. One hour wouldn't do. One hour was how long I'd sit and relax with my feet on the center console before hitting the streets and feeling around the town with my hands and feet. It was ten, fifteen, twenty bucks for an hour, and my jaw hung wide in astonishment at the pocketbook extraction. I was going to be there all night, and the only price I was okay with paying was zero. Better to lose money slow than fast. Better to lose no money at all on the stay. I made another pass down the avenue, growing a little more frustrated than the last. Fees rose and everything was warm and fused together with cowboy boots and surf shorts and it was all oversized like Texas and overpriced and cursive like California.

The bleeding sun had set, shadows now enveloping every corner of this place. Streetlights blinked on and the crowds of people transformed from families of tourists, to figures all twenty-one and up, out on the prowl for a good foamy, golden beer. The shorts were shorter and the cowboy boots rose a little higher up their shaved and sparkling legs and it didn't matter what creature was night-crawling, everyone dazzled and had twinkles in their eyes. Every bar on main street was filling, thumping music pouring from the front doors out onto the gum-stuck sidewalk. I wanted to join in the night's merriment, wanted to find a cushy seat somewhere, listen to some live tunes, drink a locally brewed stout while I bobbed my head back and forth. I wanted to land gently and let the palms hug me up tight and get my own pair of bright-red cowboy boots and sway in the shade under the moon.

I always had this Hollywood-esque idea that floated around my head like a feather. I'd be a stranger in a strange city, deciding one night to join a bunch of other strangers in a strange bar. I'd walk in, find my seat, order a picture-perfect golden pint of ale, half-inch of white bubbles skimming the top. I'd sip it a little. Then I'd see her. Boy, would I see her! Across the cantina, she'd be all alone, too. She'd have a little martini glass in her hand, watching the lead singer of some band no one's ever heard of serenade the pub-goers with a cover of *Sweet Emotion*. We would all swoon over each other and the songs would write across our bleeding hearts. Her legs would be crossed, accentuating her golden calves, feet slipped into beautiful, red-jeweled heels. She was natural— gorgeous, crimson-painted lips, deep ocean-blue eyes I could see from across the room and get lost in. Her hair fell elegantly down past her shoulders, shaded aurelian and glimmering with every head bob. She'd smile, warm like home, with dimples, grinning wide, revealing snow-white teeth. I'd melt into a puddle on the floor.

Incapable of holding back, I'd manically rise, approaching her with some fantastical confidence I'd never had. I'd wink, I'd sit, we'd laugh and cackle and I'd melt some more. Always melting around her. She'd be wonderful in her every sound. Her captivating chuckle would catalog deep into my mind, driving every joke I could muster. Anything to draw out another excited giggle. Our feet would brush under the table, our hands would glance above the board. She'd stare into my star-struck eyes. I'd stare into hers. And I'd feel something with this person I had only just met in a town I'd only just arrived in. Cursive California. Our little love story would start, just like in the movies. It was beautiful and mysterious, this expectation for the wild unknown. But if I couldn't park my rocket ship and get into the bar where all the jubilee rang out, I'd never get to meet her. And I needed the chance.

And then I saw her, on the side of the road, posted up in a steeled beauty I've still never seen to this day, and I doubt I ever will again. Standing tall, a quarter block off the main avenue, a brilliant metal sign read:

FREE UNLIMITED PARKING

I slammed my brakes, squealing off the right side of the avenue in a fit of arrival. As I frantically turned my steering wheel with one hand, I bent down and picked my jaw up off the floor of the cab—I couldn't believe my luck. Everything was extreme and either one thing or the other here—cowboy boots and short-shorts and this was free and endless and unlimited. I swung wide into the near-empty lot, jammed my rocket ship in park, and hopped out, shutting the door behind me before Mia had the chance to follow.

As I approached the backside of the ten-foot-tall beauty, I half expected the sign to read something else. This was overpriced California, after all. This was the land of the expensed, home of the homeless. I must have been mistaken, must have misread the massive black letters. No way they let people park for unlimited time spans. That's forever, and nothing was forever, not here. Parking and growing old and wrinkled under the leather-backed sun, this lot where the creatures gathered and stayed forever. This was the place, had to be the place, free and unlimited and I must be mistaken. I must have seen some hallucination that I was looking for, praying so hard for a good spot to park that my eyes were willing to trick me into anything—just to get out of the front seat, through the doors of a local bar, and into the arms of that crimson-lipped fox. There were only three other vehicles on the lot, spaced out and sullen and dark-windowed. No one was in those ships, this place couldn't be forever. There'd be more walks of life, more activity beneath the emerald green elms and hugging palms that rowed the curb. There would be more souls drawn here, had to be.

I rounded to the front side of the sign and allowed my jaw to hang wide once again. Sure enough, clear as crystal, standing on a street-lit corner of this parking lot, the steel sign rose up, beginning with a flowy cursive. WELCOME TO PALM SPRINGS. Below that, in blocky, capital characters that were unmistakably sticker-stuck to the square metal disc: FREE UNLIMITED PARKING. I pulled my phone out, tapped the camera app, angled my viewfinder up at the sign, and snapped a picture. No one back home would ever believe this if I didn't gather up some evidence. I looked at the picture, back at the sign again to reassure my luck.

I sat on the curb in front of my car. This cement stair was taller than most, jutting out of the ground two feet, making a quaint little bench as I swam around in a light alcohol-induced buzz. The night was coming to an end, as my tired eyes started smoldering, pulling my awareness and eyelids half-closed in a cross-faded stupor. Mary-Jane and shamrock-brewed bubbles floated around my head like stars and I looked up and saw them shine and fell in love a little. Down below, chicken strips and braised-'n-buttered toast were breaking down in my gut, reminding of their fried, homestyle flavor every now and then as I let out little burps and belches. I was completely satisfied on every front, even finding my beautiful golden-girl. I turned my head, gazing down the lot, as me and my FREE UNLIMITED PARKING love-sign locked eyes. A place to stay, wrap in and weep for the night. She was tall, slender, and didn't expect anything from me—the perfect one-night stand after an evening of local pub-loitering. I tipped my brow and winked and we both smiled wide at each other.

Mia was wandering around the bark and grass ribbon that threaded in between my lot and another one on the other side of the curb. She was sniffing and exploring around for a good spot to take a leak. There were no mole holes, everything was well kept and cursive. I leaned forward, resting both my elbows on both my knees, and massaged my head, kneading out some of the shamrocks and stars. I was working out the great and wide problem of life, as usual.

Suddenly, Mia let out a low growl, cutting through my intoxication. Mia never barks. Rarely ever growls, doesn't make a sound most of the time. When I first got her, it was a couple of months before I heard her make any sound at all. I was beginning to wonder if she even had a voice box, or if she had discovered that the key to life is to scream so loud your voice box steals away forever. I couldn't ever get her to make any noise, which was fine by me. I figured I was lucky to not have a dog who was overly barky and ravenous. Instead, I got one that was tame, a bit timid, a little shy, and incredibly loyal. I like to say that if I have a certain allotment of luck in this life, I used it all up on getting this dog. So I had better be careful for the rest of my time down here, because my lucks' run out. Except for the time I found this unlimited parking lot. That sure was lucky, and the shamrocks and stars kept spinning.

Mia's growl brought me to attention like a drill sergeant commanding a fresh group of trainees. My light buzz was squashed out, my eyes now wide and full and darting. Something was approaching, something was about to crash my party. Something was behind me, something sinister. I remained seated, but spun around with a jolt of adrenaline, peering down the parking lot in a panic.

Stumbling up toward me was a hunched figure. His pants were seven sizes too big for him, bunched up atop his shoes—which were also oversized with huge puffy tongues in the DC-skater fashion. His massive jeans were shaded a dusty dirt color over faded blue denim. They probably hadn't been washed in weeks, if ever. The man wore an oversized green bomber jacket, also covered in soot and stains, particularly around the armpits and waistline. His jacket was thin but puffed up due to another hoodie or three he wore underneath. Every visible article of clothing was sheened in dried mud, stained with grease, or coated in sweat. He had an entire ecosystem growing around his gremlin-grunted body.

His beard was wired, stemming out from his chin, off-shooting in every direction. It covered most of the lower portion of his face—a black brush mask filled with little bits of food and trash of its own. His hair followed the example of his beard, falling down around his face, covering parts of his eyes and cheeks and disappearing under the bomber jacket to an unknown length. It was greasy, shining in the street lamp-lights surrounding the lot.

As he stumbled closer, I watched his hands and darted my eyes around his countenance, ensuring he wasn't looking for that fast twenty. In his left hand he held a styrofoam box, which I assumed was filled with his dinner. Or someone else's dinner that he was gonna finish up. I had been asked for change many times, and normally I would be willing to send a buck or two the beggar's way—but this time seemed different. I patted Mia's head, telling her it was okay. I wasn't sure if it was okay or not yet, but the man had my awareness now, so her growls had done their job.

The homeless guy was less than ten feet away, stunted in an upright position that seemed two shambles from falling apart into a hundred little pieces. He was staring at Mia, a little weary of her alert state. Any fear I had from a physical interaction dissipated—the man was a half-foot shorter than me, and one solid punch looked like it would break every bone in his crusted body. I instantly felt a little guilt for my initial reaction and unapproachable vibe. My eyes softened. He shuffled up toward us.

"She's friendly," I said, overcompensating for my intense visage.

He approached without a word, kneeling for a moment and scratching her behind the ears, then rose back to his humpback standing position. He twinged an easy smile at the corner of his mouth and sat down right next to me on the curb.

The man flipped open the lid of his little styrofoam box, revealing a mess of loaded nachos—tortilla chips with peppers, cheese, guacamole, olives, and a slew of other ingredients that wafted over the both of us. The box was chock-full of the Mexican fare, and I briefly pondered if the man had bought the meal himself or if someone had gifted it to him. Either way, he was eatin' good tonight. He dug in, eyes black and awake, reflecting his banquet.

With the dinner box open, spilling its scent everywhere, Mia trotted a few steps to his side and sat down, assuming her typical begging position. A triple-genealogy of begging was on display for the three of us to see. I hadn't spoken words with anyone in any meaningful way in over a week, hadn't really basked in the presence of outside sentience, besides Mia. Once the man sat down, it set in how much I was begging for human contact. The homeless guy might have been searching for something similar, or maybe he did want a buck or two— he never made it clear. His words were garbled. And Mia just wanted one of those chips, coated in a thick layer of cheese and guacamole. The three of us sat, begging life and May and the western world for circumstances that were a little tastier than the ones we currently found ourselves in.

The man muttered something, forming a distorted throat noise that bubbled up through the paste of chewed tortilla chips. I couldn't piece together his words.

"What was that?" I asked.

He swallowed the blob of nacho, nodding his head in unison with his Adam's apple. "Does your dog eat human food?" he said, dipping his hand back inside the box for another bite.

"She can have a chip, that'd be fine," I said with a smile. The three of us were succeeding in our begging, the universe was rewarding our efforts. And I felt contact growing like a seed and the words of the world and the soul were traded like the wisdom of a campfire.

He held out the cheese-crusted chip between his dirt-stained fingertips. Mia slowly leaned forward, nipped the corner of the chip, then scarfed down the rest of it once she had an adequate hold. It flew past her tongue, cracked, and was swallowed before she could hardly even get a taste. She was an animal, frothing and wagging her tongue, waiting for another.

The man kept shoving chips in his mouth, chomping down on each bite with increasing ferocity. Every now and then, he'd let out an excited grunt or twitch with a vigor that only comes from the enjoyment of a good meal. He was wiggling back and forth, smooshing all the salt and cheese into his stomach and vibrating under the blanket of taste arresting his gums. This dude was really getting into the styrofoam box, really letting the food flood his veins. Most of us eat our meals while we do something else—watch television, talk to family or friends, drive, read, click through YouTube videos—but not this guy. This guy was the most mindful eater I'd ever seen. Each bite was lifted up to his eyeline, caressed with care, prepared for a parade down tongue-and-taste-bud avenue. He looked every mouthful in the eye, stroked its cheek, and approached like he was swooping in for the first kiss. It was romantic, beautiful—this guy had found his steel signpost, his Hollywood-esque fairytale. He was making love to the cheesy mess, getting intimate with the salt and olives in a special kind of way that makes an onlooker jealous. And I was, even with a belly full of shamrocks and chicken sauce.

I realized then that I make fun of Mia for never tasting her food, never taking a second to savor the flavor. But I'm more like her than I was like this guy. I distract myself from flavor constantly, yearning to fill my food-time with some other stimulus than the delicious seasonings set out before me. I wolf down my meals more often than not, animalistic and beastly. This wise old sage, dirty and homeless as he may have been, had lessons to teach in his near-sexual relationship with his food. He caressed and gazed and devoured it and I loved watching.

In between his glorious bites, I asked him what his name was and where he was from. I tried to time my questioning so he might have a second to answer before re-stuffing his gullet with more nacho. But my timing didn't matter, he wasn't going to answer. He never did, brushing off my verbal inquiry as if I hadn't said anything. Another romantic mouthful, another blissful grunt in pleasure. I wondered if he was used to this kind of flavor, or if he normally just ate leaves and gravel.

"Have you ever smoked a cigarette?" he suddenly asked me, nearing the end of his mountain of nachos. He didn't turn to look at me, just kept staring down at his meal, maintaining eye contact with the preliminary matter at hand. He tossed out the words, took in a quick breath, and resumed the feast.

"Yeah, I have," I replied.

He didn't say anything back, just asked the question plainly. Was it a right of passage, seeing if I was the kind of person who might be carrying around a pack, might give him one with a light? The post-meal smoke was setting in for him, and in all my watching, it was for me, too. All I had was a bunch of weed tucked away safely in my car. No way was I pulling that out in public, even in sunny Palm Springs, California. I had a little vape for my nicotine fixation, but I wasn't gonna bring that up either. I'm not so interested in sharing mouthpieces with random strangers. Also not so interested in having to pull crumbs of chewed-up tortilla out of my Juul. I shuddered and watched him and we begged under the pale moon.

My homeless friend gently closed his empty styrofoam box and rose to his feet. He muttered some gurgled letters that were completely incoherent through the mess of thick saliva pasted around his mouth. He hadn't been stumbling around like he was drunk, but now seemed boozed-up on the mess of food he just ate—love-drunk on the cheesy strings and guacamole swimming around his insides. He turned and stumbled his way back down the lot from where he came, disappearing into the darkness beyond the street-lit parking spaces. I watched him go the whole time, staring for a few extra moments at the black spot where he slipped out of view. I said goodbye, and he looked and said nothing and was gone away forever.

The three of us had our begging desires satisfied. I put my head back into my hands, placing both my elbows back on both my knees and kept kneading. Was that guy even real? If I had followed him into the darkness, would I find anything? Maybe he was just a figment of my imagination, a campy little character my mind invented to break the solitude

I had been immersed in over the last… few days? Week? Two weeks? I didn't know. It was May. Couldn't have been long, but felt like an eternity. I said hello to gas station attendants, grinned at waitresses that took my order at restaurants—but those people were all paid to do that, however genuine they may have been. This little guy shuffled out of nowhere, plopped down right next to me. We soaked in each other's aura for a few minutes, and before I knew it, he was gone. Had my begging gone so far as to hallucinate little greasy man-goblins emerging from the darkness? I didn't get a tortilla chip on my taste buds—that was for Mia. I had no way of knowing if the little Keebler gremlin-man was real or not. But sitting there on my two-foot-tall cement curb, I chose to believe he was. I'm not insane, it's just kneading and willful May.

Strange things happen at strange times. I was more alone than I thought, searching for some outside influence more than I knew. Scraping through a darkness of my own, grasping for a real-life moment to hold onto. Looking for any sign of that light ole Sister Eubank chirped about and I was reeling and found a sliver. But a sliver was barely good enough, escaping from one place into the next and begging for the whole picture. And I was.

When I wheeled into the cursive village of Palm Springs, I filled the stage of my mind with the perfect scenario. I envisioned gorgeous actors with crimson lipstick, golden legs, red-jeweled high-heels that clicked and took me away to the magical bluffs of Oz. Perfect shining locks of hair that fell around the delicate shoulders of my idolized woman. A love story that I'd seen in a thousand chick-flick movies. The perfect romantic love, beginning at some random bar, ending on the mattress of the local Motel 6, just like the movie of the world foretold. That prospected companionship was a sweet flavor, deep and rich in taste and feeling and I sucked on it like a popsicle. It was unique, specific, physical—maybe I was just horny. Maybe all I really needed was to have some random entity reach out through the lonely, arid desert and ask me if I'd ever smoked a cigarette.

But don't listen to me. I'm busy distracting myself from real flavors. Real moments of opportunity. Too busy carefully crafting a sirloin-steak expectation, golden-haired, glistening and sitting in some far-off place, deep on the backside of my tongue. Dear ole Sister Eubank might have been proud of my starlight second with a total stranger, might have patted me on the back for praising a slice of light amid all that solo darkness. But dear ole Sister Eubank would be wrong to do so. I'm busy fantasizing a twisted tale, fucking the brains out of some fake model fairy with perfect hair, perfect legs, and a perfect crimson-lipped smile with perfect pearly-white teeth. Locking tongues with that petite little actress. And when she'd inevitably poof into thin air, I'd be left in a confused languor, clown-colored lipstick smeared all over my face. Too bad the one who shuffled out from the midnight curtain was covered in grease, had teeth that were corrupted black, a rotting jaw from a thousand days of gnawing on a puck of tobacco. No golden legs for him, just baked cheese and unholy-guacamole and the rotting smell of a homeless hunchback come to feast from a trough of cheddar and peppers. The perfect ingredients for further stains on the backside of my gremlin friend's trousers. It's too bad, really. Too bad that every moment is tarnished with what I think I want, what I think I feel. Too bad that it's always tug-of-war between the wild inside and reality on the other side of the oak door. And I hate that, but I keep tugging, all the same, and picturing perfect moments with golden angels.

Too bad I idolize my inner Goldilocks, sitting and thinking so hard about what would be juuuust right, trying to push golden strands of hair out the top of every pore on my bald head. I push so hard and blood fills my face, bleeding from dark red into an airless purple. My eyes bulge, a bead of sweat trickles down past my temple, across my cheek, lost into the collar of my shirt. But that's my favorite necklace, the one I like to wear the most. The sweat-stained ring that darkens my clothes, starting from the clavicle and stretching toward my belly button. Harder and harder I grate my thoughts like playdough, playing at being Plato, pushing them out the top of my head, begging for them to turn gold, shimmering in the new-spring light. And it's May and growing green and deep all the time. The answers I'm out here to find, the kneading of shamrocks and stars. A breezy mane of perfect hair, born from the act of sitting and watching. More Mary-Jane, more booze, more nicotine-stick vapor. More porn, more sex, more horn-driven ferocity. More flourishing fantastic Lysergic Acid Diethylamide finales dripped on little squares of paper and slipped on the backside of the tongue for more questions yet. And questions are the stuff of life, the best ones, the new ones, not end ones. But I want answers and I'm kneading my scalp over the great and mystic and wretched problem of life.

So I push! I keep on pushing, a big red-lipped clown! Screaming bloody murder, bashing my knuckles into the steering wheel of my car, showing it who's boss. Howling like a beaten dog, tasting my salt-filled tears, looking in my rear-view mirror and stretching my jaw out wide and wild like a nocturnal beast with blood on my fangs. Keep pushing. Maybe I'll discover a new color my face can turn, I juuuust have to push hard enough. I'm almost there, I can feel it. I'll graft golden noodles out the top of my head yet, and if I fail at that, I've got a metal trigger that's not gonna pull itself. And I really do.

But the moment's gone. It's passed like time, always passed. Now we sit in another here and now. A caesura that never ends, free and unlimited. The morning after the alarm's gone off, when I know I need to get up. To move. To act. To discard expectations and address reality on the other side of the oak door. But I don't. All that pushing got me nowhere, got me nothing. Just more questions and I want answers. I don't want to wonder about taste, I want to taste it all. All that pushing—all that intaking shit trying to outthink the world for gold. For gold. All that pushing, that grafting in thought, growing golden pasta-locks—all I've done is shit my pants.

My name is Goldilocks, and I only want what's *juuuust right*. And I fucking hate myself for it.

PART THREE

Too Cold

Chapter 14

The Bloody Bench

Ocean waves lapped up against the cobblestone shore, leaving bits of moss and muffin wrappers on the face of the rocks. Above the waterline, there were splotches of gum, plastic can pack rings strung over ledges, and beer bottles of every brand jammed in every nook and cranny. It was soupy and moldy green bubbles gathered in the coves between the rocks. Ten feet down the seawall from where I sat laid an electric scooter—the kind you pre-charge with ten or fifteen bucks to zip around the city at your own pace. No helmet, no prior knowledge of the operating procedures, not one care in the world. And no one ever cared, not about these things. Drunk, bumbling, stumbling onto the electric stand, jam more money into the digital screen and ride for another ten miles to the next bar and rinse and repeat till you're swerving in traffic under the midnight thumbnailed moon, wasted and dangerous and loving it.

These little L-shaped wonders were everywhere. Gracing every street corner like a toddler's playroom, toys strewn about, tipped over and forgotten. Early in the morning, you might see some scooters lined up in little troop formations for the city's uncaring youth to ransack once again. It was some poor sod's job to drive a big ole truck around every night, in the hours no one sees, collecting scooters, charging them up, and delicately organizing them for the next transgressive day. From the evidence I've seen, you'd be lucky to find a scooter ever gently reparked in a spot off the main sidewalk, still within view of future customers. Most were thrown into bushes, twisted in the mud like decaying bodies. People just didn't give a damn, couldn't be arsed to return things the way they found them. Or at least not deliberately seek to leave things broken, destroyed, and ugly after their use. People don't care, they just wanna move their fat asses through blocks of town, one after another, to get to the place their fat ass needs to be. They don't care if they break a city investment and flip a few drivers off on the way. They sway and cackle and they don't care.

The saltwater lapped up again, reaching its sullen hand up the rock wall, grasping at the metal frame and rubber wheels that formed the broken shell of a discarded scooter. Someone had treated this little human-mover like a cheap whore—rode her good and hard for a few minutes, maybe a few hours, really gave it to her—paid her a minimal amount of chump change, then left her to the shitty, grim, salty reality of the world. Now she laid down on a garbage-covered seawall while the earth was trying to grasp her ailing bones back into the unknown depths. Her neck was already an inch or two under the water, so it wouldn't be long now. The return and cycle of it all was circulating and seeping below the surface.

San Diego sat behind me. My back was turned on the haze of towers. I stared out across the open sea. It was a grim and gray day. The sun had decided not to come out, hiding behind a hundred-thousand blankets of deep, stratified clouds, black and massive, preparing to weep an ocean of their own. It was midday, but you wouldn't know it. I didn't know it. The clock on the face of my phone was lying to me. This was the brightness of an evening shade or an early morning rise, not the dead-center day of summer-land San Diego in the muck of May. But it was. Filthy, muddy, matching the color of the papier-mache mess I had just dumped out of my cooler earlier that morning.

I slipped my little pipe out from under my jacket sleeve, already loaded full with a green salad for toking. I was in public, sitting alone on a saturated wooden bench along the seawall. I leaned forward, looked down the sidewalk to the right, then shifted my gaze down the sidewalk to the left. No joggers, dog-walkers, afternoon drunks—not one human movement, just laps and clutches of the ocean. I leaned forward a little more, cupping my hands to my face, and sparked my lighter, pulling a hearty inhale of salad-smoke down through my lungs. It absorbed instantly, charring the red meat of my throat and soul, flooded back up into the gray-matter liquid of my prefrontal, and before I could say or think a word, my lids pulled a quarter-inch down the front of my eyeballs. My head ballooned, big and bald and red, floating up higher and higher. I could see the asphalt-colored clouds getting closer and closer, beckoning me to slip beneath their stony surface and into the mystifying world of rainwater before it's been wept. I kept floating up, ballooned to teeming proportions now, up and up. Or was it down? There was no telling anymore, I might have been on my own journey to the center of the earth. Might have been on my own flight to the heavens above. I was here for the ride though, cruising the waves and feeling the froth and shooting down through the ground and up through the ozone and down again and I was turned away from the city and lost in the gray and dark blue ether. Up and up and down and up and down, let's go. And I did.

I was searching for the warmth of the sun, rising above the malignant soup painting the San Diego sky. Cracks of light were shining through, beaming with yellow brilliance, touching my skin and singing out with hallelujahs! The angels were choiring me in, clapping and praising my head-blown journey to the center of the earth or heavens or wherever the fuck I was trying to fly or dig to. I was magnificent—smiling, and laughing, staring at the little L-shaped city slicker, pointing and making fun of the rotten machination. Calling names to it, bullying the invisible bastard that thought it wise to conclude his ride by throwing the motorized wonder down to the demons of the sea. Those invisible bastards hated capitalism, and the L-shaped zipper was the poster-child for capitalism. But he paid for a ride, all the same. Paid for a zip to the edge of the sea and threw it in. He still paid, and I still bullied the thought of him, that capitalism-hating pimp. Up and up and down and up and down—I pulled out my peashooter and blew my brains out all over the moistened bench, and my blood and brain-goo soaked in with the spraying ejaculate of the sea and I frowned and smiled with both sides of my mouth.

"How's it goin' man? Care if I join you?" some angel broke the singing silence.

Pop!

My head-balloon burst. Dammit, Icarus, why do I have to fly so close to the sun? Or to the boiling center of the earth? Or wherever I am—I sure ain't anymore.

"Ummm… yeah, dude, f-feel free, have a seat," I said, trying to widen my eyes a bit.

A man was standing several feet away from my bench, looking like he had just been on a jog. A little necklace of sweat ringed around his light-gray, sleeveless hoodie. He was a fit guy with bulging calves and defined arm muscles. A styled mat of dark brown hair topped his head, still kempt, even after a sweaty, humid jog. He had one of those magazine-model smiles, pearly-whites peeping out from behind his thin lips. He looked like a nice dude, seemed friendly enough. Mia hadn't even growled—my little energy reader back at it again, reading everyone's vibe. And his was welcome and we were friends in a moment.

The man sat down. I grimaced as he planted his ass right in all my brain-goo and blood-chunks that were busy soaking into the bench. Hope that doesn't stain, too late to tell him now. He was sitting and slowing his breath.

"How's your day been so far?" he asked, turning his eyeline out over the water.

"Not too bad, not too bad. Just been relaxing, enjoying my time in San Diego. Never been before," I replied. Well, that was a lie. Enjoying San Diego—wasn't so sure about that yet. It was all dreary and nothing was happening just as I thought it would. Not here.

"Never been? Really! Well it's one helluva place," he exclaimed, intent on filling me in on the wonders and cursive of this southern California getaway. "Where are you from, then?"

"I'm from Utah, actually. Been traveling on the road for a bit now. Everyone told me to go check this place out if I'm headed south, told me San Diego was the place to see," I replied in a lackadaisical manner, inadvertently displaying my undecided disdain for this place.

"Yeah, it's one of those spots you gotta check in on when you're traveling. Weather today has been complete shit though, no denying that."

"Ain't that the truth. Just gray and gross. So you're from around here then?" I asked, assuming his San Diego citizenship.

"Nah, I would never live here!" he cackled at the suggestion, "I'm from Austin, Texas!" he stated with a proud voice—a Texas boy through and through and he sounded off, loud and proud of his cowboy-boot heritage. I could see it in him, plain and fierce.

My high mind was trying to figure it all out, stumbling around this conversation with assumptions left, right, and center. He loved this place, but didn't want to be associated with it, but still, it's a place you gotta go and see when you travel. All the same, it's California, it's southern, cursive California—where the women run wild, lift their tops up, beaches stretch the entire length, and movies are made, and Hollywood roars, and everyone makes their stake in the world of media magic, and everyone is an actor or an activist. Ah, I get it now.

"Jesus Christ, I'm with ya!" I blurted through my convulsed amusement, "Gas and milk are five bucks a gallon, this place'll nickel and dime you to death."

"Amen, brother. A-fuckin'-men."

We were both laughing now, slapping our knees and talking shit on this concrete monkey-jungle. Clearly our home states had several points up on California. No changing that. Amazing how hard the ice can break once two strangers find something they both dislike. And we were both disliking, bullying all the souls within and snickering about our far-off homes.

"So what are you doing down here then?" I inquired with a questioning smile.

"Well, I'm a flight attendant. My plane's pitt-stopped here overnight before we take off this afternoon," he said, massaging his calves and knees, attempting to break down the lactic acid buildup from his run.

"So you were just here one night then? Is that pretty normal?" I asked. He had my attention—I'd never met a real-life flight attendant that wasn't on the job. They're always so nice and never have time to tell you anything about themselves other than the name on their shiny airplane-shaped tag. They hustle up and down skinny rows, pushing those skinny little carts, doling out little snacks and juices, all before disappearing to some front- or back-end recess of the plane. I hadn't thought about their lives outside the aircraft. I must have thought they just live below deck, spending the majority of their life at thirty-five-thousand feet. I might have been high and ballooning now, but this dude always was. Those singing angels and muddy clouds were the backdrop to his everyday experience. He made Icarus look like a hack—flying up side-by-side with the sun every day, never popping, never tumbling out of the sky into the black reaches of the sea. His wings were spectacular.

"Yeah, the crew I'm with right now leaves from Austin and touches down in San Diego a lot, so I get to spend a night or two here almost every week," he said in an exhausted tone.

I liked thinking of myself as a vagabond, spending my nights in different towns, looking for little rivers to sit and sing next to. Uphill hikes to drag Mia up, outward views to snapshot and ponder on. But this guy? This guy made me look like a hack. His towns weren't side-by-side, they were thousands of miles apart. He had a choir of angelic sunshine and rivers of blue sky to sit next to. He was an authentic vagabond, a real obsessor of movement and his boots had the mud and grit of the Texan desert and the tanned-out soul of San Diego.

"Wow, so San Diego is sort of a home-away-from-home for you then?"

"Fuuuuck no. This place kinda sucks, man. I mean, the girls are pretty, the sun shines most of the time—but you can find that shit anywhere," he said with a chuckle, now massaging his upper thighs. "I mean, don't get me wrong, San Diego is a cool place. It has nice beaches, good nightclubs, ya know, the whole California experience. But it's just not... I don't know. Not my thing, not my scene, ya know?" he said, shifting his gaze from the ocean to me.

"Ahhh dude, I think you're sayin' exactly what I'm feeling," I replied, shaking my head with a so-what-that's-life shrug and grin. I ought to check my pipe—is this guy real? These figures are popping up out of the rough and reading my brain like a script, repeating back to me the things I think I know, but not sure enough to say out loud yet. "I think I hate this place," I said, surprised to hear the sounds slip out from behind my lips. Maybe I'm hearing juuuust what I want to. But I said it, and it tunneled into his ears and spurred like a bronco.

The man leaned back on the bench and let out a deep cackle, howling out a belly laugh that was filled with genuine humor, real exhilaration in his reaction. I must have said something funny. I chuckled along with him, smiling a bit bigger than I had in a few days. My cheek muscles could tell. We laughed in spite of the gray-and-grim scene that stretched across the sky. Cackled like a horde of hyenas that just stumbled into a den of lions, nervously backstepping out of a foreign joke we never remembered signing up for.

"Well dude, what the hell are you doin' down here then?" he slipped in between his chuckles. He hung his left arm up on the backrest of the bench and stretched his legs out halfway into the sidewalk.

"That's a good question. I don't know—everyone told me to check it out, remember?"

"Yeah, well… fuck everyone. You just gotta do what you're gonna do, and go where you're gonna go. And if they don't like that, if they get to smack talkin', then you find some new everyones. Ya know what I'm sayin?" he said matter-of-factly, making eye contact again.

Yes! I knew exactly what he was saying, I felt what he was saying like the rain was starting to fall. He was script reading again, peeling the words right off the surface of my overexerted spaghetti brain. Saying stuff I thought about but was too scared to say out loud. This Texas boy was giving me permission to be whoever and whatever the hell I wanted to be.

"Jesus Christ, I think I'm with ya, man."

"Course ya'are. We both need to learn that lesson, sounds like. You know how weird it is tellin' your Texan family and friends that you wanna be a flight attendant? Ahh—that's women's work! Ahh—why'd ya wanna leave? Ahh—get a grip, Texas boy!" he replayed the conversations and side-hand remarks that had no doubt consumed a substantial chunk of his brain space. Replayed them all in one quick sentence to a stranger on a blood-soaked bench. It was all Texas, just like cursive California. Everything was Texan in Texas, big and whole and filled out and he had a life to live up to. Bulls to wrestle and lasso. They were boots-on-the-ground in Texas, not Icarus, thirty-five-thousand feet off the dirt. But he was. And one quick sentence was all I needed to be right there with him. Both our brains were blown out now, mixing and congealing in a meaty stew. No way the bench could absorb much more, but there's always more to come. "God damn, it's like they thought I was tellin' 'em I'm gay or somethin'," he said, rekindling laughter out of resentment. He rolled his eyes and massaged his calves.

"But they got over it, didn't they? How long did it take them to figure out it was your life and not theirs?" I asked in a hopeful, humorous tone.

"Course they got over it. Sometimes you gotta find new everyones, but not when it's your family. Those ones stick like glue. Ehhh, but that ain't too bad, though. Ain't much of a concession if ya ask me," he replied, working through the lesson himself as he said it. And he was sayin' it.

"Yeah, I guess you can't pick your blood-and-bones family. Suppose you just have to teach 'em how to accept things that aren't so normal," I said, trying to understand what I was attempting to say. Sometimes you gotta teach yourself a thing or two just by saying it out loud.

It was quiet now, as ocean waves lapped up higher on the cobblestone seawall. The scooter was descending further into the water, almost overtaken by the salt of the sea. I wondered if the waves would be powerful enough to drag it off the rock. I guessed they wouldn't be. That tomorrow morning, that same L-shaped discarded refuse would still be sitting there, still be left for dead, used and abused. We both gazed across the horizon. The silence felt appropriate, while both our gears turned and the blood on the bench soaked a little deeper and we circulated.

"What's your name, anyway?" he said, breaking the quiet with a question that normally starts a conversation, but in this case, was ending one.

"Christian. And her name is Mia," I replied, pointing my sticky-weed finger down at my mutt, who was lounging in the grass to my right, watching groups of seagulls take off and land. She was too busy to listen, tending to flights of her own. "And what's yours?"

"I'm Anthony," he said with another big grin. We both leaned back into the bench now, finishing out the mind-mixture that had thoroughly absorbed into the softened cracks and splits of our wooden bench. "Ya know what man? We're gonna be juuuust fine," he said at last, holding his stare on the gloomy horizon line with a big toothy grin.

"What makes you say that?"

"Cause... you're here, aren't ya? I'm here, aren't I? At least we're both doing this shit. Most people just sit around their whole lives, thinking they know what they want. But they never take the time to chase it, never take the time to figure out what they *don't* want—you know, what they *don't* like," he said. He seemed taken with his own words, especially the don'ts, just as I was. Between the two of us, there was a third entity using our mouths, reading both our brain-scripts back to us. And we were silent and knew it and listened.

I nodded in a stoic agreement, eyes wide, committing to myself not to forget that.

Well, I'm out here, aren't I?

It was some flipped-and-twisted version of the gambler's sunk cost fallacy, taken to the biggest scale. Placed in the mold of life—I'm here, I'm down here, feet resting on the pavement, eyes bloodshot and stapled to the horizon. I'm here, and I wasn't before. I was up there in the angel's choir or down there in Hell's ovens before. I was somewhere before, but now I'm here. Before all of it, any of it. Before I was yanked from my mother's womb, before I drew a first breath. But now I'm down *here*, I might as well do something with this. Whatever this is. I've already come this far, searching and sifting through every grain of sand, admiring the ones that look juuuust right—ignoring the ones that don't.

But I'm here, aren't I? Might as well keep investing, keep gambling with my life. Keep finding the *shit* Anthony is talking about. Keep discovering what I don't like. Maybe at the end of that road, I'll accidentally stumble into something I do. Something I do. Yes!

"Well, I guess you're right. It sure would be a lot easier to do nothing every day, than something. Anything."

"Exactly, man. It might be cliché to say you've only got one life, so live it. But the ones who shake their heads and call that cliché are the ones who don't understand what that really means," he said, staring so intently at the dark thread of smoky silver connecting the sea and skyline, his face emotionless—a puppet producing age-old wisdom. His mouth was moving.

"Anthony, you ever think about how much time we *don't* have?"

"All the time, man. All the fuckin' time," he said heavily, combing his fingers through his hair. Maybe I was just ruminating in my dying high, but my eyes started leaking some sea salt of their own, moistening under the weight of time-theory. I quickly faked a yawn so the pair of tears forming could have some bodily logic behind them.

My new friend glanced down at his watch, "Speaking of time, I gotta go get showered so I can make it to the airport on schedule," he stretched his arms and legs, groaning out, "Duty calls, I guess. Would hate to get stuck in this town!"

"Can't think of anything worse!" I replied, shaking my horizon stare and watching him as he stood. Anthony turned around, stuck out his hand, prompting a parting handshake.

"Well, Christian, it's been a pleasure gettin' to talk for a minute. You're a pretty cool guy—you're gonna be alright."

I rose off the bench and met his eyeline, enthusiastically shoving my hand into his, shaking it firmly. "It really has been nice getting to chat. I appreciate you joining me on the bench for a little while. I probably needed that a lot more than you know. You have a great flight, man," I said, releasing his hand as he turned toward his hotel.

As he stepped off the curb and jay-walked across the street, he gave a little two-fingered peace wave over his shoulder, a final friendly gesture before he was gone. Sucked back into the mass of the western world. See you later, Texas. And I was here again, alone but for Mia, sitting on a bench under a canopy of grime and gloom. Two human brains blown out, blood-red and crimson stains painted all over the wooden bench surface. Chunks of meat here, an amygdala there, bits of cerebellum and cerebrum scattered all over the seat and sidewalk. It was a visceral murder scene of thought and emotion and I stewed in it and let it soak my bones for a moment.

I was pleased with the disgusting mess, a little uneasy about how to clean it all up before I found my rocket ship and reseated myself in the captain's chair. And what would passing joggers or midday walkers think? Probably call the police, "Yes, 911? There's a fucking goon splayed out on the side of the road, ranting and raving about time and things he loves and shit he hates. What should we do? Oh, and there's, like, blood and brains everywhere, and he's skipping through it all and playing in the repulsive mess like a child."

Can't have that. Gotta get lost real quick. Maybe if I leave a bit of the mess behind it'll help the next bench-sitting horizon-gazer work through something. Who knows. Who cares.

I looked over to my right, just in time to see Mia hunched back, crouched, taking a shit in the perfectly cut Californian grass. She had turned away from me, but her head was swung back over her left shoulder, and she was staring directly at me, nonverbally saying to cover her while she got vulnerable in this public space. I drew out the roll of scat bags, unrolled them until I reached the first perforation, and tore one off.

San Diego was a bust. The more time I spent siphoning through that machine, the more discontent I grew. It felt foreign—and not in the fun, exploratory, adventurous way. It was confusing, loud, and rude. People honking at every corner, yelling at random strangers for the smallest infractions. Navigation was impossible, with every wrong turn extending the destination route out another few miles along nonsensical one-way streets. Beggars were on every corner and they pan-handled and hung cardboard signs around their necks and there was no light in their eyes. I bought a drink, some new bearings for my longboard, and a little keychain, and that cost enough to rethink the entire financial decision to visit in the first place. Everything felt like an overdose of sunny-ville, picturesque, cursive California. Maybe it was the vibe, maybe it was the people, maybe it was the doomy-gloomy sky that made me uncomfortable. Maybe

I was getting homesick and everything about San Diego was in juxtaposition to what I wanted to feel. Land of the expensed, home of the homeless. Where dreams went to believe they were alive, but just got lost among the crowd. Where dreamers went to scream their dreams amid hordes of other screaming dreamers. And everyone was all still asleep with lightless eyes.

I was zig-zagging through the streets, cutting across random municipalities of San Diego, soaking in the little cities surrounding the towering one in the middle. I had no aim, no current destination to make progress towards. I knew I was going to spend the night here—one more night in this place before I took off north tomorrow. I had given up on using the map finder on my phone—there were millions of people, millions of cars all rushing the streets in a real big hurry. Outwardly, this place was an eyes-half-closed, dude-sayin', joint-smokin', laid-back, beach-vibing, Bob-Marley-worshiping, every-little-thing's-gonna-be-alright fantasy land that practically ran on the fumes of weed and dreams. But just under the surface, barely taking any stoke at all, it exploded into a cocaine-induced, anger-mismanaged, discontent, fit-throwing hell-scape that offered no free parking (or even cheap, at that), no clean streets, and no safe lots. It felt like everyone might smile at you, might offer a little compliment, then stab you in the kidney and sell it if given the chance. I like keeping my kidneys un-perforated, ready and able to sort through the bubbly contents of the occasional beer, thank you very much.

I glanced in my back seat and saw my overstuffed laundry bag. I had slumped it over there so I would remember to address the dirty clothes problem. I had put off cleaning my clothes for too long, the bag now crammed tight with stenching, sweat-out gym shorts and undies, shirts, and heel-holed socks. Loosening the cord to that bag would release a devilish avalanche of taint, one whole male locker room crammed into the contents of a single bag. I think some of the clothes were still a bit swampy and damp from their time on my body, be it yesterday or a week ago. Packed in there, no time to dry out, just like California. Everything was just like California and I was starting to hate it here in the south and west and I wished for the open and vast wastes of Mojave.

I pulled into the Ocean Breeze Laundromat and shut my engine off. It was an adorable little building, one block off a road that ran along the San Diego coastline. It was cool outside, and the structure was living up to its name. A wafty wind brushed down the street, carrying with it the smells of sea life and salt. The side of the building had a massive mural of dolphins and flowers and waves, vibrantly painted over rough cinder-block bricks. It stretched down the entire side of the structure, portraying the same scene a hundred-eighty degrees behind me. This one froze in place, though, while the one down the street was lapping over and over against the sand and rocks, flowers blooming up through the dirt. Either way I looked, I could hear the sounds of swirling water and smell the scent of fish and salt.

I hoisted my massive bag of filth over my shoulder and walked into the laundromat. Picked a washing machine that didn't seem too grimy, quickly dumped my swamp into the metal bin, and realized I needed coins. What year was this—coins? Fine. Thank God there's a machine down the row. Fed two bucks in, got a pile of quarters out. Buck-twenty-five for a load of wash. Fine. Shit, I needed detergent. Hot water wasn't gonna do the job on these fell deeds that might get up and walk out of the wash bin themselves if I didn't hurry. Another machine down the row, selling little boxes of Tide powder. Buck-fifty for a box. Fine. Quarters in, soap-box out. Back to the washing machine—all the articles are still in there, they haven't wandered off yet. Count my quarters, only two left. Dammit all, not enough for the load. Back to the coin machine, dollars in, quarters out. Back to the washing machine—one more stoop to make sure everything was on the up, looks like it's all still there. Dump the powder, slam the lid, hit start.

Whew. I leaned back on the machine as it started wiggling back and forth, gaining speed in its revolutions. Whisking out all that human-juice. Shit, I was still wearing my hoodie, the one I desperately needed to scrub clean— probably one of the dirtiest things in my collection. I turned around and attempted to lift the lid for the late joiner. Locked. Of course. I could cancel the load, but I'd have to pay the buck-twenty-five again and my bank numbers were plummeting. I shook my head and cursed my stupidity. Dumb-bo, just can't get this right, can ya?

I conceded to the car, where Mia sat, scanning every window, watching every pedestrian as they passed. The movie of the world was still beached and gloomy. She was resting on her blanket, which was covered in dog hair and little streaks of dirt from our expeditions outside of the rocket. That needed a solid scrubbing, too. I started doing some scanning of my own, noticing dog hair and dirt on most of the blankets we were using. One blanket, another, and another, Mia's doggie bed, my beanie hats, the little travel towel I had used to dry the sweat off my brow a hundred times. Several handkerchiefs—all needing to be cleaned. I quickly realized I had enough for another load, and the sooner I got it in, the sooner both loads would be done around the same time. I gathered my arms full of extra articles to wash and stumbled back into the Ocean Breeze laundromat.

Dollars into coins. More than enough this time. Enough for the drying, too. Soap from the soap machine. Fine. Into the washer go the hairy devils, pulling my hoodie up over my head, coins in, button's on, more wiggling. Another sigh of relief. You know what I don't like? Laundry. Life ain't easy being this dumb. At least you make it look good. Outside, a jet was roaring overhead, soaring east down the span of the continent, and I waved and hoped Anthony was waving back. Keep going, Icarus.

Chapter 15

This Stupid Car

I notice that many of the day's events were not interesting, or even enjoyable for the most part—with all the driving, cold weather, parking problems, garbage food... all being completely mediocre. And yet, I don't feel as though it's been a bad day. It feels like any other, a day that I can remember with a smile, all the same.

I flipped through the back half of my little brown book, eyes darting across the blank pages, yet to be filled with scribbles and scratches. I got to the final cover, resting the book on my thigh. It shifted automatically back to the last written leaf, where I had strung a silk cord across the page as a bookmark. I read it aloud this time, "A day that I can remember with a smile, all the same." Psshhh. Okay, little Keebler-elf fairy boy. I shook my head.

Shears of wind beat against the side of my car, rocking it back and forth, testing the give of my shocks. The gusts were relentless, howling across the sagebrush and rocky hills that spanned out for miles in every direction around me. Blowing hard, it felt like the gale would use the kayak atop my car as plane wings, lifting me and Mia off the ground to soar above the desert for a while before crushing us against one of the stone giant mountains that sat still on the horizon. Either that, or it would simply tip the car over, roll us down into the sandy ditch that sunk to our left. It wasn't plausible that the car would sit as still as those mountains, not under this intense pressure shift. Wind battered the side over and over, lapping against the car like the waves beating that broken scooter into the sea. How long till we get sucked under the sand, used and abused and lost out here in the middle of nowhere? Lapping wind, slamming, crashing, screaming over and over, one assault after another. I wanted to join in. It was aggressive and trying to wipe everything away.

My eyes were turning a jaundiced shade of yellow again. Pissing into this wind would be awful—but duty calls. The car cabin was cold, a foreign feeling compared to the rest of my expedition so far. It was usually a blistering heat that magnified through my windshield. Mia and I weren't panting, inhaling water to cool down anymore. These were new times. Mia was curled up in the back seat, tying herself into a little furry knot to keep warm. I was wearing a coat over my hoodie, beanie pulled down far over my ears and eyebrows. I jammed my hands under my legs to warm them up—few things worse than grabbing your pecker with icy fingers. But duty calls.

I swung the door open and stuck my left leg out. The door swung back, crunching my shin in the doorframe. Son-of-a-bitch this wind. Why don't you go blow someone else, you dickhead. I shook my head. I shook my leg, wringing out the pain of a banged-up shin.

This time I kept my hand on the door, shoving it wide and barricading it while I hoisted myself out of the front seat. Mia hopped out behind me, instantly regretting it as more abusive gusts plastered us against the side of the car. The door slammed itself shut, and I was just grateful the driver's side window didn't shatter. It was brutal out here. The atmosphere had a hole poked in it and all the frigid air was zipping out into space and trying to yank us along with it.

We made slow progress down into the gravel and sand ditch, about fifty yards from the car. Once we were down, the gully and its scattered boulders provided a slight respite from the wind. Zipper down, piss-propeller out—not into the wind, but with it now. Let's at least try and be smart about this. Mia was wandering around, sniffing for a spot to mark. She didn't waste much time, already getting exhausted while attempting to stay sturdy on the earth. Her forty-pound frame could be blown away with ease by one of these wind-slaps. Should have a leash on her, at least. This wasn't the wastes of Nevada or the cliffs of Yosemite, but it felt dangerous and she clung to the crackled roots woven through the pebbles. What a sorrowful scene that would be—my little mutt whisking in circles up into the sky like some wicked-witch-of-the-west horror scene from Oz. Up and up and down and up she'd go and be lost and lever-pulled to the great beyond and I'd truly—genuinely—be alone. Best we get back into the car before we both get pounded near to death. And we did.

It was cold and getting colder. The wind sucked any ounce of heat that attempted to make itself felt in this place. Any beams of sunlight trying to mediate the cold with warmth were met with castigating blasts and cyclones. It showed no signs of stopping. I had one little bar of cell service, so I tried Googling a weather report—this was commonplace. The air never sat the hell down and was still for a moment. Toddler mentality was all over throughout California, couldn't escape it if I tried. Everything was always going somewhere, anywhere but here or there, and moving all the while. Swift like cursive in the golden state and nothing felt so golden anymore. It was cold and getting colder.

Late afternoon, and I was going to spend the night here. That's at least five more hours of howling bullshit until I can close my eyes and try again tomorrow. I pulled out my phone, tapping the power button to see the time. 4:37 p.m. I sighed, tossing my cell back into the console in between my two front seats. My left heel was impatiently tapping up and down, waiting for the doctor to come out of his cave and beckon me back for an appointment. Diagnose these otherworldly howls, different and horrid from the groans of the Mojave. Where was it all going, why couldn't the air just stop and be still and quiet and allow for life, for the movie of the world to resume? I leaned my head on my knuckles, elbow propped on the arm rest of the car door.

Habitually, I shoved my hand back in the console, checked my phone again. 4:38 p.m. And here it felt like three minutes since I last looked. I threw the phone back in the console, little harder this time. Madness was creeping over me, inch by anxious inch—up the back of my neck, across my scalp, red devil, impatient, angst flooding my face, crimson-tipping my ears. It was all chaos out there, all still and rushing chaos. There was no dust to blow, no trees to split and break. Rocks and boulders sat in the wind and shrugged and showed no care for the hole in the atmosphere, the hole we were all getting swallowed into. My rocket was vibrating and shaking back and forth and I felt it wildly and we didn't move, just braced down and prayed hard.

What the fuck am I doing out here?

There was no appointment with the doc, nothing to wait for. I could freeze like a rock in place, wait a hundred years, wake up, and this land would still be the same—windy, cold, visually beautiful in its own way. Still stricken by the racing breath of the planet. It was awful. Nothing would be different, I wouldn't have missed any appointments, it would just be the year twenty-one-nineteen and I'd still be asking my prevailing question.

I was going mad—it was lock-stepped May and I was somewhere in the Alabama Hills. The worst part was that I couldn't pinpoint what was making me so angry. So discontent with the here and now and everything before. Every gale that beat against the car made me a little madder, as if the world was wronging me through its natural presence. Just by being out there, on the other side of the glass, going somewhere fast and meaning it. I looked around everywhere for something to point my pissed-off finger at and blame. Nothing I was running into was what I wanted, just piles and piles of what I didn't. I was petrified, unable to engage with any of the activities I had prepared for this exact moment. Play some harmonica. Read one of the twelve books you packed. Write in your little brown book. Play the Nintendo Switch you haven't so much as glanced at yet. Listen to the Game of Thrones audiobook. Whittle a piece of wood. I was shrinking and hated all the things I brought along for the ride and wanted nothing to do with any of them and my car kept shaking and I kept sitting heavy.

None of it sounded good. Didn't feel like touching even one of those things. They were all like laundry—stinky, swampy, dank, and dull. Only thing I wanted to do was sit and hate and brick my brain with more Mary-Jane and shove another tortilla with mayo and chicken sandwich meat on it into my fat fucking face and be really chafed about it. And I was.

Routine becomes Habit
Habit becomes Lifestyle
Lifestyle becomes Belief
Belief becomes Stone
Stone doesn't break.

I peered out the window, still resting my skull on bloodless knuckles. Beyond the glass and howling wind, there were little rock knolls dotting the desert top. Occasionally, a lot of knolls would gather and form rocky plumes that folded up on top of one another, building up in smooth, round little formations. Some would stack high, towering over the sandy surface—little stone mini-giants sitting crouched like playing children at the feet of the daddy mountaintops that lay beyond. Scattered sage and yellow-flower bushels were spaced across the scene in near-perfect gaps. At the base of the bigger towering knolls, the foliage bunched up, hiding away the spot where the rocks sunk deep into the ground. It was all perfectly still and petrified as rushing winds breached the lowlands and tore at the seams. It was all happening.

Beyond them, beyond the knolls and little bushes and flowers and sand, rose enormous peaks. So high, their tops disappeared into the descending pearly-white clouds. The ravines and ridgelines were flooded with snow, wind blowing off the outer layer of fluff like a smeared pastel painting, center-stage and moving in real-time. Gray stone lay beneath, jutting out in some spots, revealing the jagged and rough surface of these slumbering behemoths. They were utterly magnificent, stealing away words and thought and worry, if only for a moment. They apexed one after another, each ridgeline pointing out, then retreating into a graded mountain valley, then back out, then back in, veined with snow.

So high up, out there in the atmosphere, so high they were stabbing the clouds with their sharp spearing snow-caps. Where the snow transformed into stretched and billowed clouds, I couldn't tell. It was all one swirling scene, moving, mixing, windblown into a new picture a few minutes later. New parts of the mountain face would reveal, and old sections would disappear behind the advent of additional cotton-clouded blankets. Then the old parts would peek back through the stratified, heaven-formed windows. Nothing would repeat in the same manner, always changing and molding over the caps in a more ghostly way than the last. It was all happening and it was all still down here under a firmament of moving parts, rushing parts, parts all swirling like whipped cream, sweet sugar, and milk across the movie of the world. And I was watching, struck by whimsy and the feeling of being drawn out into the black of space.

Another sheet of wind broke against the car, splitting forward and aft like a river around a mossy rock. The wheels dug in, not moving, not sliding, cemented in place.

Pearly willows whisping off
The tops of snow-touched peaks
Brushing out into the swimming blue
Stratosphere, deep and vast
Beneath a sea of desert bluffs
Knuckled boulders heaped and bundled
Little russet goblins climb
On each other's shoulders
Scuttling off into the hills
Lost, still as stone

I gripped my pen, lifting it off the page. Another chicken-scratched sheet. For a moment, I forgot about the endless gales, the knolls, and the cold. Now my fingers ached, stark-white and frozen. I lengthened them, stretching them out wide until my wrists and palms started shaking, then clenched them back in, forming a fist. I repeated this a few times, trying to pump some blood back into my fingertips. It was working, but only for twenty seconds or so, before the cold slipped back, frosting my joints once again. I cupped them to my mouth, exhaling a puff of belly-air through the chilled sausages, attempting anything to bring them back to life. I don't know what for, all I was doing was sitting, staring, still as stone in a tundra topped with sand. Freeze me solid, cryo-sleep tonight. I rued it and pictured it and shivered at the thought.

I pulled out my phone again, clicked the power button— 4:54 p.m. Back into the console. I shook my head. Even a burst of creative chicken-scratching didn't drag by a noticeable chunk of time. Nothing would at this rate. Maybe time was freezing up too, stretching seconds into three-minute slugs. Drawing out hours into agonizing days of idle anger with no logical purpose. I'm pissed and I'm jamming my finger at rocks and rockets and Mia and the icy air and everything but the one thing that's really pissing me off—me. Don't say that out loud, though. Just gonna piss me off more. It's not my fault, nothing I can do about it. Just gonna jam those bloodless knuckles under my chin and think some more about how mad and cold I am. It was cold and getting colder all the time.

This stupid car. What kind of rocket ship am I running? A crew of two, an incompetent captain that wastes away in the face of decision. Cars don't blast off into the unknown, scooting around Mars, through the stars, around the moon. They don't run on rocket fuel, they barely pull a few G's, unless you're getting slammed by another and spinning out of control. Cars have wheels—rockets have giant bays that blast billion-degree flames, propelling tons of steel up through the atmosphere. Cars have thin little windows that can shatter and crack from just a little pebble-flip on the freeway. Rockets have reinforced glass, thick enough to withstand the sucking abyss of space. This stupid car wasn't withstanding anything.

Why would I think transforming this stupid car into a little tent-on-wheels would be a better idea than buying a van or a motor home or a trailer or one of the other twenty wheel-based locomotives that people live in. You know who lives in cars? Homeless people. They find a nice spot for 'em, park 'em, and find their closest twenty friends, pile in and fuck each other in a great Olympic-style orgy. They stack and stab needle after needle, filling the floor of the front seat with empty spoons, vacant syringes, smoked-out roaches, cigarette butts, and dried up beer cans. They shatter the windows and never bother to fix the mess, living with glass splinters in their underwear for who knows how long. Sit in one of those cars and you'd be lucky to escape without getting the newest car-lab concocted sexually transmitted infection. Or disease? It once was STD now they say it's STI, and I feel like it's all the same. Maybe it's an "infection" when you get genitial warts in the bombed out, jerked-off carcass of a long-dead Subaru. Whatever it was, it wasn't here. I'm idle and dulling and wracked inside from swathes of living out the wrong fantasies, living in cars, wishing for home and this isn't it.

This stupid car—I might as well leave it here in this spot, let the sand build up around the tires. Maybe a couple hillbilly goblins will sneak around and join me and we can all dawn our homeless hats and act the parts and participate in some intimate Olympics. Maybe that would be a better use of my time rather than sitting here, knuckles sinking further and further into my skull—they're almost poking out the back of my head. Goblin friends, any friends, even the fiendish ones, I'd take 'em now, more than I would have before. Crawl in, there's room. That is, if you can get the door open. Watch your shins.

Cars are meant to be a midway point. A physical middle ground handing my body off from my house to my workplace, from school to my house, from the grocery store to my house, from my house to the bar. I set foot in this cabin when I'm going somewhere, not when I'm just existing. I'm not in here to just be. But I am—boy, am I! I'm in here with sights on the horizon somewhere, with the wheels listing, radio blaring, heat blowing hard. I'm in here to go from one place in the world to another and that's always been the primary case. This stupid car—now I'm just in here and the sand is building up, my tires are sinking into the ground. My beige exterior doesn't look any different from the tanned surface of a million little knolls scattered across the surface of the desert. It doesn't look different, and it might not be, all the same.

In one ear and out the other. My time, my apprehensive time. Checking clocks, tapping my feet, waiting to get somewhere that I'm going. That's what cars are for, after all. I've been trained on that front since I was a little baby boy. Strapped into the car seat, never just for fun. Always going somewhere, always moving. Mom didn't chest-strap me in, just to sit in the back seat and hang out. She was taking me places and I knew it. I felt it, as the rumbles of the engine vibrated under my little baby butt. I went to sleep and woke up in a new light, spans of time completely blown by without recognition. Car time had a beginning, a middle, and an end. Now my wheels are disappearing from all the sand blown around, wind splitting front and back, moss growing on my steel chassis that's fast becoming a surface of stone. The moss was growing—on my casing, across my forehead, crawling into my ears and I can hear it stretching its little green fingers around my drums, whispering idle songs.

This stupid car. Going nowhere. Even when I do command it to move, it's never with one place in mind. There is no middle ground out here—it's all the same. When I finally stop for the day, I don't get out and walk inside, plop on the couch and flip the T.V. on. I don't have a kitchen to make a sandwich in, don't have a bathroom to propel my piss into. Don't have a real bed to snuggle on, don't have a living room to laze about. There's no middle ground. San Diego handed me off to the Alabama Hills, with no definite destination in mind. The Alabama Hills will hand me off to the next place, wherever it might be. When I get there, my wheels will stop rotating, they'll sink a few inches into the dirt and I'll sit on my rock-hard ass in the captain's chair and I'll think real hard about what's going on out there, beyond the thin glass, beyond the steel-stone casing. I'll knead and wrinkle and watch the movie of the world and struggle against time to solve the great and diabolical question of life. But I'll still be sitting, still angry and pissed and crimson with some madness I can't put my finger on in the front seat of my car. Front seat of this box that's always taken me from point A to point B with more reason than growing moss. But the moss is growing and I can hear it.

I turned around and crawled into the back seat of this stupid car. I'm not sure what made me do it, maybe some internal realization or desire to shift my perspective. I had pretty much punched directly through my own face, so all that knuckle leaning wasn't getting me anywhere. I scooted Mia over and fluffed up my blankets and pillow, forming a comfy little seat to relax in. I leaned back, gazing up between the two front seats, fighting the urge to reach back up and snatch my phone. I pulled Mia in closer, tucking her onto my lap and wrapping her in a fleece blanket like a burrito. She was tired or cold or annoyed or all three at the same time, I couldn't tell. She happily cuddled up on my lap, basking in the shared bodily warmth. I held my gaze between the two front seats, out the front windshield, out across the plains of frozen desert, straight into the sharp faces of the Alabama Hills. My hand stroked and scratched the nooks behind Mia's ears as she drifted back into an early evening slumber.

I felt as though I was on an endless flight between two places—some vacation destination and home. A flight that took off and never had plans of landing. A rocket launched for the moon, sailing on passed, with no goal in mind, no touchdown, no north star to aim for. No first step for self-kind, just infinite rocketing. Rocketing and rocking and soaring idle through space and time.

Cars take you from one spot to another. Rockets take you from the Earth to the Moon, or to Mars. Things that move and have seats take you places. That's not just routine or habit—that's belief, that's fact. But I'm hovering in the middle-land, lost in a box, frozen in the hands of the middleman. A package ordered by the universe, by God, by something in the midnight stratosphere, but never delivered. Forgotten in the back of an angel's FedEx truck, always wheeling around, following the delivery of a thousand other boxes, seeing them placed on their sweet little porches. But never mine. My box sits still in the dark in the back, shoved in a corner. Forever stuck in the place between the points. Cemented in the moment between one phase ending and another beginning.

What the fuck am I doing out here?

I raised my hands up and shrugged. At the same time, I cut through the silence of the cab, lifting my voice above the shaking wind. "This stupid car had better start being okay with me hanging out inside of it."

Mia's eyes blinked open from her nap, darting up at my face in a sort of dumb-founded amazement. She was right, and I knew it instantly. All the anger I had built up, constructing and excusing and blaming and pointing at every little inanimate thing around me. All the blood that had flooded my ears and forehead, all the pissed-off discontent, all the idle madness I had been training—little devilish soldiers I lined up one after another, facing out toward the world, ready to slash and kill and destroy everything before them. Suddenly, all their screaming, anguished faces were turned around, looking right at me—their stupid commander. Their spears were raised, guns directed, arrows at the ready, all angled at my ignorant, tongue-tied face. They had triggers to pull and I let them. Sometimes you gotta teach yourself a thing or two just by saying dumb things out loud.

Their bullets and spear tips and arrowheads ripped through my flesh, and I sat there and stared at the face of stone giant mountains and I was stone myself. The sand built up around my wheels, higher yet. It was cold and getting colder.

The world put me in this position, reinforced the idea that cars take people places. The world taught me how to jab my fat finger into the face of everything around me. The world taught me how to be the victim of this idle madness. The world taught me that homeless people live out of their cars, slam needles into their forearms, fuck like donkeys in the backseats of scoured Subarus. The world taught me to be lazy, taught me to live in the space between one thing and another. The world taught me to live for caesuras, taught me that outsets are too hard to stake. The world jabbed its even fatter finger right into my impressionable clay forehead and made a big fat hole and then filled it with all my feelings. Told me to use that as low-grade dumpster fuel, told me to use that as my inspiration, my motivation. Oh, these stupid feelings. These stupid feelings that dictate my very soul. The world told me that cars take you from this place to that place, and that's the purpose they serve and there's no other reason and if you think there is, you're stupid. I kept on, and the world was telling and I was a victim to it and it was the heaviest transgressor.

But the world was stark-brazen, categorically, clear-blue-sky, ice-sliced, jagged-mountain, undoubtedly, dumb-foundedly wrong. The world taught me this doctrine—and I let it. Yet here I was sitting in my car—my rocket ship—lounging in the back seat, in the space between two places. The car didn't have an opinion about it, the car was steel and dust and metal and cloth and rubber and waiting under a white and snow-dusted sun. I'd better start being okay with hanging out inside this thing. And that's it.

I grabbed my little silver pen, unbound my little brown book again, and wrote a little theory down three pinstriped lines.

What if when I'm feeling lost
In the stillness of all this stone, I smile?
And then move my hands and feet, of course.

I wrapped the elastic cord around the leather casing of my little brown book. Slipped my little silver pen into its rubber-band sheath. Tossed the book into my front seat, grabbed my phone. Immediately slid it into my jacket pocket and swung open the back passenger door with enough force to signal to the wind that I didn't care if it wanted to blow or not. Blow me away, dickhead. Mia jumped out behind me, grinning ear-to-ear. It was cold and getting colder in the frigid ides of May. Somewhere near inside or far out on the frozen sand, a stone was starting to break. I shoved my hands into my pockets and started walking.

Chapter 16

Tar-Covered Hands and Feet

Pine trees scattered the woodland, each one spaced the same distance apart. Their trunks had no variation or curvature—spearing straight up into swaying canopies, high in the sky. The woods were thick, blotting out the evening twilight behind a trillion little needles, dark and green. The smell of sap permeated the air, caked to the sides of every trunk in massive, sticky, golden blobs. The forest floor was barren of bushes and other foliage, layered deep with a trillion more brown, decrepit needles fallen from years past. The layers carpeted the ground in a spongy mat, covering holes and divots with just enough dead-fall that the ground looked flat. The legs of my little black and blue everything chair cut through the layers, jamming down into the hard, frozen dirt. My butt hung only an inch or two above the sea of needles, as I stacked and angled various logs, forming a teepee in the fire pit. Blood ran down my thumb.

The wood seemed mostly dry, but it was hard to tell. The bundles I had gathered were so cold to their core, I wasn't sure if it was water frozen on through or if they were just matching the temperament of the outside air. Their little wooden souls had better be up for burning tonight, a fire's the only thing hot enough to stem this creeping freeze.

My fingers had lost all their tan coloring, appearing now as the hands of a dead man—white and devoid of life. Little splotches of dried blood rimmed my nails, forming red smiles that peered back at me while I ripped and split the wood for tinder and kindling. I had no gloves, no protection from the biting cold. No protection from the splinters and rough surfaces of the wood I bundled. I could hardly feel my little ice-boxed sausages anyway, so all this shearing of stick and flesh was just a visual bloodletting that I hoped wouldn't leave me sore tomorrow. But I knew it would. I tried not to care. Tried to pretend I was a mountain man of old, like all the badass bearded tough guys I'd seen on the big screen. I pulled the bark and skin off a fist-full of twigs, shredding them into a potent ball of flammable fuel. A picture kept fluttering across my mind as I sheared another set of sticks and placed them at the ready.

A black-and-white image I had seen and somehow internalized so deeply into my brain, I was recalling it over a decade later. A little rectangular picture taken a hundred years ago. A man standing on the banks of a sprawling mountain, pine trees surrounding him on nearly every side. He's dressed in brown leather garb. I assumed it was brown, while the picture showed everything as a light shade of gray. He has a long-sleeved leather shirt on, with little tassels falling down his shoulders, around his chest in a V shape. His leather pants are laced up the sides, like a pair of shoes tied tight and secure. And those little brown moccasins—how could I ever forget those foot gloves. Stretched like Saran wrap around his feet, halfway up his ankle, before turning over and flapping down. They were the perfect shoe. I imagined the man running through the woods like a gazelle, racing smoothly with long strides that were balanced and weightless. Sharp rocks, jagged stones, poking tree branches, a trillion pine needles—none of that a match for the perfect mountain shoe. The image stood stark.

The man had one of his feet up on a fallen tree trunk, and he was turned toward whoever it was snapping the picture. A mountain man pose in mountain man clothes. His beard was massive—so full it was almost a challenge to find the button of his nose. His mouth was completely lost in the mess of gray and white wires, scraggly and unkempt—but that seemed like the whole point. A mountain man beard, the perfect face blanket. Right now, I would give a thing or two to have a beard like that. My chin was frozen, my lips were cracked and had little pinstriped lines of dried blood running down them. I could feel my lips, but my nose was numb and dumping golden blobs of its own down onto my shoulder. I grabbed my handkerchief and forcefully rammed another snot-rocket into a mess of other freshly dried goo. Wish I could grow a beard like that mountain man. Maybe my nose would thank me for it. Maybe it would just end up being another trough to catch snot in.

The mountain man had sullen eyes. Eyes that had seen a thousand peaks, knew them all like the back of his worn and dirt-coated hands. His eyes replayed a hundred tales of bear-fighting, lion-tracking, and rabbit-noosing. He looked like he'd gone toe-to-toe with the beasts of the woods and won on every occasion. Afterall, how could he be standing there, in my brain, if he'd lost a battle with a grizzly? That leather might be tough, but it was no match for a bear-claw. He might have escaped, might have shot it with the oversized musket he held in his right hand, its butt planted right down into the soil. His eyes told the story of the never-ending game—survival-of-the-fittest and he planned on winning. A game he planned on playing until someday, he lost. But he was playing hard, all the same. His eyes made it clear that he wouldn't let his lever be pulled while resting in grandma's hand-me-down rocking chair. He was a mountain man—it was the mountains that would gobble him up someday. And they did.

On top of his head sat a coon-skinned hat. The black-and-white shading of the image detailed clearly the alternating ringed stripes painting the puffy raccoon tail pinned out the back of his head like a carnal ponytail. It brought the whole outfit together. Brought the entire ensemble of the traditional mountain man to bear in a beautiful chorus of adventurous hunting, mountain stews, hide tanning, log-leaping, animal-fighting fury. He was constantly leaping and living off the woods and he was wonderfully strong and his tale was an answer to a riddle.

I remember the mountain man like I saw him five minutes ago. I was in elementary school and we were flipping through the pages of our American history book. Every other page was just another one filled with a billion words that I didn't want to read. More pictures, more stanzas of historical importance—importance that didn't resonate with me yet. Natives gathered around campfires, dancing and banging on drums. Lewis and Clark and Sacagawea all paddling down a river, looking forward into the bleeding horizon of the West. A big-muscled man pounding a golden spike into the railroad, linking two halves of the continent. Soldiers barricaded in a trench, ready with gas masks and rifles in the heart of World War One. Flipping through the pages of that book, a conglomeration of American scenes and sorrows, victories and villains. Somewhere in the middle, there was this little black-and-white photo of a mountain man, standing stalwart on the side of a ridge, dressed in the perfect garb. Donned with the perfect hat. Gripping his trusty musket, horn of gunpowder dangling off his hip. Skinning knife tucked under his strapped-leather belt. I wanted to be like him.

So I kept shearing bark off twigs and sticks and logs with my bare hands, shrugging when I reopened the dried-out cuts that covered my fingers. The blood just told me I was doing it right, suffering just enough to be like him. I didn't want this to be easy, and I didn't have many alternatives. No gloves—arctic mountains, pines and night-time approaching. I held out my hand, empty, sliced, skinned, and bruised. It was steady—unshaking in the icy climate. Pearly-white, a dead man's hand. It was still. Twinges of pain and tiny drops of steaming blood reminded me of my livelihood. They felt right, well-timed. Felt desired. And I licked them clean.

I pulled out my Bic lighter, leaned forward, and sparked the bushel of bark, dead pine needles and twigs. Instantaneously, it ignited, glowing red-hot and vibrant against the drab backdrop of the forest. The ribbons of flame reached up through the teepee I had built, hugging around logs and smaller sticks, daring them to take light. Slowly, they took the dare, crackling and bursting under the intensifying heat. The warmth bled out from the core of the fire pit, blasting my face, chest, arms, and knees with a familiar blanket of hot fervor. This was true warmth, not some pseudo-heat generated by the man-made gears and cogs of my car's engine. Not the body-generated calidity that comes from wearing four jackets, like I was. This was energy sucked and sent out in a magnificent exchange, as true and defined and real as the sun on a sweltering day in the Mojave. I was high up, mountains sloping all around and the fire screeched.

I turned the Bic lighter over in my hand a few times, rubbing my thumb down the side of the smooth exterior.

That black-and-white mountain man didn't have one of these. He'd be gobsmacked seeing how easily fire could shoot out from the little round metal hole on top. One flick of a wheel, one press of that little red horseshoe gas leaker—flame. He'd have to strike rocks on one another over and over until he could get one spark to sing off into his precariously prepped pile of tinder and kindling. Then came the immediate blowing he'd perform, puffing up his cheeks, backing the embering bushel with his calloused hand. A lot of steps for him to produce that undiluted warmth. One flick-and-hold for me.

The logs of my teepee were all ablaze now, sending wavering orange light up against a backdrop of pine trees. The outermost ring of pines glowed like a circle of ritual worshipers, leaning in, hovering their sprawling arms above the flames. The breeze swayed them back and forth, in toward the firepit and back out again. Their branches moaned out creaking groans—swaying, hovering, waving all the time. Summoning woodland demons from outside the perimeter. To come and gobble me up, like the mountain man I was pretending to be. Or to join me in my quest for warmth, join me ringside as we'd all absorb as much heat as our bloody bodies could take. Save some for later, store up some of that radiating passion for below-freezing sleep hours. And they would be.

Past the worshiping pines, was an infinite darkness. The sun had set, twilight dissipated, and streaks of velvet midnight painted the unknown. Gazing up from my fire-stare, my eyes couldn't dilate into the black curtain. Back to the flames, back to the darkness, eyes never adjusting to either. Blazing fingers wagged before me, bright and flaring amid all this opposite. Shadow-driven claws reached out through the space between the trees, as demons started spawning from black-holes, crawling out one after another into my little camp. One trickled up under my four layers of jackets, beneath my shirt, prickling up my spine and around my neck. I violently shivered an invasive chill—a physical vibration to rid the scent and seizure of tainted thoughts. Shaking all the same, the mental shades remained. Daring me into the darkness, daring me like the flames dared those logs to burn. Daring me to step out beyond safety, get gobbled up by the mountains. There were things out there, demon-things. Creatures more sinister than sin itself, just give them a toe, a pinky-nail dipped into the pond of tar. I was alone and my eyes grew wide and wild as the folds of California threatened.

A toe dipped and I slipped, head-first under the surface.

Great grizzlies were out there, sniffing around for a meal, for a warm sack of blood to drink on. I'd heard of these attacks, seen videos, seen DiCaprio get mauled and ripped ass-to-elbow in *The Revenant*. They say you're supposed to fall down and play dead, after interlocking your fingers behind your neck. Lay face down so the grizzly's knife-like claws gouge out the muscle and meat of your back, instead of ripping out your heart or the soft jelly of your tummy. They say the bears like live game, they like the challenge, to play with their food. So play dead, and they'll slice you up, but not before they get bored and drag you back to their lair for snacking on later. That's when you're supposed to run for your life.

I had a strong rocket ship though, no grizzly could breach that. Right? Fuck me, they definitely could. They're brilliant. I've seen movies of people getting ripped up by bears, but I've seen videos of bears slipping their claws under car-door handles and opening them, too. I'd just lock the doors, then I'm safe.

They'd shatter the windows next, maybe crawl up on the hood and sit their six-hundred-pound ass on my windshield. That wouldn't hold. Then they're in, clawing at my kicking feet, savoring the screams and shouts, playing with their food, just how they like it. And forget Mia, she'd be done for before any of this could play out. She'd go on the offensive, jump at the furry demon-bear as if anything she could do would matter. Just a little chicken-wing snack for the grizzly bear. Just more animal meat—the bear had plenty of that. Fish, deer, wolf, elk, moose—dog-breast wouldn't be that different. But human? Human meat would be sweeter. They say the forest service hunts down bears that attack and eat humans, because once they have the taste for man-flesh, it's too succulent to ignore. As if their whole lives, they ate bland oatmeal with no brown sugar, and now they've had a breakfast of bacon, eggs, pancakes, and syrup. Once they've had that delicious meal, there's no going back. They hunt. And I was the menu.

They're out there, they smell the bead of sweat dribbling down my cheek like a shark sniffs blood in the depths. I'm sitting too close to the fire. They smell the reopened cuts under and around my fingernails, the blood drips that should have dried out by now, but no. They'd get high on that metallic scent, just to get a swish of it around their teeth and tongue, just one taste. They're out there, they're coming—and they wouldn't give three-and-a-half shits if I applied maggot-fiend ideology to their encroaching demon-hood. I jump out, scream loud, rip my pants and shirt off, and tell them how I'm gonna fuck 'em up, kill their cubs, beat their grizzly-wives. How I'd arrive in the middle of hibernation with a baseball bat or a peashooter and do 'em in. Do 'em in good, right in the fucking face. Yeah, the grizzly, right in its thick skull. No way. I'd just be making it easier for the bear, taking off my clothes so he doesn't have to pick them out of his teeth once he's done. I'm the maggot invading his forest, and he's hungry. He's coming and he's angry and I'm sweating and I taste exquisite. Fear is the seasoning on my meat.

My many knives, my nine-millimeter, my dog, my car, my fear—I'm well-to-do against a bear crawling out of the shadows. Better off than I'm giving myself credit for. The forest service might show up in the morning, crimson palm-prints stained across my windows, trails of frozen blood leading off into the woods. A dead dog, an empty magazine from a nine-mil that did nothing against the invading grizzly. Several jackets torn up, dangling from the doors of the car, bits of cloth and meat and fistfuls of fur guiding the investigators to some nearby cave, where'd I'd be, resting easy in the stomach of a slumbering bear. I'm well-to-do against the coming beast. Maybe Mia will sense it before I do and give a little growl and we can both saddle up in the rocket and get out of this mountain jungle before it's too late. Let the fire burn, burn down the woods, the worshiping pines, the lair of a thousand dark-dwelling demons. Burn it all out, black and barren in revenge for something that never even happened. Revenge for putting those tainted thoughts in my head. They're hunting, he's hunting. And I'm all alone.

I'm well-to-do against the beasts, but not against the tar that's taking root in between my ears. More Mary-Jane, more pipe-fulls, loads of green and sticky salad—renew the lonely paranoia, ass hanging an inch off the ground on top of a mountain I've never been to before.

I stared at the same dark hole between some pine trees for several minutes, attempting to shirk the blindness of my fire-gazing. There it was—forty yards out, slumping between wooden poles, carefully stepping on the silent carpet of pine needles, one stealthy maneuver into another. One tree trunk to another, peering around the bark, two little glowing holes peeking out at me. Monstrous and midnight, staring at my blood-flooding face. It was probably licking its black, leathery lips. Playing the game, the adrenaline chemical seasons the human meat. Just stare a little longer, the seasoning isn't ripe yet. It knew I could see it, it was frozen still, trying to get me to believe the tar-night curtain, rather than admit to the reality of a grizzly come to feast. It knew, it was smart, it was prepping for a delicious dinner, an easy kill. And I was.

I fumbled around my coat pocket, holding my vision on the frozen beast, nestled between the trees, our eyes locked on one another's in a deathly staring contest. Empty pocket. Shoved my hand in another one, empty too. Inside my second layered jacket? Empty. Right side, second layer pocket—there's my Bic lighter. No good, unless the grizzly-demon's fur is caked in hairspray. Doubtful. Third layered jacket, left pocket—nothing, same with the other side. Empty. Where was the flashlight, the knife, the mountain man camping equipment? Scattering dirt around my feet, not feeling any objects that might have slipped from my pockets. Holding my gaze. Feeling to my left—tupperware container with a half-eaten loaf of bread on it. Not good enough to tempt the beast away from me. Wasn't even white bread—some cheap wheat shit. Holding my gaze. Left pants pocket—my cell phone. Sure, call someone right now, give them the trauma of listening to someone be devoured alive. Right pants pocket. My god-beam flashlight. Always the most obvious, last place you look. Hands not so steady anymore, pulled out the torch, clicked it on, turned the intense beam straight at the spot where the eyes were staring at me.

Nothing. Just the remains of a fallen pine tree. Mia was lying by the fire. The sudden shift from darkness to illumination caused her to perk up, staring out to where I shined the light. She hadn't previously been alerted, and for some baffling reason, I hadn't even thought of looking to her for a signal. Nothing. Nothing was out there. It was just me, the brushing of a breeze filtering through the pine trees, the crackling of firewood. I shook my head in disbelief. I knew there was nothing—but I dove headfirst into the tar pond all the same. Well-to-do my hairy, frozen ass.

The mountain man image came flooding back into my mind. His hunting musket, his knife, his beard, his perfect mountain shoes, pants, and shirt. That coon-skinned cap that barely drooped below his ears. I wanted to be like him. Calm and collected in the face of the wild world. Able to hunt and wrestle with the biggest beasts that shuffle around the woods. I wanted to be just like him, calling the mountains my home. Living off the land, charting the western frontier, moving his feet and hands. Obsessed with vagabond living.

I had three jackets and an oversized coat on. He wore a little leather shirt with tassels. I had two beanie hats on, pulled down past my ears and eyebrows. He was donned with a coon-skinned cap that only blanketed the top half of his ears. I had pants with two hip-side pockets, two cargo pockets, and at knee height, zippers that turned my pants into shorts. Innovation. His pants were laced and had no pockets—just leather and unbreathing from bottom to top. I had tough, thick-skinned hiking boots on, soles built an inch thick, protecting the bottoms of my feet from the stabbing rocks and branches and prickles of a trillion forest needles. He wore those perfect mountain man shoes—little moccasins with the top flopped down, soles a centimeter thick. Just a centimeter thick, maybe less. Jagged stone—hell, even the tough point of a fallen branch might shred into those things. Running through the woods like a gazelle in those? Psshhh. Okay, little Keebler-elf fairy boy. It was all romantic and I was falling in and out of love.

The image was burned into my mind. Romanticized, flourished and fabricated on the wheels of a simpler time. Nothing about that mountain man moving his hands and feet was simple. Fires took ages to make, sparking two undusted rocks against one another in hopes a wily spark might land in the perfect spot. I flicked a little switch and had flame for as long as I needed it. Those little leather clothes would just leave him freezing near to death on abnormally cold nights. The leather would sop up his sweat and rot out his skin under all that unbreathable material. The pads of his feet would be wrecked—diced up and sliced in a thousand ways from all the missteps he'd make on journeys across mountain tops. He drank from rivers and springs and got Giardia and roiled with beaver-fever and didn't know why. I had jugs of filtered water and WebMD. I had fleece blankets, a minus thirty-degree sleeping bag to keep me warm, crafted with duck feathers and other shit that I'll never even begin to understand. If he was lucky, that mountain man might have the pelt of a bear, or deer, or some other animal he had to go and manually kill and skin himself. Our western worlds couldn't be further apart.

I had a bin filled with grocery store food—hot dogs made of pig assholes and elbows, cans of chunky chili, loaves of bread, bags of everything-in-one trail mix, jars of creamy, smooth peanut butter. My cooler might have been degenerate, but at least it kept things cold for some amount of time. That mountain man didn't know what a fridge was, didn't have access to a portable freezer to store his hunted animals. I had fresh eggs and a gas stove to fry them up on at any moment. I could make a breakfast of coffee, eggs, and bacon in less than thirty minutes. It would take him days to obtain those ingredients on his own. I could drive my rocket ship twenty minutes down the road and be in Mammoth Lakes, California—get a Starbucks coffee, a hot meal, jerk-off in a local motel room, see a movie on the big screen, shit in a porcelain toilet, fall asleep at the public library—all in one evening. And cursive California would call that an uneventful Saturday night. And they do.

The mountain man's movie was staring between pine trees at dark beasts that might be lurking beyond, but he had no flashlight to see the truth. His caffeine-fueled equivalent was adrenaline-induced games of survival. The world he lived in was a far sight from the one I inhabited. His living wasn't simpler, not by a longshot. Mine was. I had time to think so hard I could grow golden locks of hair and shove my fist straight through my face from leaning on it.

I didn't want to be like him. His life was a living hell. He fought daily, tooth and nail to survive and rise to the occasion the next time the sun peeked up from the east. He hardly had time to ask the question of whether or not today was the day the mountain would gobble him up. He just woke up and started surviving. Started moving his hands and feet. I didn't want to live the life he did, the one I was so drawn into romanticizing. The one where a single shot from his musket at the demon-grizzly in the shadows would leave him having to reload the gun for two minutes, just to hopefully land the next bullet before getting mauled. No rocket ship to retreat to, no steel chassis to guard him from the beasts that lurk in the endless shadow. Not that one, never that one. I didn't want to be like him. I had time to fall in and out of love and see it all happening.

It wasn't his circumstance that I had fallen in love with. Not his clothes, his hat, his beard, or his gun. It wasn't the little strapped leather belt he wore, or the knife tucked under it. It wasn't his desire to live in the mountains, wasn't the stories of him playing those survival games. It wasn't him fighting great and wild bears, or trapping rabbits, or fishing trout to feed himself. It wasn't charting the Western front, mapping out the frontier for the rest of everyone to follow into the wilds of the golden state. It wasn't any of his actions—that was just the shit. The never-ending list of shit he had to do every day in order to continue drawing breath. In order to continue surviving. To continue living. All the extra steps.

I thought I had fallen in love with those things. That shit—the stuff that paraded as fun. But I hadn't. I was star-crossed with something deeper than that, something that drove all the mountain man's shit-doing. I was obsessed with the meaning. I was taken, utterly and completely gripped, by the fact that he did it anyways, all the same. In the face of snarling bears, striking rocks, garbage shoes, freezing weather—he still did it. He moved his hands and feet, when at every single step, it would have been infinitely easier to give up. To stop finding the things he didn't like, in hopes he'd stumble into the ones he did. Easier to hear the beasts and run away. Easier to stay home in the log cabin next to the fire, then venture out in the pouring rain. Easier to drop the gun, and buy his meat from the local butcher. Easier to let someone else come along and do the dirty work, then it is to tread out, find a new path, find a new stump to put his foot up on. But you don't get your picture taken that way. You don't get your image plastered in the world's history book by staying home and staying comfortable.

No one cares about the hands that are soft, free from cuts and blood, devoid of callus and grime. No one cares about the soft feet that are kicked up on the ottoman, socks off, toes wiggling in the heat of the fire. Those feet, those hands—they don't go anywhere. They don't move. They're stone. And stone doesn't break.

I didn't love the things the mountain man did, the hard survival things. I loved his hands and his feet. It was those body parts that led him to a stump, with a photographer, into a picture, into a history book, into a classroom a century later, into my head, into my long-term memory, on the top of a mountain amid pine trees at midnight in Mammoth Lakes, California.

I slammed the back passenger side car door behind me, making sure it sealed tight. Leaning forward into the cockpit, I jammed my car keys into the ignition, and twisted them a half turn, flipping on the battery, but not the engine. A little "ding" sounded and some dim lights blinked on, both inside the cabin and out front. The thirty feet in front of my rocket ship illuminated, revealing nothing but frosted, dead pine needles and the trunks of several trees. No creatures, no eyes peering back. I reached over and pulled all four window switches at once, rolling them all up, closing the inch or two they had been cracked for ventilation. My hope was that mine and Mia's body heat and breath would cloud up the car interior and help retain a few degrees of warmth. Even at the cost of it smelling like dog farts and armpits.

The temperature was dropping, and my fire had died out after I deathknell-ed my yellow stream into the embering coals like a true boy scout. My only wish now was to burrow into the five blankets I had and pray for the white morning sun or sleep to come before the shivers took root. I lined each blanket corner-to-corner, shoved Mia down in between my knees, and cloaked us in a mound of fleece sheets. The pillow was stiff and brisk against my cheek, as my face warmth started heating up the memory foam pad, sinking my skull in, one inch at a time. My eyelids drooped, and to my ultimate surprise, I drifted to sleep. It was a snooze of hands and feet and I dreamed of Bill and Lucy gracefully dancing with fear and death and asking me all the perfect questions and I never had the obviously right answers.

Sunlight scattered through the branches of the pines, bringing with it clues of warmth, but nothing to root out the biting cold of a frosty mountain morning. I yanked the stacked blankets off my body, realizing that I hadn't felt Mia stir even once through the night. She was still tucked tight between my legs, curled up in a little dog-knot. For a split second I wondered if she had suffocated under all those blankets and my legs, with the car windows up, no air ventilation. I poked at her. Nothing. I jabbed my finger at her back, under her shoulder blade, and cracked her name in my raspy morning voice.

She stirred, lifting her tired eyes out of the knot. That musky, tightened look you get when you rise from a long slumber and everything in your face and brain is stretched thin and the world is too abrasive and early. She looked a little annoyed, like I had just interrupted a deep hibernation. She tucked her head back into the knot. I crawled out of the car and rammed my frozen toes and ankles into my rigid hiking boots. I beckoned Mia out of the car, and she begrudgingly obliged, stumbling out of the cabin and into the dirt. She trotted off into the woods, sniffing for a good mole hole to rain on.

I sat down in my everything chair, still sunk in the pine-needle floor of the forest, right where I had left it the night before. I pulled my little silver pen off the spine of my little brown book and flipped open to a fresh page.

Holy flipping shit did it get cold.

I scanned the adjacent leaf of my book, where I had written the afternoon before.

The mountains are home.
Home. What does that feel like?

I smiled at my freezing misery. Home. Apparently home felt like Christmas temperatures where my nuts have to suck so far up into my abdomen that I can't find 'em. Apparently home was shredding my fingers on icicle sticks for tinder and kindling and they're sore now. Apparently home was layered blankets, foggy windows, vicious shivering, and black holes where grizzlies hung out and waited to crunch your bones. I grew up around mountains, they were home. Massive, jagged outcroppings from the earth. Rock and dirt and bush and tree, rising in elevation. That was home, that had to be home. And home was feeling rough.

My gaze shifted up to my four open car doors. I had swung each one wide in order to circulate out the tainted air that fermented overnight. Each window was veiled in fog, every square inch coated in exhales. Mia and my deep sleep-induced respiration covered every glassy surface in a sheen of micro droplets. So many beads gathered on the surface that streaks had started forming, running down through other smaller ones. My ole rocket was mourning under the sunrise. It wept and wept and streaks bled and the chilly, high-altitude air tried to wipe it all away, breezing through the front and back lungs, doors jarred wide.

These tears weren't on the outside, but on the in. They weren't the result of pounding rain in a withering Las Vegas parking lot. They weren't heaven's tears, crying for me, encouraging a moment of decision, a staked, dedicated outset. These ones were sadistically produced by my own guts, my own lungs, painted all across the windows, now streaming down over and over again, crying for the misplaced, misled, hopeless romantic that I was. And the white sun was knocking at the door and waiting to smear the mess clean.

Along the way, attempted outsets and inward-focused actions became the product of my own outside tears. Things I did to prove to everyone else that I was in control. Movements I made as evidence that I was a person who created, crafted—someone that deserved a picture in a history book. Maybe if everyone thought of me as a mover and a shaker, I'd somehow stumble into being a successful one. Those insidious beliefs had sunken deeper now, as trivial matters like mountains and failed attempts at solving the mystic riddle of life became the product of inward agony. Inward it was, peeling me apart. They were prying and I was watching it all happen. These are mountains, I should feel at home in them. What did home feel like? Home is in the mountains. But home was feeling rough and foreign, and I was alone at the peak, slopes on all sides and miserable still. What did home feel like? Home is in the mountains.

A backward answer, inked onto the page in order to condemn the shambling boulevard of zombies, the dusty booming dunes, the congregated blood-clot that called itself San Diego. Another set of words that could prolong my caesura, for juuuust a little longer. San Diego wasn't good enough for me to start living, nor was Las Vegas. There was a glimpse of meaning deep in the Mojave, where I found myself dancing. But I was alone there, too. And the math and answers continued not to add up. I wander and search and I beg for the perfect place, the perfect seat to sit in, an adequate moment to stop and be haphazardly struck by this thing called inspiration. When blue-lightning blood would flood my veins and I'd be consumed with this thing called motivation. Together those two energies would fornicate into the great western dream in everyone's mind called success, and I'd be happy then. I'd be at peace. I'd have found the right place. The right time. I'd have found the right stump to set my shitty little moccasin on and beckon some struggling artist to snap my photo for the ages. I'd be history, and boy would I!

I told you that if you're reading this, don't. All the blood and brain-goo that once soaked a random bench in San Diego is now soaking into you. Filling up your pores, running down the creases of your fading smile, leaking down your neck, belly, legs, and toes. You won't get away from it, can't wash it out. It's gonna stain your pearly-white clothes, and if you're horribly lucky, might stain your skin and bones a confused shade of gray. I'm just a court-jester in the middle of nowhere, atop an arctic mountain where the sun is always white and never sees the cuffs of spring. My ass hanging two inches off the ground, suspended above a sea of stabbing needles. Idolizing the nature of some ancient geezer with a huge storied beard and musket that barely works in his right hand. I want to be like him. But not the survival parts, just the hands and feet ones. I'm falling in and out and in love with it and wishing I could reach back through the pages of that elementary history book and talk with the backwoods brawler, see what made him tick, see what made those hands and feet move. That was it, that was really *it*. The answer to the great adversarial, rotten, fascinating problem of life. It was all a problem.

I want to be a mountain man, big and brawny and winning the woodland game. And I'm sitting petrified at the sight of black holes I can't see into. Inventing eyes that are seeing back. Mountains are home, and I'm freezing and hating every second of it and for some reason choosing to continue north, where it's only getting colder. Always getting colder. I'm slicing my own fingers up and smiling because it makes me feel manly. And on this morning, the sun's showing the cuts from last night and they're swollen and aching and I'm feeling rough. But those scars aren't going away, those little bloody smiles rimming my nails. And the story I'm living about how I got 'em won't be a tale worth telling. Served up on a big silver platter, reminding me that I don't give a shit about how I feel—I'm just gonna move my hands and feet anyways. Then jam a resin-pipe three feet down my throat and breathe Mary-Jane in a mainline IV and write one-liners down pinstriped lines that facade the deeper questions of movement in a world that's built on dreams and the sights of the horizon. When I'm tired of that and loathing myself, I'll say this place isn't good enough and I'll drive somewhere new because the hell-baby made of inspiration and motivation will surely be waiting there. It's not my fault this mountain top isn't producing the vibe for mental exuberance. Sitting and watching the movie of life, writhing and wondering why I can't find some light in this shady journey. Looking down and seeing my hands and feet and they're covered in a thick black layer of tar. And ole Sister Eubank would see them too, and she'd scorn them and call them sin and repulsive and be disappointed.

Several lines below my pseudo-revelation of the mountains being home, I scratched another little blurb with my little silver pen and frowned at it.

Book idea (again!? It's fine)
HOME

Again? A folder on my laptop had over twenty different files, stacked atop each other in a leaning tower of bullshit. The folder was called *Book Projects*. I even pluralized it—I knew I'd never land on any of them. But hey, maybe if I turned the file into a common whorehouse of ideas, I'd fall in love with one of 'em someday. Doubtful. Whores give themselves up for the exchange of currency, to make ends meet. My file folder was doing the same. Pimped out ideas that were all just a few pages long, several opening stanzas of some intricate thought, never given the courtesy of a full review. I would hire a new pound of flesh, take it to the back room, draw the velvet red curtain, sex it up for a few minutes, hit the part where you gotta start learning more about it, the part that got hard—forming a relationship with it—and I'd give up. Unsure that I could produce anything real from the interaction, I'd throw it back into the brothel of other used and abused ideas. Move along. Next pound, please.

Again? Yeah, again. I'm back. The cathouse knew me by name, knew me by my scent, my words, my aggressive starts and quick finishes. I couldn't last more than two minutes, and I never tried to. So promiscuous with my own ideas, fleeting one into the next, building my leaning tower of half-starts: *A New Freedom, Alive & Well, Outset, Project Circulate, Threads, Birds of Nature, Deadtrack, Never Eat Soggy Waffles*—just a few of the harlots I had played with in bed. Each one got to the point of asking me to whisk them away from a life of shallow expenditure. They all wanted to have meaning more than a title in a file on my laptop—several pages of toying, but never anything more. When the going got tough, I conceded. Left the bed, the crimson-draped room, left the brothel all together. They knew I'd be back, but it'd be for a new girl. A new idea, a new document with some new catchy name. They were always right. The catchy names were a dime-a-dozen, and I was supplying it all and living in the space between the decision and the outcome. I was feeling rough and shallow.

Again? Double clicking the folder, seeing the pile of ooey-gooey ideas—I thought I was getting somewhere. So I was fine. Again? Yeah, I'm back again. And it's fine. I'm fine. I don't need to form a relationship with these threads of thought. It's fine. I can land my shitty little moccasin on the tree stump and demand my picture be taken without getting truly intimate with these ideas. Who needs expertise, who needs to finish something to be successful? Again? Yeah, again. It's fine. I'm telling myself it's fine. It's gotta be fine. There would be a better time when I could sit and pick through each of these ideas and make something useful out of them. There would be a better time to swing by the whorehouse, pick up my favorite girl, and take her out on a date. And instead of climaxing and running off, I'd ask her questions about her life. There'd be a better time when I'd ask and I'd sit and I'd listen to the answers and I'd learn something that I didn't know before. The top of a freezing mountain wasn't the time. The stretch of zombie boulevard wasn't the time. The wide-open desert, the teeming city— these weren't the times. These were the wrong times, not the new ones. Just end ones, in between ones. But the time will come someday. Again? Yeah, again. And it's fine. And I want my picture taken now because look at all the whores I've been with. Again and again and it's fine. Maybe if I retrace the word *HOME* a few times it'll remind me to run steady with one of my favorite show girls when I come back again. Dark pen strokes, over and over, again and again—when I'm back and I'm feeling good, I'll pick this one apart and I'll learn about what home really feels like. But I'm fine, and for now, I'll just say the mountains are home, and I'll let that trifling little thread dictate the course of my future. Because this isn't the time to figure it out. Again? Yeah, I'm back again, here to find a new idea for a quick one-two shag. And it's fine.

Fine and willfully blind in May.

Chapter 17

A Blue Dream

I dug my teeth into a brick of rainbow-colored rice-krispie-treat. It was marshmallowed together, Fruity Pebble cereal as the centerpiece of flavor. The block was spongy and broke apart with ease. I was grateful for that—too many times had I been duped into crunching down on the ricey treats, tantalized by their soft appearance, only to be greeted with a rock-hard surface. Too many youth soccer practices with sugar-coated concrete grit as the capper. I remember eating them anyways, soaking one corner in my mouth for a minute or two until it was soft enough to gnaw on, breaking apart in my little mouth. The stuff of a dentists' nightmare. Processed particles of sugar and spice and everything awful seething in between my little teeth. I wouldn't need those little white chompers much longer anyways. Adult versions would find their way stabbing through my lower and upper jaw soon enough. Just for me to eat more garbage.

This one was soft, and as I pulled the treat away from my mouth, strings of white mallow stretched out between my lips and the rest of it in my hand like a grilled cheese sandwich. I went in for another bite, then another, and finally, popped the rest of it into my mouth, licking my thumb and fingers clean. Bits of mallow were wedged in my teeth, colored in every shade of the rainbow. I leaned over so my face filled the rearview mirror and stuck my tongue out. It was dark purple. I rubbed it against the roof of my mouth, trying to suck the chemical hues off the surface. Back in the mirror, it looked the same shade as before.

I shoved the wrapper in the side compartment of my car door, the same place I jammed every piece of trash in my car until I made a gas station pit-stop, where I'd empty fistfuls of receipts, plastic packaging, and McDonald's burger wrappers. More garbage. I twisted my keys in the ignition, spurred up the engine to my rocket ship, and wheeled off down the road.

The heat was dialed all the way up, as my engine started dumping warm blankets across my face, chest, and chilled fingers. Snow covered the ground outside. Banks of brown and black and white frost piled up on both sides of the road, stacked and then restacked as snowplows passed every few hours, shearing the most recent fall off the blacktop. Bits of mud and black asphalt that chipped under the weight of heavy truck-driven shovels dotted the snow like scoops and scoops of cookies and cream. It was slushy and the world hibernated under the drawing curtain of late spring when the snow seeps into water soon enough.

I hadn't expected snow, wasn't dressed for it, didn't have the camping equipment for it, didn't want anything to do with it. I grew up in a place that was winter half the year long—forlorn November till foolish April, and that was if we were lucky in Northern Utah. A thousand icy mornings, waking up at six o'clock, donning three layers of coats, gloves, scarves, sweats under my school pants—it got old after a while. Ask me back then, I'm not sure it ever felt new. I don't know anyone who enjoys weathering seven-degree wind-chills before the sun comes up. But we did it every morning, five days a week. Had to get to school on time, had to take the bus, had to make the drop off or pick up before the bell. Whatever function we used to get to school, we did it. I did it. My mom did it. My sister did it. It sucked. But hey, I wanted mountains now, and mountains don't relax at beach temperatures. They're always cold and getting colder.

The snow was still racing past me, brimmed on the right and left. I hadn't foreseen any snow. It was May, snow was supposed to be a thing of the past. It was May. This was cursive and dreamy California. It was supposed to be edging off spring, about to dive full-force into summer. More snow. More snow that made no sense, and I kept going north. North because mountains were north. North has a nice ring to it. North gives you the illusion that you are inherently heading in the right direction. Following the North Star, following a passion, a directive—north couldn't be wrong. Impossible to lead me astray, north was the way I was always supposed to go because, well, it's north. It just felt right. I drove north and imagined seventy-five degrees.

Once you hit the West Coast, you only have two options from there. Or three if you want to backtrack east. But really only two: north or south. Once you hit the coast in Southern California and you don't have a passport, you really only have one option: north. So I went north, and I drove through the Alabama Hills, and saw snow far away on some razor-backed mountains. I barreled into Mammoth Lakes and camped and saw little mounds of snow off between pine trees, rising only two or three inches off the ground, nothing to be concerned with. I went north and kept going—and now? Now snow was everywhere, and I hadn't even seen an Oregon sign yet. Did it even snow in Oregon? It sure did here in Northern California. But Oregon? I'd never been, other than driving through when I was so young, I can barely recall anything except everyone telling me they pumped gas for you out in Oregon. I didn't believe them. Seemed like a childhood fallacy someone spread just to be contrarian. Like babies being born from women's ass holes, or blood being blue inside, but turns red the second it makes contact with oxygen. They pump your gas for you in Oregon? Yeah, right.

OREGON WELCOMES YOU!

A big green sign flew past me, and suddenly, there was snow in Oregon and cursive, ailing California was a thing of the past. These were new times and the West Coast land of sleeping dreamers lay behind me. I smiled wide and the fruity pebbles between my teeth glimmered and bobbed like a magical flag as my rocket ship trekked into a new place where things were unknown and begging for discovery. I was here for it, looking and numbing up all the while. If they pumped your gas for you in Oregon, I'd find out soon enough.

Green fields were everywhere, turf with little rubber pellets embedded under the surface, goal posts and football uprights jabbing up into the sky, soccer nets and howling kids. Ten, twenty, thirty, forty, fifty, forty, thirty-yard lines on my left and right. The same field copied and pasted five or six times in every direction. Youth soccer leagues were dueling on several plots, parents rising out of their camping chairs to point and shout—run faster, kick harder. Ref whistles screeched, stopping, starting, stopping play, calling fouls, signaling half-times. Black chain link fences lined the fields. Chain links coated in rubber, no grating against these. Only bouncing. Just like my head, bouncing up and down, walking down the yard lines of a field not in use. Where was Mia? In the car? But I was at a park, the single best place for her to get some out-of-car time, where was Mia? Why did I leave her in the car? I turned around, my little golden rocket parked a hundred-and-fifty years away. Ten yards forward, my head is bobbing. My feet against the turf, how are my knees and feet and thighs looking? I straightened out, stopping my supposed shaggy-waltz, trading up for a composed pace. Looking down at my feet, my tennis shoes were damp. Looking down at my feet, and now my hands. Black cord wrapped around my right palm. My eyes followed it, out and around, tangled and at the end of it Mia pranced alongside me. I turned back around, ten more yards back to where I was, and another twenty after that.

Up on the hill before me, a rising mansion, a holy house put high on the hill, painted in contrast to the gray, overcast sky beyond. Windows lined the outward facing walls, shaped in squares and triangles, some with little balconies in front of them. Lines of rising columns, a magnificent structure, reflecting the images of trees, atmosphere, and other, lesser buildings. The hill rose up and up and out past the green fields, emerald bushes and forest green shrubbery coiling together in some parts, leaving others barren. The spaces devoid of foliage produced beige weeds, dirt and stalks of wild wheat. The hill kept growing, lifting the heavenly house up into the stratosphere, its shining windows beaming back the sun's breakthrough glints that found their way through blankets of misty clouds.

Thirty more yards, down past the furthest set of uprights, head bobbing up and down, house of the rising sun spearing higher up all the time. Whistles raked the air, the game must be ending on one of these bright green rectangles. Left and right and back and I can't find which plot is concluding action. Not wanting to be in the middle of an exodus of soccer moms, half praising their kid for winning, half groaning for taking time to watch a loss. Maybe they'd all be happy, walking to their vans with trophies, in victory or defeat. Maybe there was no winning or losing, each goal being one scored for both teams, regardless of the net the ball flew into. That pissed me off. They would score it like that, those fun-loving, competition-loathing, participation preaching prats. Give every kid a trophy, a medal, a golden statue to make them feel like they actually did something, even if they lost ten-to-one. Just fold up those kids, head to knee, hand to elbow, ankle to ass, and put 'em back in the womb while you're at it. I must have missed the sign on the way into the park that said ALL WEAK BITCHES ALLOWED. We give out trophies for farting on the sideline here. I knew it, I could feel it in the air when I got to this place. I'm frowning and wondering why Medford, Oregon of all places.

In college there was an article I read in a sports psychology class that told stories of new soccer leagues in Oregon that brought trophies to practice on day one and handed them out and made everyone feel like a million-and-one bucks. Just for showing up in their little stretchy shorts and numbered shirt, shin guards strapped upside down and all. Those kids could have their shoes on the wrong feet, tripping up and down the field, and they'd still get a two-foot-tall trophy at the day's end just for occupying a space on the team. More than likely, for occupying a space on the substitution bench. And that pissed me off.

I got a trophy when I played soccer as a kid, but I only got it when my team won the local championship. That trophy was baby-blue and sparkly, with a badass little golden character on top that was slamming a soccer ball with his foot.

It was two feet tall, and it sat on my nightstand for years. I looked at it, and I remembered the dinner my coach bought us after we won and how he grabbed our shoulders and wagged them and patted our backs and said how proud he was of us. And he only did that when we won.

Once during that same season, I got possession of the ball, and started tapping it with my feet, full sprinting for the net, and when I looked up, I was heading for the wrong goal. It was my own goalie who was looking at me with a horrified expression. My coach, my dad, my mom, and every other parent on my team screamed, trying to get my little ass to turn around the other direction. Prior to committing the ultimate sport betrayal, I heard them and listened. I flipped around and dribbled back down half the field and fought my way through defenders. I scored my first goal in soccer and I felt fan-fucking-tastic. I remember being screamed at for going the wrong way. My success was a great feeling, my failure stuck with me and I never went the wrong way again. Not on the soccer field. I didn't get a trophy for messing up, I got one because my team and I learned from our dumb mistakes and went on to beat every other team in the league. I didn't get a trophy for sitting on the sideline with my pants full of shit, whining about how the cleats cramped my toes. I got a trophy for practicing every day and winning. And I was proud of it.

These kids were gonna get trophies for doing whatever they wanted and expect that same treatment once they got to school, to college, into the workforce, into adult life— everything awarded for doing anything. Every moment a shiny, glimmering existence deserving of praise. Did these coaches not see the little hellions they were creating? Green fields everywhere, filled with a thousand little bastards and their bastard parents, all being raised to believe that every utterance their body made was special. And that pissed me off. My head's bobbing and I'm standing still. There's nothing going on, no whistles anymore, and the house of the rising sun has flown so high it disappeared. I swayed and bobbed under the swampy sky.

My engine shut off, and I stepped out onto the parking lot asphalt, closing the door behind me before Mia could follow. Looking down at my feet, my shoes were less damp. My pants had a few dirt smudges on them, as did my mustard-colored hoodie. I looked up and read the sign to myself as I passed under it—GOODWILL. How appropriate. I felt like I had dressed for the occasion, ready to peruse worn and weathered clothes for no reason. The door swung open, after I realized it was pushed by my own force, first pulling and wondering why it was locked. Down at my hands, shaking my head, nearly plastering my bobbing face against the glass. The lines and letters wavered.

People—Oregon people, unwashed people, cleaned people, a sea of bodies in a Goodwill, all floating through the isles, picking through dresses and coats, century-old hats probably riddled with lice. Unstacking and restacking ancient dish sets from great-great-grandmas house, toy kitchen sets made in nineteen-eighty. Rows and rows of books, emanating the age-old page smell from their tanned and curled-out leaves.

Underwear and socks, lined down an entire aisle, hung on little two-clip hangers. Who buys used underwear and socks? Several white pairs hung too, and I wasn't gonna dare a peek, not sure I could live seeing someone else's racing stripes up for general sale. They say Goodwill doesn't wash their donated clothes before lining them up for public browsing. I shuddered. Pairs of undies with paisley, flowers, trains, cars, swirls, and unicorns. Socks that rose to the knee, halfway up the calf, or just to the ankle. Some that pulled nearly all the way up the thigh. Sexy underwear, work underwear, lounge underwear, sports undies, spandex, and swimming suit liners. Some for seventy-five cents, others for five bucks. How many genitals sweat themselves out into the tainted, unwashed cloth lining the aisle? The question made me quake a little, and I shook my head again and bobbed it further down, around, and into the next row.

What was I looking for again? Anything at all? Maybe it was nothing, just an excuse to walk into a building and see some faces up close. Maybe just to greet the cashier when I buy something I don't need. Maybe to get a smile or cheers, a greeting or reminder to have a good day. Down an aisle, up another, shuffling past a family shopping for baby clothes. Past another looking for kids shoes. Screaming kids, sleeping kids, distracted kids, moseying adults, and thrift-store fashion-seeking teenagers and a head bobbing up and down and up and down and up again. What was I looking for again? Maybe a new hoodie, a long sleeve shirt, or a real coat to weather the cold. Was there snow outside? It didn't snow in Oregon. Maybe it did, I don't remember seeing any, but it sure was chilly. It would probably be wasteful to buy another layer. I have blankets, and no way am I buying a sleeping bag from Goodwill. That might be worse than buying a used set of undies or someone's jerk-off sock to put on my foot. Perhaps nothing would be worse than that. I buy my socks brand-new, thank you. I rubbed and kneaded my forehead, lamenting the aisles of thought and bobbing that led me to that sinister climax.

The ceiling rose twenty or thirty feet above my head, supported by giant steel beams bent in archways from the side walls. It was a colossal warehouse of low-priced shit, one man's garbage becoming another man's treasure every five minutes. Head bobbing left and right and up and down and up, I was in the exercise section now, perusing treadmills that looked like they'd been run into the ground. Dust and thirty-year-old caked-up WD-40 rounding every spin-wheel, rogue wires and cracked cup holders adorning the electric faces of ellipticals, stationary bikes, and blown-out rowing machines. Nothing looked like it worked. No cords flowed from the backs of the ancient creatures, no ability to test worth here in the store. Maybe they just need a good manual tug. I sat on one of the bikes and rammed my dried shoes in the foot buckles, and tried to spin the wheel. Stuck. Maybe it was locked up? I hopped off and stooped to a crouching position, peering up under the seat and down below the metal wheel. No buttons, no switches to flip. I stood and leaned against it and shook my head. They were pedaling junk that quite literally couldn't even pedal. And it wasn't. I frowned.

What a joke. I thought this place runs off the goodwill of people donating working garbage for tax write-offs. It might be garbage, but it should still be working garbage. Functional. The wheel should spin, at the very least. Really living up to the stationary bike name, this one. Maybe someone would buy it and put it in front of their television and sit there and that would be enough. Every step checked off to get to the point of physical exercise, only to be met with a locked-up wheel. But they'd be sitting on the bike and maybe that'd be enough. Maybe they'd think themselves into losing weight, peddling the wheels of that bike so damn hard in their mind that a bead of sweat would streak down their forehead. I shook my head. I'd take the jerk-off socks before I'd take this broken goal-crusher. No I wouldn't. None of this was from the goodwill of anyone.

I walked out of the exercise aisle, glancing over at crusty couches that were a decade past their expiration date. Plastic-leather cushions, cracked, revealing tufts of foam and stitching. Lazy-boys with worn out, sweat-through armrests. Broken recliner handles. Stains every four inches on every surface from god-knows-what. Dog piss. Cat puke. Drunken spit-up. Blood stains, maybe wine spills. Jerk-off socks became seaman-seats. So many smears the original color just reflected someone's stained life story.

Through the couches, seats, and chairs, three-legged tables, and vintage wardrobes. I'm back in the clothing section—coats and jackets and sweatshirts. And there it is. I pulled a faded brown vest off a metal hanger, sliding my arms through the sleeveless holes. It matched my mustard-colored hoodie perfectly. I lifted my arms and found the side pockets, noticing a little hole with white stuffing poking out. Not too bad. I palmed left and right, feeling around for the little white price tag. I caught it in between my two fingers—$3.99. Sold. I bobbed up the aisle, towards the cashier, joining a few other folks ready to check out.

"What ya getting?" the woman behind the counter said, her fingers tapping the table's surface. Her wedding band was clicking against the metal. Fast and ticking half-seconds.

"Oh, uhhh. This vest, sorry," I pulled off the vest and tossed it up on the counter.

"This all?" she quipped back, flipping it over while thumbing around for the price tag.

"Yeah, that'll do it."

She scanned the item in, her machine chirping out the departing call.

"That'll be $4.19."

I rammed my debit card into the little keypad device, punched my PIN, and slid the card back into my wallet. The woman bagged up the vest and pushed it across the table.

"Have a good one," she said, with a flatline expression, looking past me toward the next customer. Wherever her goodwill was, it wasn't here. Wasn't in my bag, or behind the table, or on her lips, or in the sound of her voice. Onto the next person hoping to find some treasure among the trash. Ole Sister Eubank would have been proud of this place.

I smiled wide, revealing my unbrushed teeth. There might have been pieces of fruity pebble in the nooks between, but I didn't care. "Thanks, you have a great day yourself!"

I swung open the door, and a mixture of heat and cold washed over me. The sun was lower in the sky, its radiant beams slipping between dark and swollen clouds. The blood-orange light glazed over my face, and I stood for a moment, eyes closed. My nose and cheeks stiffened up in the icy breeze swirling around the storefront.

Clubs adorned the windows. The kind you see on a pack of cards, three round circles atop a base. The shapes were white-lined against blackened glass, shaded so dark, they acted as mirrors to those on the outside. The street reflected into the glass, cars racing by down the avenue, blurred and streaked across the pane. Then they stopped, one vehicle sitting behind another, red brake lights glinting off the black windows. The street light must've changed. Green to red. More drivers lined up. I watched them in the window reflection, drivers tapping their fingers on their steering wheels, living for the next green light, knowing where they were going. They were waiting and they knew their next move and I watched the movie of their ghostly reflections.

Under the clubs, there were big, blocky, white letters, outlined in bright red and roaring into the street—POKER ROOM.

I swiped my thumb around the screen of my phone, picking my way around Google Maps, learning a little about the city of Medford. Where the hotels were. Where the local restaurants were. Where the library was. Apparently, where the poker room was. Poker room. I didn't know there were such things outside of Nevada. But here I sat, looking in dark windows straight back at my naivety. A poker room—that sounded like a fun use of my time. A worse use of my money as my bank numbers just went down. Maybe there would be some local folks who'd share some good stories. Did they have blackjack? I'd play some blackjack in a heartbeat, only if it's five bucks, maybe ten bucks. Fifteen a hand would surely be my max, right? Only if they have blackjack, though. Poker room—maybe they'd only have Texas Hold'em. Was that on my table of options? I knew how to play, but not with strangers. Only with my friends, and even then, I'm no good. No bluffing, no high-end strategy that I was ever able to follow. I liked blackjack because it had a set of rules and basic strategy you enact for the best statistical outcomes. Hold'em was a little different. Money I'd win or lose was money belonging to someone else, not the house. And in hold'em, often enough, it's money I'm losing, not bills I'm winning. This is a poker room.

My heart was beating faster as I imagined playing and losing over and over to some scruffy do-no-goods beyond the blackened windows. I'd fold and fold and fold, losing my bankroll purely off antes to a sour group of Hell's Angels. Then I'd get a good pair of cards, finally. I'd start my betting, and some would fold out themselves. The gig is up. It wasn't hard to tell when I finally had a decent hand, because now I'm playing. Betting up, tossing chips. I'm in with my stellar hand. And then someone at the other end of the table would go all in. All his chips, his little towers of striped blue and green and black pushed into the middle. He'd look down the felt table at me, smugly peering over the top of his smoky glasses, knowing he had me, good cards or not. And that's where the game beats me. The all-in foible.

Scared money, money that wasn't much for betting, but for my meals, my gasoline, endless bags of ice for my shitty cooler. That was the money I would be playing with. Money that deep down, I knew I couldn't really afford to lose. I might have some good cards, might have a good pair, but he might have one better—and the full river hadn't even been laid out yet and now I'm sweating. Now I'm staring holes through the faces of my cards, and a bead of saltwater is plowing its way down my temple. And he sees it and knows he's got me. Now I'm shuffling the two cards back and forth, putting one on top of another, rotating them above and below and above and below and my head is bobbing even harder. Bobbing up and down and up and down, pulsating, heartbeat picking up. I'm somewhere I shouldn't be, doing something I have no business doing. The poker room—take me to the confession box, let me bleed my secrets out and forget I ever had this idea. I must hate my dollar bills if I'm willing to give them to a beatnik biker like this. I must hate my money, and I must be a little bitch at the same time. Can't I have my ante back? Can I get one of those wins just for participating? I don't want to lose, and now I'm quite literally invested. I must have missed the sign under the club outside, in big blocky letters that said NO WEAK BITCHES ALLOWED. We bet in here, with real money and there are no take-backs. I was falling in and out and in love with the clubs.

My knees were tapping, up and down in unison with my rising heartbeat. My heels were clicking off the pavement of the sidewalk, as I stared at the black windows, my butt planted on a hard metal bench outside. I wasn't inside, wasn't holding cards, hadn't bet a dime or dollar yet. But I wanted to. Maybe they have blackjack inside? That one's easier to control the ebb and flow. Easier to opt out and opt in or bail completely if things get a little out of hand. Control. They'd probably have blackjack inside—that's the game for me. I'm much more in control with that game. Heartbeat bobbing, head bobbing, floating up and toward the dark glass door. I pushed it open and was Daniel in the lion's den and swaying. I walked in and the scene renewed and the movie switched tracks and I wavered and bobbed like mad.

Long oval poker tables with red felt stretched over their surface filled the room. Every table had a horde of giant office chairs surrounding it, each with an old, wrinkled man planted in the seat like a garden of ancient herbs. Most had lengthy, wiry beards of gray and white. Some were black, some were tied and weaved and braided. Some guys had bandanas on, covering their foreheads, tucking back and taming mats of hair that extended past their shoulders. They had dirty jeans on, cowboy boots, big belts with accompanying buckles. Some even had leather vests with various badges and pins tacked on. Clouds of smoke puffed out of some of their mouths as cigars and cigarettes embered in between their middle and forefingers. A haze of burnt tobacco filled the poker room. I didn't need a stogie of my own, I was getting lifted off the second-hand smoke flooding this man-cave that was way too small. Poor ventilation didn't help. It was warm. It was muggy. Low murmurs echoed around the room and the sound of flipping poker chips and swirling drams of ice and alcohol clanged around every table. They were all growing steady in their chairs, as old as time itself, pinned and buttoned and here for it.

Several old sets of eyes peered up through the smoke at me as I timidly entered the lair. They didn't smile, beckon, welcome, or address me. Just peered up, measured, and returned their gaze back to the card game laid out before them. I was so far out of my depth, I went from frigid Oregonian air to drowning in a sea of sin and wrinkly old man-farts, smoke, liquor, chips, beards, grease, and grime. I had a little vest of my own on, but it wasn't leather, didn't have four decades' worth of made-up accolades pasted to the front of it. I had no biker-gang nickname. I could feel my heart beating in my head as I searched for something. What was I in here for? Not Texas Hold'em. Blackjack, that's right. I scanned and saw nothing but rivers, flops, and turns presented in the middle of every table. No stagnant bets, communal cheers and jeers from wins and losses against the house. No blackjack. Just hold'em. And they were all holding 'em.

"Hey dude, you got your ID with you?" grunted a man from behind a little podium to my right. I hadn't noticed him while I stood, bobbing in my boots. Scared money, no cash, just my credit and debit cards. My ID. I have it. I won't win against these veterans. These old fogies shot and killed people in Vietnam. Shot liquid death from flame-throwers into grass huts and down dirt tunnels, pulled the triggers of M-16s, threw grenades into bunkers, and shit in buckets and swamps and got Tuberculosis and survived and now spent their days grunting and flipping chips and drinking Jameson and laughing with wide-open mouths, revealing their seven brown and yellow teeth. These guys were the real deal and old as the moss on the Oregon trees. I'd never killed anyone, but they had and you could see it in the folds around their eyes.

"Uhhhh. ID? Ummm... Let's see. I do have it. I'm just... ya know, I think I'm good, man," I said, fumbling indecisiveness around my bobbing brain. I turned around, stepping back toward the shaded door. From this side, you could see out just fine, like looking through the right side of sunglasses. The bench I had spent time fretting on was just beyond the door.

"Alright man, suit yourself," the doorman grumbled, moving his eyeline back down to the tarnished pages he was reading. A book nestled between his fingers, its bygone leafs curled up and wavy from years of humid bag-toting. He flipped a crinkled page.

Edibles and Extracts. Big white letters were plastered to the window. That window was attached to a tiny building. It was only one story tall and had a flat green rooftop. I pulled my phone off the little stand mounted in my rocket ship and unplugged the auxiliary cord, silencing the music. Over my shoulder, I chanted my usual refrain.

"I'll be right back." I'd always be right back.

Mia was lying in the back seat, sprawled out and enjoying an evening nap. She swung her head toward the cockpit, locked eyes with me, and gave a nod. Just like always. He'd be right back. Just like always.

The door slammed shut behind me, and I started walking toward the little gray building with a little green roof. It was on the street corner, so small it was nearing shed status, rather than a full-on business building. It was bland, boring, undecorated, uninteresting. The door was plate glass, this time with visibility to the other side. Beyond its exterior were a set of bars, running top to bottom. You can tell a lot about a place by whether they have bars on their windows or not. You can tell a lot about the local culture. The local crime scene. The local attitude. Bars were usually not a great sign. Bars meant that someone somewhere in the space of time decided guerilla warfare was worth it. If locks are there to keep good men from making mistakes, not to keep criminals from doing crime—glass is there to do the same thing. But glass is no lock. And in this place, it wasn't.

My shoes were a little damp again. Halfway across the parking lot, all the wetness from my day of bobbing was flipping up droplets onto their woven tops. A little bit made it down to my socks. Just a little damp, enough for me to notice. Enough for a little squish. I was bobbing, staring down at my two feet, up and down, down and up, now at the barred window that was actually the door. To the left was a big sign—EMERALD TRIANGLE DISPENSARY.

Behind the words was a simple green triangle shape, its right side incomplete to allow room for the overlap of the shop's title. Ah, that's right. Entering the motel room of Mary-Jane. Emerald sounds nice, must be nice, gotta be nice inside. Nicer than bars on the window outside. Nicer than the dead-beat gray and boring green roof outside. Edibles and extracts were inside. What's an extract? Extract what? My bobbing brain out of my ice-tipped ears? Extract my soul from my bobbing body. Extract me out of the world and into a shed on a street corner in a city called Medford. Charge me hourly to use the Mary-Jane sex dungeon. I pushed open the barred-up door-window and crept inside.

It was darker than I thought it would be, even smaller than it looked on the outside. There was a narrow aisle behind several glass display boxes lining the walls. Each display case was filled with wonky pipes, screw-ball bubblers, penis-shaped bongs, scientific beaker-looking smoke bubble producers, straight-lined one-hitters, lighters with blasting colors of every shade, Grateful Dead inscriptions and Bob Marley smiles. Nothing was gray and boring like the outside, it was wild and psychedelic and everything was tie-dye. There was tupperware full of green flowers, sticky-icky crystals teeming and gleaming in the light. Dragon farts, honey-waffle-ice-cream-supreme, brown-couch-kush, pixie-dust dangles, original-gangster purple-shaded graphite flingers, face-melter-scream-shaker, ooey-gooey-nincompoopery, elven green-leaf, chocolate-cream-weed-in-a-dream. Mary-Jane was upping her game, testing the names and brands and art and laying it all out, swinging her legs open on the motel bed. Get over here you weed-head-motherfucker, you know you want some of this. My eyes were wide and my bobbing jaw hung open like a kid in a candy store.

I waltzed from one case to another. Overcome with endless choice, too many wonderful plant selections to pick from. And that wasn't to my fancy—fridges filled with weed soda. Weed soda? Orange bubble cream THC-infused soda. Bubble drink to bubble-bob your head, feet, legs, and hips. One of these, a fifth of vodka, and your ass is glue. Pre-rolled joints, pre-loaded one-hitters, two-gram vape cartridges, everything under the sun and stars and moon, round and round and back to the sun again. Think of it, they had it in this little shed, with a little green roof on a little corner in a city called Medford. The freedom of the west crammed tight behind gray cinder blocks and it was all legal and waiting for me to choose.

My head was bobbing. My feet were damp. I was supposed to be right back. Now I faced the hardest choice yet. Pre-rolled joints or vape cartridges? Maybe try a weed-soda? A new pipe and some regular old flowery buds looked nice. My head is bobbing. Mary-Jane, you sly dog. Poker room didn't take a dime, and now you're laying there and you say it's fine, and you say what else are you gonna spend it on, and you know what that feeling is, you know it gets you juuuust right. Mary-Jane, you sly dog. Much more of this and my feet are gonna start stinking, my head's gonna bob right off its axis and roll down the street with a big Bob Marley grin frozen to it. Mary-Jane, I'm supposed to be right back and it's been five minutes? Maybe ten. Couldn't have been fifteen? Fifteen was the maximum amount. No more than that, right? I should get a trophy bag of buds just for walking in the door, willingly cursed with endless-choice syndrome. Signing up for the motel room, playing with the temptation. Yeah, I should get a trophy for that, just for playing the game. Just for exercising a lack of self-control. Control. That's right, control. Perfect, complete control. I had that. I'd seen that somewhere.

Not so easy to get a piece of this wallet, a cup of the hot-dog-water floating around my brain. Bobbing. Head bobbing. Boiling? Bobbing. Control, that's what it was. Not so easy to get me to splurge. No more than fifteen a hand, I was good at that. I spent four dollars and nineteen cents, never even hit that four-twenty lottery. Nope, not me. I had control, right here, hands holding the edge of the glass case, nose three inches off the surface, eyes glued like sticky crystals to the magnifying glass they had positioned over the little green buds. Wouldn't get me, it was four-nineteen, not four-twenty, remember? You remember. Wasn't time for more. Mary-Jane, close your legs, have some dignity. Try moderating your promiscuity for once, why don't you? You thoughtless whore, you sly dog. Not gonna get me. I'm better than spending scared money. It's only four-nineteen, not four-twenty, remember? I remember.

But I'm in here, aren't I?

"Can I get one of those vape cartridges, and a quarter ounce of the Blue Dream, please?"

It was dark, chilly, and my socks were soaked. I yanked my left sock off, then my right, and wiggled my toes, trying to return some feeling to them. I shoved the wet socks into my dirty clothes bag, doubtful they would be dry again until they got a run through wherever it was I would do laundry next. They were the primary ingredients for the science experiment I was building in my dirty clothes bag. Not just the cherries on top, but the real meat of that magic smell. I was parked, sitting in the back seat of my tent-on-wheels. Head bobbing and it was all swirling like ocean water.

I pulled a long-sleeve shirt over my head, and a pair of sweats up around my hips. Next came the dry socks. The wool socks. There was some instant relief. I sighed, smiled, closed my eyes for a moment, and let my head bob some more. Sunshades jammed in the windows of the car, my little slumber cabin was ready for sleeping. The parking lot outside was well-lit with streetlights. Beyond them was a vibrant sign, glowing through the misty rainfall—AMERICAN RED CROSS.

There were lots of cars around, parked in their individual little stalls, grazing on the asphalt. Another hospital parking lot tonight, safe as can be. The safest. No one would inquire here, and if they did and if some shit started, the Red Cross folks were right there. Ready to help. They would help control the situation, if one were to develop. Control. They would do that, right? Control. I needed to do that, have some of that to get to sleep now. My head was throbbing, bobbing, beating. It was bigger than the case it was kept in, trying to expand like a balloon, stretching around the confines of my skull, bulging out my temples and eye sockets, jabbing through my ear canals. Bobbing.

For my back windows, I used two special car door socks that stretched over half the door, covering the glass panes. They were mesh, and when you looked through them from the inside, you could see relatively well out. But when you stood on the outside, trying to look in, it was much more difficult. They were nifty little sheaths. What's more, they allowed me to roll my windows down during evening hang-out times, and the mesh let cool air in, keeping all the bugs and pesky mosquitoes out. It was drizzling and crisp outside, so for now, the windows were rolled up tight.

I stretched my toes down into the bottom of my sleeping bag, wiggling them some more, trying to stir up some heat. Mia was tied in a knot again, her nose buried under her back leg in a feeble attempt to keep warm. I tossed a blanket over her, tucking it down around her little shivering body. She made some happy grunts, untucked her nose, and gave me a wet lick across my cheek. I scratched behind her ears, and she tilted her head back, half closing her eyes in a little doggy ecstasy. She gave me another lick. I patted her with my palm and laid my head down onto a frozen brick of a pillow. Slowly, my bobbing head started sinking into it. Rain pattered against the roof of my rocket, leaking down the windows, dripping off the sides of the vehicle into the reflection of the midnight stratosphere. The world wept and my rocket grazed. A hundred, a thousand machines were grazing. Licking sweet rainwater off the shiny blacktop like a popsicle. Grazing all night, maybe all day today. They were grazing and my head was bobbing, pulsating. The clouds stratified across the velvet sky reflected off the watery pools gathered in the lot, running down the cracks and ravines, searching for a grate to pass through into the underground abyss. But the grazing machines needed to be fed, needed to be cleaned and polished. I could feel my slowing heartbeat echoing across the miles of space in my brain. A drum sounding the day's end. Bobbing and beating, the sound ricocheting off every round angle of my skull. I tightened up my eyes and thought of leaping sheep. Everything was spinning a bit too much, rotating around the darkness on the backs of my eyelids.

I drifted into a fragile sleep, rocked into dormancy by my circulating frame and the slams of my brain's heart—bobbing, bobbing, bobbing.

Tap. Tap, tap. Tap. Tap, tap… tap, tap.

"Hey, you in there. Hey dude, I know you're in there."

My eyes peeled open, wide and crazy. Left, right, center, left. Darting around every window, still laying on my back, head blown out all over my pillow. Suddenly, a beam of intense light broke through the window next to me, piercing through the mesh window-sock, right into my wily, tired, bloodshot, bobbing eyes. I raised my hand to shield against the invasion, and adrenaline started dumping like buckets into my veins. Heartbeat picking up, pounding over and over, I could hear it, taste it, smell it. My vision narrowed, I panicked for a half-measure, turned over, started reaching for the peashooter, the knife, the axe—which one would be best here? The nine-millimeter would do the trick, just show it, tap it against the glass just like whoever was outside tapping that fucking light-stick against the window. Tap him back. And if that doesn't scare him off, then maybe some louder tapping is in order. The Red Cross is outside, just a shot to the shoulder and I'll drag him inside and they'll stitch him up and that'll teach him not to go poking his big fat fucking nose in places he shouldn't. Just a tap back against the glass and he'll get the message, won't he? He would. Maybe he had a peashooter of his own, maybe he'd use it less on the shoulder, more on my bobbing brain. Then we really would have a red, wormy mess on our hands. I reeled and tried to figure it all out in a moment.

Tap. Tap, tap. Tap, tap, tap.

"Hey buddy, I know you're in there, I can see you."

Son of a bitch, this guy. Take that flashlight and shove it up your ass. Damn thing's so bright I'd be able to see the light coming out your mouth. Maybe the knife was a better move, show that I'm not fucking around, but I'm also not one trigger pull from killing. I'd never killed anyone. It'd be some sparring in a wet parking lot, one of us was gonna give the machines some man-flesh to graze on tonight, you keep that tapping up. Mia was starting a low-growl. She must have smelled the adrenaline, tasted it, sensed it, did whatever dogs do when they see their owner's eyes open so wide and wild they're getting ready to fight or flight. Flight? I hadn't considered that one. Maybe I could jump out the other side door with Mia and sprint off into the night. But my car? My rocket? My tent-on-wheels? I can't leave that, not for this bastard to pick through. Too many valuables, too much stuff I need. I don't even have shoes on and it's fucking raining and my head is bobbing. Flashlight beam so bright, I was either going to go blind or get a sunburn. He was using it to get his visual, how well could he really see me? Using that dumb light-stick to control the situation. Control. Control. I needed some of that right now. Control. Slow down, no nine-mil, no knife, no axe just yet. But maybe, if the time calls for it. Control. Slow down, what would happen if you just slowed down.

"Hey dude, you can't park here overnight unless you're going inside to visit someone."

He lowered the beam long enough for my messy eyes and mind to adjust. He had on a security uniform, a light blue button-up shirt with several shiny badges, one of them being that little Red Cross symbol. He was plump, wearing a traditional cop hat, complete with a belt adorned with a taser, hand-cuffs, a baton, and other security tools. He'd been watching me, not just outside the car, but on some security camera somewhere, behind closed doors. I thought myself clever, pulling into the parking spot, not getting out of my car even once, covering my windows, and passing into a slumber. While I thought myself clever, he saw an Oregon bum traveling the road. And I was.

"You gotta move your car, man. You're gonna have to park somewhere else, these spaces are only for employees or people visiting someone in the hospital."

"Yep, I gotcha. I'll move. No, worries. My bad for parking here. I'll leave right now," I shouted while crouching up over the middle console and planting my butt in the driver's seat. No shoes on, no jacket, still in my jammies. Head bobbing sideways, I felt like someone had ripped my noggin off, turned it upside down, and placed it back atop my neck and it was all wrong and splitting inside my cranium.

"Sorry man, for waking you up. Rules are rules. You might be able to park somewhere else though, maybe a hotel lot or something. Sorry about this."

"No worries, I get it. I'm outta here," I said abruptly, twisting my keys and throwing the shifter in reverse. My hands were shaky, and I felt frail on my adrenaline come-down. I backed out of the parking spot, wheeled across the midnight blacktop, and sped off down the road away from the Red Cross. I hated it there. And here.

The little white letters of my car's clock read 1:43 a.m. What a joke. I shook my head. No smiles, no laughs, no self-deprecating humor, just a self-deprecating belief. And all the questions came flooding in again after the bobbing started slowing its pulse to long, drawn-out slugs against the inside of my wrung-out bones.

What the fuck am I doing out here?

I was sitting at a stop light. Red. Bobbing. No other cars behind me, none to my left or right, or out across the intersection. The rain kept coming and the light stayed red, its crimson aura leaking outside the lines in the fog and mist of the night. Why did I park there? Why did I choose that spot? Of course they keep watch of a hospital parking lot, of course they do. Why wouldn't they? Of course they only let customers stay there. Customers. As if you walk into a hospital to buy an ailment. Customers, stalls for grazing, just for our customers, our ailing, bumbling, baffled, broken customers. Red light, still red. Of course a hospital has security, of course they have those big-brother cameras watching their machine grazing-grounds. How long did he keep tabs on me, knowing I was in my car, knowing I was probably about to fall asleep, knowing that I wasn't gonna leave till morning. He knew, so he came tapping, of course.

I hate it here. I just want to belong somewhere. I just want to have a place to hang my hat, what the fuck am I doing out here? I just want a direction, a goal to orient myself towards, I promise I'll give it my everything. I promise. Now is the perfect time for that, I know it. Now, at 1:44 a.m, the red light is still red. Every night, every day, wandering, bobbing up and down and up and down, and I'm no closer to learning about where I want to go. I can't even keep up with the stupid journal I started. Where's my little brown leather book? Where's my pinstriped lines and my little silver pen? I'm ashamed of my inability. That's what it says on the pages, down those damnable lines. I'm ashamed at my failure to keep up with myself, running a thousand miles a minute. Maybe around the next corner I'll find what I'm looking for. My purpose. What I'm looking for. What am I looking for? The words, the topic, the genre, the answer to the evil, denigrating problem of life. I'm out here, aren't I? I'm out here and every fucking day I'm finding everything that I hate and I'm bobbing all the time and can't seem to just slow down. A thousand miles a minute and sitting and watching, all the same. I'm looking for what. For the answer to the question and wishing it to be packaged right. I'm looking and searching and finding endless bobbing. I'm looking for the perfect moment. I hate it and I'm asking and yearning for it, but the movie is silent and I'm idle and waiting and that fucking light is always red. It was still red.

The streetlight turned green.

I screamed. I slammed my foot to the bottom of the car, gas pedal shooting from upright to flat in a quarter second. I screamed and howled, I felt blood gurgling in my throat, my mouth, I tasted it, I smelled it. I fucking hated it. My wheels screeched, my voice broke, and both kept wailing all the same. Twenty, thirty, forty, fifty, I wanted to run this stupid fucking rocket ship right into the next light pole, maybe reach eighty miles an hour first, just to confirm that I wouldn't come out the other side alive. Hit that steel beam so damn hard I'd blow straight through the windshield and rake across the ground like a meat-crayon and there'd be no doubt my lever would be pulled, and I could finally have a direction to go—straight up into the midnight stratosphere. I took my seatbelt off. Sixty, seventy, eighty-two—I raced past a sign that read forty-five as the speed limit and slammed on my brakes and lurched into the steering wheel and it all wretched to a halt. No one was around. No cars. No people. Just rain, pattering off the roof of my rocket. Hot streaks of salt were streaming down my cheeks and my tongue had a metallic taste on it. My knuckles were ice, gripping the steering wheel, frozen in place. I stared at the reflective road as the light rain transitioned into a downpour. Up ahead, there was a collection of backlit signs—all Marriott hotel properties, intermingled with several restaurants and mall shops. Hotel. The fat man said something about a hotel. My head was pounding and cracked like a raw egg.

I pulled in, found a parking spot on the backside of the hotel lot, and turned off my car. I glanced around at the tops of the light posts, checking for security cameras. The usual practice from now on. No cameras to be seen. There were well over a hundred cars, they wouldn't notice mine, wouldn't notice me. I hate it here.

I leaned my head against the steering wheel, and the tears kept coming and through them all, I wailed the words that were stuck like glue and it was only mine and Mia's ears that heard them. "What the fuck am I doing out here?"

I sat back, noticing a colorful wad of packaging in the pocket of my car door. I snatched it up, head bobbing, and unfolded the crinkled wrapping.

FRUITY-PEBBLE EDIBLE BAR

I continued straightening out the wrapper, reading the notes printed on the plastic.

100MG EDIBLE MARIJUANA SNACK

I finished opening the casing, flattening it out across my thigh. There was a little diagram on the underside of the packaging, displaying how to separate the fruity bar into little bite-size sections, dividing out ten small ten-milligram portions.

START WITH ONE 10MG PORTION

WAIT 45 MINUTES,

EAT ADDITIONAL PORTIONS AS NEEDED

One ten-milligram portion? I ate the whole fucking thing. And my head was bobbing.

Chapter 18

Great Expectations

I think about my future and I'm scared.
My expectations for my life terrify me.
Nothing is certain.
What is it that's really scaring me?

I was sitting in my black-and-blue everything chair, little silver pen in hand, little brown book in my lap, spilling ink and frowning all the while. A hundred yards away, waves were lapping up against the pier, lightly breaking against the rocks and wood beams anchoring a maze of docks to the bay. It wasn't purely saltwater, as the ocean mixed with the Umpqua River, diluting the salt content. Seagulls gathered together, soaring overhead, wings stretched wide as they lofted lazily on the breeze billowing in across the water. Occasional bleats echoed down the pier as a seagull found some piece of trash to snack on or argued about mating priority. Beyond the birds, Mia, and myself, there wasn't another living thing to be seen.

I rose up from my seat, extending my arms up above my head in an attempt to loosen my muscles that had been sitting cramped in my rocket's cockpit all day and now were jammed in my chair. A walk would do me good. Get these calves, thighs, and ankles juiced up a bit. My back was stiffening, which always made for a rough night of sleep. I grabbed the black leash from the passenger-side door, clicked it on Mia's collar, and started shuffling down the massive, empty pier.

There were hundreds of parking spots, some plain and some with electrical hookups for motorhomes and trailers. Some were outlined simply with three sides of a yellow rectangle, with no other services in place. Others had spots where campers could plug in poop-hoses and flush away all the sewage they gathered in their mobile homes. Each spot was numbered. I looked back at where I had parked, realizing that my vehicle was most likely hovering right over one of those numbers. Numbers meant assignments. Assignments meant fees, price tags. Price tags meant renting, and I hadn't done any of that. Vagabond parking might be met with a ticket. I paused, turning around for a moment, stepping back a few paces toward the car, then stopped again. I wasn't going anywhere far, and this lot was massive and there wasn't one other car parked on it. If someone came to boot me, tow me, or ticket me, I'd see them from a mile away. I'd be able to get back and get moved if need be.

I turned around and picked up my gait, walking away from my rocket ship toward the far edge of the pier. The sun was buried behind layers of dark gray clouds. On an average overcast day, you might be able to pinpoint where the sun could be by the emanating light concentrated at one particular spot in the sky. This was not one of those days. My best guess was that the sun was in the western atmosphere somewhere, hiding out above the ocean waters. Western was a good guess, that was where the sun was always going, and I'd followed it as far as I could. Unless I wanted to start swimming. It was early evening, everything was drab and gray and black and dim. Behind me was a little coastal city. More of a village, called Winchester Bay. It sat depressed on the Oregon coastline and was rank with a murder-mystery vibe baked into its crust.

Earlier in the day, I had thumbed through pictures of towns, looking for any place that looked unique and worth visiting—Winchester seemed to fit the bill. But all the pictures online were sunny, filled with light and smiles, campers, villagers, visitors, seafood, and sailing boats. None of that was here and now, no one was out, no one was smiling, no boats were floating, and I had yet to see a Winchester Bay native. And it was dark and getting darker all the time. More clouds slipped from light gray into shadowed plumes, heavy with rainwater, yet to fall.

Behind the small grouping of seaside structures, hills rose, covered with deep forest-green pine trees. The drab ocean flipped from gray with glints of blue into a sea of endless green with hints of brown. It wasn't like the woods in Mammoth Lakes, where each tree was spaced out from its neighbor—these trees were rammed together, growing off one another, covered in vines, bushes, and other overtaking foliage. It was impossible to see into the undergrowth. As the hills rose up, they met a dense layer of fog that was sifting down over the ridgeline. A cloud that slipped too low and was now being grated in between a million little pine needles. The mist was wafting, leaking down the hill, being pulled over the forest like a woolen blanket. It hadn't yet reached the village. But it would, soon enough.

Sixty-eight, sixty-nine, seventy, seventy-one, seventy-two. The parking spaces were passing under my feet, one after another. These ones had no hookups for campers. No spickets with running water, no poop-portals to empty their stew. Just regular old parking spots. Eighty, eighty-one, eighty-two, eighty-three. I wonder how much it costs to park here. Maybe they allowed for overnight stays? Of course they did. Why else would some of these spots have hookups? Probably not cheap. But no one is here, no one is hooked up—right now they're making nothing from these little vacant rectangles. Maybe they had off-season pricing. Ninety-eight, ninety-nine, one-hundred, one-hundred-one. The row ended. I paused, looking back. Why end on a hundred-and-one? But it did, and I furrowed my brow and kept walking.

The end of the pier was twenty yards to my front, and past that, a river-ocean mixture escaping out to sea, somewhere out there where the mellowed sun was hiding away. The breeze picked up, whisking frigid air across my cheeks and bare neck. I shuddered. It wasn't as cold here as it was in Medford, but it sure as hell wasn't warm either. I stooped down and unclicked Mia's leash, letting her wander around freely. No one was around, no vehicles, no people, no campers, not one soul. I was all alone. Not one blip of movement. Just me. Just Mia. Even the seagulls had taken flight to somewhere they could catch a few final rays of sunlight, far away from this dreary place. It was dark and getting darker all the time.

I shifted around, looking back down the rows of empty parking spaces at my car. It was alone, the only one on the lot. Hundred-and-one spaces away, I stood, alone, the only one on the lot. I looked down at my feet, at the blacktop under them. Why alone? Always alone. Always out here, doing things alone, smiling alone, writing alone, driving alone, walking alone, watching alone, listening alone. I sat down on the asphalt, tucking my legs under one another in the crisscross-applesauce position. I picked up a couple little pebbles scattered on the lot around me, rubbing them in my palms. They looked like remnants from a time when the blacktop was laid. On the outside, to the naked eye, they looked just like all the other millions of little stones embedded in the bitumen surface. Each pebble encased in the asphalt was a little different than the last, some were smooth and round, others were jagged and angled. Some were a little bigger, some were tiny. Altogether, they were similar enough. Rocks melded together forming a massive parking lot. Empty. The pieces sitting in my palm were no different. But the pieces sitting in my palm were missing one important trait— they weren't linked with each other, weren't cemented in the earth with a thousand, a million, seven-and-a-half billion other stones. They were alone. I was alone. The last soul I spoke to was a fat man with a blue button-up shirt who was telling me to get lost, waving an invasive light in my face. How long ago was that? Long enough. It was still murder-mystery May and the sun was flushed out like the eves of December.

Alone now, sitting crisscross, alone now, alone then, always alone. I untied my legs from their applesauce formation and tucked my knees so deep into my chest, I thought they might pop out my back as angel wings. It was dark and only getting darker all the time. I hoped they would pop out, fly me away, above these hanging clouds, up higher to where the sun and seagulls were calling. It was all nooses and everything hung heavy and dead.

I looked back down the row. Back at space one-hundred-and-one. Back at the pebbles in my palm. Back down the rows at my car. I wanted to go back to my rocket, fly it over the mountains, across trophied Oregon and cursive California, savage Nevada, the great-white salt flats of Utah, back to my grid in Logan. Back to the place where things made sense, back to where I could be alone or be with friends and family. Where I could recluse in my room and play video games all day, or emerge and coexist with people I knew. Where I was only alone when I wanted to be, with people when I wanted to be. With people I knew, people who knew me. I wanted to sink into the black goo that solidified those little parking lot pebbles together, stiff and sturdy. I hate it here—it's just dark and getting darker all the time. The Western Front waned before me and I wasn't chasing the sun anymore. Not unless I wanted to start swimming.

What was waiting for me back at my car, in this village, under these blankets of fog? What was waiting for me tomorrow? What town, what part of the road? What was waiting for me tonight, where was I going to sleep? What cafe or restaurant was my dinner going to be eaten at, where was breakfast in the morning? Where was the next place to take a piss, to do my laundry, to get my gas pumped? What was waiting around every single corner, at every single step of the journey? I didn't know, couldn't know.

What was waiting back home? My grid. My lovely grid. The place where things were planned out, the place where order ruled, street names made sense. Where dinner was in the fridge or pantry, ready to be made, and breakfast was two eggs, two pieces of toast, and two sausages. Every morning. A cup of coffee, swigs of water, a bathroom break at my own toilet, flipping on my computer tower switch, clicking to whatever video game was in season. Every morning. Booting up chat applications, poking fun of friends while blowing up little cartoon comic characters on my digital screen. Every morning. Ripping my Mary-Jane robot-penis vape over and over till my eyes were bloody and boiling, then dripping eye drops in just to rip some more and get away with it. Every single motherfucking morning. The same bed in the same place, under the same roof, in the same bedroom. Pulling the same food out of the same fridge, sitting at the same kitchen table, watching the same television, binging the same shows—over and over and over again.

Back home, every morning going to school, injecting an education into my brain-meat, scribbling notes, asking questions, returning every day to the same house with the same people. Eating the same bowl of ramen noodles, getting the same four-for-four at Wendy's three days a week, smoking the same weed, glazing over the same eyes, speeding through it all. Planned and organized, one number after another, just like these parking spaces, one after another. Ninety-six, ninety-five, ninety-four, ninety-three. No skips, no deviations, one after another. Lined and laid on a grid of their own, just like home. Nineteen-hundred north, eighteen-hundred north, seventeen-hundred north, down the blocks, the city blocks, one after another, square after perfect little square, all the way down to main street. Back up one-hundred south, two-hundred south, three-hundred south, up and up, block after perfect block. And it was.

Back home, where everything was certain. Everything was at ninety-degree angles. Everything was only something to talk about, something to think about. Ideas were thrown around the classroom, traded among friends, laughed at, scoffed at, picked apart, loved, hated. Everything was something to write on a page in a book—an emotion, a mental response. Back home, where empty pages of my little brown book became as cozy as the frilly carpet, a place where I could toy with hypothetical bullshit and leave it at that. Hypothetical. Certain that nothing on the page would leap out and rip my head off and spew my brains and blood all over the desk. Where everything was just a preconception of action, just a thought about what could come, what might be. And now I'm out here, and it's getting darker and darker all the time, and all that certainty is gone. Nothing is just a nice-sounding idea anymore. Life's coming, and it's coming fast and vicious, and year after year I keep thinking it'll slow down and give me a minute to catch my breath and let me keep playing endless hours of video games, eating endless bowls of ramen noodles, shoveling mouthfuls of rotten shit into my face every single day because it's certain and I love that. I miss that. I want to know where my next piss can be propelled. I want to know where my next dinner is going to be eaten. I want the numbers to line up after each other. Fifty-two, fifty-one, fifty, forty-nine, forty-eight, forty-seven.

I miss that certainty. Certain. What a luxury I had. Where has all of that gone—certain that I'd have a home to go back to, that same kitchen table, those same video games, that same nicotine fix or Mary-Jane addiction, the same job, the same classroom. Luxurious and certain and always knowing where and when things would happen. My own porcelain throne to sit atop every morning as many times as I want. Clean and shiny and sparkling. A bathroom to shower in for free, hot water to stand under for free, every morning, everyday whenever I wanted. So certain at the dawn of every morning what I could and would do that day. Up and down perfected street lines, edged with perfected sidewalks. So luxurious and safe and cozy, I love that, I miss that, I want that. That's what waits for me at home—order and certainty, my favorite drugs. What I can't live without, what I need mainlined straight into my dried-up, beaten, and broken veins. Things foreseen, just like the numbers in this parking lot. Twenty-eight, twenty-seven, twenty-six, twenty-five, twenty-three, twenty-two.

I paused. Twenty-six, twenty-five, twenty-three. I backtracked several spaces and walked down them again. Twenty-six, twenty-five, twenty-three, twenty-two, twenty-one, twenty. There was no twenty-four. Where the ever-living fuck was twenty-four. I walked over to the other side, looking at the parking spaces that mirrored the ones I had been walking down. One-seventy-five, one-seventy-six, one-seventy-seven. What is going on—where is twenty-four? I continued my pace down the row toward my car. The numbers kept falling, one after another, in perfect order, until I reached the spot where number one would be. I leaned down, looking under my rocket ship. In big, bold, yellow paint was drawn number one. No twenty-four. I stood up and rubbed the scruff on my chin. How do you mess that up? Who taught these Oregonians how to count? No twenty-four. The numbers were supposed to be one after another, in perfect order, down to the last digit. And there was no twenty-four. There was really no twenty-four. That's where sideline trophies will get you—missed numbers, uncorrected, uncared for. Where was twenty-four?

I slammed the car door behind me, sitting tentatively in the driver's seat of my car. Mia was in the back, panting, looking out the window for any visual stimulus she could find. The movie of the world was switched off and it was dark and getting darker all the time. I wanted to go home, fly home, teleport home. No more Oregon, no more gas bills, no more fourteen-dollar showers at truck stops, no more roadside overnighters, no more pissing in bottles in my backseat while I hoped no one was watching, no more stinky armpits or dirty clothes science experiments. No more coin-operated washers and dryers that leave my apparel damp no matter how many times I run the cycle. No more McDonald's WiFi,

McDonald's McDoubles, dirty fingernails, and moist sneakers. I wanted to go home, fly home, up over the blackened clouds and encroaching fog, up over the seagulls and breaking sun, the beams of warmth that were somewhere out there. I wanted to go home, back to the same house, where the same people were, so I could eat the same bowl of ramen noodles and play the same video games. I wanted it and swooned at the thought of it.

Why not? What was stopping me from making the thirteen hours and thirteen minutes drive back to my grid? I could be home and in my bed by tomorrow afternoon, snug as a bug, comfy with clean clothes and soaped pits, washed sweatpants made of fuzzy fleece, long sleeve pajama shirt on, slippers and dry socks. I could have all of that by tomorrow afternoon. A clean shave, a scrubbed bum, a place to pee that wasn't a used Powerade bottle or shit-flecked gas station bathroom. I could take thirty-minute showers, as long as I wanted. I could sit on the floor of the shower, let the hot water sprinkle down off my shoulders all night if I wanted. I wouldn't worry about what grime was crawling around or growing on the shower floor, it was my shower, it would be my own filth, washed away, cleaned, shiny and white and pure. I wouldn't have to wear sandals in the shower anymore, it would be my shower and I could stand in it as long as I wanted to, and it would be so warm and cozy like the carpet frills of home. I wanted that, wanted it like a meth-maggot-fiend wanted his next bloody fix, wanted it like a zombie-shambler wanted their next drink, wanted it like a whore wanted her next buck, wanted it like Mary-Jane wanted to skull-fuck me into oblivion. I wanted it. I wanted it and it was dark and just getting darker all the time.

I could do it. Thirteen hours and thirteen minutes and I would be there. I would be home. Why not? I could do it. I've driven further for longer before. I've driven from Georgia to Utah straight through. That's thirty hours of non-stop driving. I've done it. I did it. I could do it. What's thirteen hours compared to thirty? Nothing, that's what. Not even half. I could do it, and the same people in my house back home would smile and laugh and ask me about my trip and we'd talk all night and I'd share stories with them about the surface of Mars, and cowboy coffee, and the Mojave Desert, dancing and dancing, and the booming dunes, and homeless people in Palm Springs, and my friend Anthony, and freezing my tail off in the northern California mountains, and how they pump your gas for you in Oregon, and… and… and we'd laugh and I would tell them what I did and… they'd laugh and they'd smile and they'd pat me on the back and wag my shoulders just like coach used to, that's what they'd do. They would hug me and tell me how cool that trip must have been and when I tell them about what I did they would love me for it. They would wag my shoulders and pat my back all night, and smile and laugh. They'd give me trophies, armfuls of 'em, two-feet-tall, three-feet-tall, five-feet-tall trophies, shiny, and sparkling and baby-blue, just like the one that used to sit on my nightstand. They'd bury me in rewards and hugs and kisses and pats and wags. I wanted that. I'd be in their history books, a real mover and shaker. I wanted that.

I would tell them my stories. The stories of the times I moved around, used my hands and feet. What were those stories? You remember that time I danced? That time I… that time I cooked some coffee? That time that I was hiking uphill? That one time that I ran into a casino pinching my pecker, looking for a place to pee? I had a lot of stories, didn't

I? The time I sat and watched... the sun set. The time I saw a hawk flying, or the time I walked out of a casino without placing a bet. The time it rained, the time I sweated in the heat, the time I sat and watched... the time I sat and watched... water fall down the windshield of my car. The time I sat and watched... a security guard politely ask me to vacate the lot. The time I sat and watched. I sat and I watched. Sitting. Watching. Are those my stories to tell? I sat and watched it all.

If I don't go back with some greater purpose than other people will think me a fool.

I wouldn't be a fool, I would sit around and tell them all about my journey. And they'd wag my shoulders and pat my back, wouldn't they? We'd smile and we'd laugh together and it would be the greatest of times. Greater purpose. Sitting and watching. Thirteen hours and thirteen minutes and I could be back to luxurious certainty. The same house, the same shower, the same toilet, the same computer and keyboard and mouse, the same bed, the same people, the same breakfast, lunch, and dinner. Certainty. I wanted that. Flick the needle, test the pressure, jab that sucker into my main vein and flood my blood with it—certainty. Eyes rolling back into my head, face flush, limbs weak and rag-dolled. Convulsing, overdosing on certainty, give me the drug, give me that fix, I wanted that.

Thirteen hours and thirteen minutes. Home in no time. I jammed my keys into the ignition. I paused. I hesitated. I couldn't turn them, couldn't start the car, couldn't will the engine to life. C'mon. Thirteen hours and thirteen minutes. That's it, that's all you gotta endure and you'd be home. Turn the fucking keys.

My right hand hung on the inserted key, and my left hand, open palm out, slapped my forehead over and over. Screaming, howling again, shrieking—c'mon you bitch turn the key, go home. Slapping, slamming, tenderizing my forehead, my eyes, my cheeks, over and over, open palm slapping, closed fist punching now. Over and over, another punch, another punch. C'mon you fucking dimwit, turn the keys. Do it. Stinging skin, sweaty and boiling, punching and slapping over and over, an avalanche of brutality at my own hand. Right hand still hanging, lynched and lifeless from the key. Spit drooling down my scruffy chin, dribbling down onto my hoodie. Metallic in my mouth, on my tongue, punching and beating and slapping over and over. You bitch. You can't do it, can you. Why can't you do it? Home, you want that. You know you want that, you know that feeling, you know you want that feeling. I pulled the key out of the ignition, threw it into the backseat, and buried my face in my hands. It was just dark.

What is it that's really scaring me?

To be thought a fool of. To be thought of as anything but marvelous. To be thought of as a clown, a jester, a soul-searching, spirit-journeying bimbo. To be chalked up as a feeling-chaser, going from one mainline fix to another. Nothing ever good enough for me. Scared of the images formed in everyone's mind. Scared of what they'd think. Scared of their projection, of not living up to it, not being what they want me to be, not being what they see me as. Scared of being the punchline, scared of going nowhere, being no one to anyone. Just scared. And I was.

When did I start believing in side-line trophies? When did I start believing that I deserve something for doing nothing? How were brownbook theories supposed to form under the weight of fearing judgment? And I was afraid. Afraid of running out of money, going home, having nothing to show for my time on the road. Afraid of what they'd think. They have great expectations for me, they know what I'm good at, they know who I am, they know what I should do—and I'm listening. I'm taking notes, scribbled across the chassis of my very soul. They're building the skeleton, and I'm trying to fit inside of it. I've gotta fit, what am I otherwise? I'm scared, I'm afraid I'll be too small, too big, too fat, too long—I want to fit juuuust right. I can't go home, I have to find my purpose. Out here, at the bottom of a piss-bottle, off the side of the road, in a YMCA shower, in the cold, in the heat, in a vacant parking lot, in an empty village, in the dark. I've gotta find it, I've gotta fit. And it's gotta be out here under a rock somewhere.

They have great expectations for me, but mine are bigger and bolder. And they scare the shit out of me. And none of it is certain, and I think about that all day, every day. I think about their great expectations more than I think about my own. I think about the skeleton they're building, I imagine fitting into it, with no extra room, no bulging between the boney bars—juuuust right. I imagine that and it makes me smile, and I imagine them wagging my shoulders, patting my back and smiling and laughing with me. I fit their bill. I imagine that. I want that.

Then it gets late, they get tired, they go to bed. The party ends, the welcome-home concludes, and the next day blows in like a wrecking ball. The sun peeks up east, hours pass, and I sink back into in-between moments. Times when no one is here, when I'm alone. When the lot is empty, the parking spaces are devoid of life, and I'm walking down them. No party, no smiling, no laughing, no back-patting or shoulder-wagging. The in-between times. I remember what we talked about, the stories I told about moving my feet a little bit. They hear them, they know I traveled, drove, walked, and sat. But only I know what I thought about all of it. Only I am left with the brown-book theories I formed. Unexplainable, emotional, mentally charged, confusing bits of brain-soup. Maybe I'm a fool for taking the trip in their eyes. Maybe I'm a clown for sitting alone, for dancing in the desert, for disliking San Diego, for eating a hundred milligrams of THC in a fruity pebble bar. Maybe I'm a spirit on the wind, looking for something I'll never find, searching for a high ground that will always elude me. Maybe that's what I am judged as. Fine.

And then again, maybe fuck what they think about me. Their Goldilocks skeleton that I'll never fit into. Their perfect boxes, the stories they know, the sliver of life they've seen me live. Their great expectations? What about mine. What about twenty-four. I don't want to be the pebble sunk into the bitumen, the black goo that solidifies all the rocks in place. I want to be in the palm of my own hand, rolling around, under no one's mindful eye other than my own. I don't want to be in perfect order, in a perfect grid, lined up perfectly street block after street block. I want to be number twenty-four, laughing with everyone at the party, dressed as number one-hundred-and-one at the end of the row. Out of place, odd, screwball. Completely mad. A random ending, flying out solo at the end of a long list of parking spots.

I wanna sit with the stew that's too hot for a while. I wanna burn my mouth on it so I learn what that feels like. That's what I really want, plugged and drugged into my veins every day. I want it like ole Sister Eubank wants darkness surrounding her light. I want it like Grandpa wanted cancer.

I want to dance with it like Bill and Lucy did, let it soak into bones of my own. White bones, boring bones—I want bones that get restless and ask the world for more and get a little dark under the disgusting, magnificent problem of life. And that's *it*. And none of it is ever juuuust right, but all the same, I want it. And I want to be grateful for it, and I'll say it. Always.

Fuck you, Goldilocks.

Chapter 19

Idle Mileage

The bottle was filling, one inch, two inches, then three. I gazed out the back window of my rocket ship, scanning down the road left, then right. No rumbling F-150s were in sight, no joggers, or dog-walkers. Four inches became five, then six. To my right, there were several empty parking spaces. To my left, three or four more spaces, an empty Honda Civic, and then two more spots. Behind me, vacant storefronts lined the sidewalk, all of them either closed or out of business. I kept swiping my view back and forth, making sure the owner of the Civic wasn't returning yet. Not many options on this storefront in the first place unless they were here for a dentist appointment. One of the shops had a woodsy sign decorated with bears and pine trees surrounding letters that signaled the place you get your chompers checked. Seven inches rose to eight, and I was starting to wonder if this Powerade bottle was too small. Everything was woodsy, cabiny, foresty—the high-mountain theme was strong here. It was cozy, like all the Keebler elves poured out of the woods at once and built this little town as a shrine, a beautiful bridge between the natural and the man-made. Eight inches and rising. One spurt, another, a shake, and one warm waft of piss-scent floated past my face. Yuck. I shuddered, snatched up the bottle cap, and screwed it on tight. If anyone asked, it was Just Powerade. Maybe dehydrated, lemon-flavored Powerade. Maybe they'd buy that lie long enough for me to find a dumpster to bottle-flip my porta-potty into. Everything gets a bit more complicated when you're on the road.

I crouched back over the center console and planted my butt back in the cockpit of my ship. Engine on, gear in reverse, no cars, I backed out, and turned the corner of the block. Down the sidewalk, there was a city trash can. I swung back into an empty space and hopped out of the car, grabbing my corrupted Powerade. More left and right head swinging, searching, making sure the coast was clear. I jogged over to the garbage and dumped my bathroom break into the bin. Mission accomplished. From what I could tell, no one saw my degeneracy, no one would have the evidence. Then again, you never know when you might be the subject of the next viral YouTube clip. Look at this guy, bottle-o-piss, thinking he's sneaky, tossing his waste into the public can. Look at this guy. Gross. Always kicking my potty-problem down the road.

Everything takes more time when you're on the road. Bathroom breaks become bathroom goals. They cease to be a quick little action you do in between activities and start becoming the activity itself. The first flutterings across my mind when I drove into town weren't where I could munch on the best food, get the best brewed beer, hike to the coolest views, or visit the greatest landmarks. Those things didn't matter. I'd get to them. What mattered was if the gas station had a public bathroom. Where the local library was, so I could take a quick trip inside and dump my guts. Some cities have public restrooms in their parks and that was always a dream. Especially when they were clean. Magically clean. Spotless. That's a one-in-a-million score that feels newsworthy when you stumble upon it. Few and far between.

Gas station bathrooms were always the worst. Had to be the worst. Gas stations in Oregon are confusing. There are way too many people working there. Standing around, waiting at the pump for you to pull up and roll your window down to tell them which gas you want. They'll take your credit card, pick your Ethanol level, and tap their foot while you wait in the driver's seat. Sometimes they even ask if you want any snacks. When the pump clicks and the gas stops flowing, they'll hand you back your card, and with big toothy grins, rub their dirt-covered fingers together, waiting for that glorious tip. A tip? For what? I'm well capable of pumping my own gas, why do I need to pay you to make you feel like you have a job that's worth having? More of that sweet, sweet Oregon sideline trophy bullshit coming into play. I can pump my own gas. There only needs to be one person, two max, working at this stop. And they have eight little yellow-jacket stringers out here under the gas station pavilion, rubbing their fingers, pressing pump buttons, swiping credit cards—and for what? Here's your trophy, sir. For doing the work that every other person in every other place around the globe does on their own.

In Oregon, you feel awkward when you open your car door and step out onto the blacktop at a gas station. But I've gotta piss sometimes, and these sideline trophy holders sure as hell aren't gonna pump that for me. Here, I'll tip you extra if you unzip me, angle my propeller, and clean me up. I don't think so. I might be a Mary-Jane mind-bended husk, but I can still hold Peter and get most of those drops in the toilet bowl myself, thank you. Sadly, I think those station sideliners really would take the extra couple bucks to stand behind me and pump my piss. Oregon—land of the free, home of the sideline trophy-chasers. It was in the air.

I drove through this great beaver state, up and down, scrawling the surface in search of a place to park my wheels for a while. All this movement, spending one day in one place, one day in another. Always driving, peering through the front windshield, always wheeling to somewhere, from somewhere. Giving myself the illusion of accomplishment—look how far I've come. The odometer on my car has risen several thousand ticks from when I first set out, and that's gotta mean something. Up and down, I'm searching for something, and if you asked, I couldn't tell you what. But I'm driving, feeling around in the dark, giving myself the illusion of accomplishment. No idle miles, no thumb-twiddling, no sitting and watching—I'm moving. Fast. At sixty miles an hour, seventy, sometimes eighty-five miles an hour down the road, spending fuel, watching the mile ticker go up while the gas ticker goes down.

I drove and drove, and then I found myself in Sisters, Oregon. And I stopped. Around every central city block was free parking space after free parking space. It was foresty, cabiny, woodsy, everything was built from pine trees, and green and beige and mountainous and smelled like morning coffee and cured leather. Every business had a great brown grizzly bear as its mascot, or a black bear dipping its paw into the honey jar. There were little beavers with their oversized tails smiling their gigantic two front teeth, and marvelous stags standing with puffed chests on cliff edges. Every billboard and sign was decorated with these Keebler-friendly characters. You knew you were in the mountains. There was no denying, no hiding the fact. So my wheels stopped rotating, and landed. I wanted mountains, and here they were. I nestled in the north and west places of the world and was smelling and tasting it all.

When I think of home
It may not be the sheetrock walls and plaster ceilings
That come to mind
Nor the covered porch and paned glass
That fill my memory

But green hills blowing, rising pines against the azure
Rolling mountains and sheared cliffs
Jagged and disjointed from an ancient earthen stir
Forests of infinite wander
Lapping tides of tree and brush
Out there, across the western set
Of sun and stars

My pen was leaking, etching my identity down row after pinstriped row in my little brown book. The mountains—I was home. The air was crisp, steeped in the scent of sage and pine needles, tree sap, and fresh soil. Sisters, Oregon. I fell in love a little. I looked out the window of my car. The sun had risen higher in the sky, drawing down onto the chassis of my ship, lending some of its warmth to the inside. I shed one layer—my massive marshmallow coat—down to my brown vest and mustard-colored hoodie.

Today was an important day. Today was the day that a dear friend of mine had committed to joining me for a brief time on my journey. Today was a day that I'd get some real company. Company that wouldn't be silent like Mia was. Company that would talk back. Matthew was driving up from Utah, meeting me out here in the suffocating woodlands of the northwest. Today was that day, and I could feel the excitement. And tomorrow we'd be mountain men together and tread new paths. Home was reaching out and finding me, embracing me, giving me my mountains, my thin air, my altitude, and my real in-the-flesh friend, Matthew. He was real and coming to meet me in Sisters, Oregon. I didn't have to go back; home was coming to me. Home. I wanted that, craved that. Friends, laughter, talking, making jabs, making things real, sharing, telling the stories, getting my back-pats. I wanted that. And it was coming to me.

I returned to the pages of my little brown book. More scribbling. This home-away-from-home was drawing out prompts. Questions that needed answering, questions that were sitting under the surface of my skin for long enough. I chose to keep my wheels where they were, and now a confusing set of puzzle pieces was bubbling up. This place was just ambient enough that I felt the next chapter of the world was about to unfold. But I needed to organize the one I'd just raced through. I feared forgetting, feared losing the threads that I'd been tugging at for the past month. I had arrived in a place like home, flipped the light switch on in my mind, and found a giant mess. Clothes, toys, papers, chairs, bed sheets and blankets all thrown around the room. Nothing in order, a toddler had ransacked the whole scene with his little two-year-old desire to try every part and parcel, but never found anything he liked. Dumping every bin out onto the floor—at least he was discovering the things he didn't care for. But the room was a disaster, and landing in my mountain home, I now had the charge of picking through the mental pieces. This puzzle fits together somehow.

I go

  go

    go.

What would it mean to slow down?
What am I ultimately supposed to find passion in?
What steps should I be taking in order to obtain the future I want?
What kind of career do I want to create, what kind of life do I want to live?
Where is home?

The questions were coming, and I scoffed and hoped writing them spontaneously would reveal some answers. I started drawing out boxes on my beige brown-book paper. Four big boxes that took up half a page each. These puzzle pieces were gonna fit together. Somehow. In bold letters, I marked the first section—BOX NUMBER ONE.

What the fuck am I doing out here?

When I set out on this journey, I believed it was permanent. I convinced myself that this was life now. Life on the road. Life away from the place I grew up. Life outside the grid, outside the perfect lines and city blocks. I was never going back, I never wanted to return to the comfortable routines of the same bed, same food, same porcelain throne every morning, the same roof over my head, the same surface greetings with the same people. I was going to live out there, live out on the road, traveling my way into a digital nomadic existence. My ticking time bomb was the money in my bank account. That's how long I had to get my writing projects profitable. It had to work because there was no other option. I was going to give myself no other option. Feet to the fire.

Feet forever to the fire. No more woolen socks covering idle, comfortable toes. No more time spent staring at the page. I was gonna move my hands and feet, and I was gonna be rewarded for it. I wasn't going to borrow #vanlife from anyone, I wasn't going to be temporary. I wanted to own it, live it, be in it. That was the plan. No in between times, no end ones, always new ones. Outsets. I was going cold-turkey on cutting out the comforts of home. Cold-turkey on the luxury of certainty. Fuck the withdrawals, I had said. Said before I even left. Said while I was still atop a toilet of my own. Said while I was snuggled up under my fleece blankets in my foamy bed under my shingled roof. Back at home.

Now I'm here, now I'm in Sisters, Oregon. On the back half of a detox looking into the past and laughing. Permanent? How could I permanently piss into Powerade bottles, permanently hemorrhage money on gas, permanently spend breakfast, lunch, and dinner at McDonald's? Now I'm in Sisters, Oregon and I'm sweating out my sins. This place reminds me of home. Detox doesn't last forever. Detox from the same. Time away from the same. Was that why I was out here? No consequences, no kids, no girlfriend, no school, no responsibility. Nothing. Time to flip every toy-filled bin in the room of my brain and make a huge fucking mess like a toddler and not care. Time to find out what toys I hated and which ones I enjoyed. Time away. Detox. Detox.

I finished packing a tight green puck of Mary-Jane in my little green tube, leaned over under the sightline of the front car windows, and sparked my lighter. One deep inhale. One deep exhale. Rising back to baseline. Detox—that seemed right. Detox from all that routine shit at home. Day after day of the same video games, the same bowl of golden ramen noodles. Detox. Just time away from all that stuff. Time away from it. And here I was, away from it. I'm living up to the detox, just by sitting here, rooted in the front seat of my car. I'm living up to it, my detoxing. I'm out here just to exist away from that stuff. Away from the great expectations of everyone back home. All I have to do is be out here, and the detoxing is doing its work. All I have to do is gather enough idle mileage and I'd be set. Idle mileage. Box number one was filling up fast, scribbled with the dealings of detox. So long as I was out here, that was good enough. So long as I was gathering idle miles, that was good ee-nough.

The car was warming up as I stirred my pen and the sun baked through the metal exterior, and it was bubbling and emerald outside. I floated. BOX NUMBER TWO—I penned and re-penned the capital letters across the top of the second square.

Writing. What am I supposed to do with it?

Samuel Taylor Coleridge once opened his mouth and said, "Prose equals words in their best order; poetry equals the best words in the best order." His nephew wrote that down, probably having no idea that a hundred-and-ninety-two years later, some schmuck would be sitting in the front seat of a magical four-wheeled machine that grazed on asphalt, scratching it in pen strokes down pinstriped lines. What's more, those words from eighteen twenty-seven would mean something. And they did.

My head was hovering a bit above baseline, looking at the ink of perfect words piecing together in their perfect order. What am I supposed to do with that? I could do it, words in their perfect order. Bill reinforced that I could do it, Lucy made me believe I could do it. I could do that, I would do that with my pen and the keys on my keyboard. Why couldn't I? Perfect words in their perfect order, in poetry, in prose, in whatever the hell I wanted. Everything I etched was perfect already, everything I bled was straight from the heart. I'd soaked benches with that goop, soaked my front seat, soaked the desert sands, left bloody bread-crumb trails behind me every step of the way. That would be enough, should be enough. I ballooned.

I'm supposed to lay my head down in the crotch of my elbow, align it perfectly with the lines in my book, and let the gray matter flow like a golden river. In college they said it was a stream of consciousness, but I wanted a river. I wanted rapids, raging white and wild. I wanted messy, dangerous, drown-me-below-the-wake waters that sucked me into the eddies if I tried to swim for shore. I'm supposed to press my head so fucking hard into the page that I fall in, and that should be good enough. The words spill from my fingertips, from my heart, from my brain—that's what they told me, that's what they said when I sat in class. I don't want streams, tributaries, little trickles of authentic living. I want a gushing firehose, a broken dam barging through the cement levees, through the desert sand, through the hordes of zombie shamblers, through the ones dressed in black, groping at the undersides of idling cars. No brooks, no streams—just an avalanche of rapids. I want to be the Colorado River unleashed. Those were the perfect words in their best order, that authenticity. Who could look at that and think otherwise? I didn't.

What am I supposed to do with it? My ticking time bomb is ticking all the same. Digital nomad? I'm supposed to be a digital nomad and my raging waters are here, in this little brown book, wetting my pinstriped lines, kept in secret—my eyes only. If you're reading this, don't—the same first line in every journal I've ever had. My waters are raging, and maybe if I tell people that, they'll pat my back and pay me money just for believing it. Just for the fact that I'm doing it. To them, just for the fact that I'm saying I'm doing it. I've gotta make money, and this is gonna make me money. It's got to, that's what it's gonna do. What am I supposed to do with it? Make money, become profitable, practice, practice, and more practice whirling the rapids with my pen that will surely generate revenue. And there was no doubt in my mind that would be enough.

I lifted my hand from the page, flicking out my fingers, sore from scribbling. My hand was cramping down the backside of my palm. I locked my fingers together, bending them back to the point where three or four cracks and pops sounded out from my joints. I'm solving puzzles left and right, and I'm not even on LSD. Next thousand-piecer, please. BOX NUMBER THREE—penned, re-penned, then underlined. The wizard resumed and my eyes were young and ocean-blue.

Work. What do I do for money right now?

Scrolling and scrolling, a million little squares racing past my eyes. For months before I left my grid, I flipped through Instagram catalogs filled with pictures. Followed the biggest and best van-lifers, showing off their journeys, displaying their magnificent Ford Econoline conversions. I double-tapped the shit out of those real-life paintings, giving as many amens and heart-shaped-validators as I possibly could. They were wonderful, adventurous souls, and I wanted to be just like them. They achieved the peak of digital nomadic life, living in their little boxes, working out of coffee shops, planning meet-ups with their fans. It was all so doable.

What I never did was go back in time, scrubbing back to the birth of their Instagram timeline or YouTube video feed. I never checked how old it was, I never cared. They did it overnight, they got their validation and success out of the gate, and that was enough. They got those hundreds of thousands of followers and fans just for outsetting, just for signing up on the dotted line of van living. That's what they did, and I could too. That's all it would take—opt-in for the digital nomadic existence, and the dollar signs, the fans, the commenters, the validation and adoration and back-pats would follow. That would be enough.

But I've been out here, every day plotting another data point on my graph of endless wonder, and I'm lonely and I've got a ticking time bomb sitting in my bank account. Those numbers are just going down, a deadly one-way street leading to zero and beyond. Debt. Debt for going on this trip? Debt for sitting here, drawing boxes and looking out my foggy windows? My windows are getting foggy. I jammed my keys in the ignition, turned on the rocket ship, and flipped on the airflow, adjusting the vent switch so the air would blow up past the front windshield. No fog or streaks, just clear and crystal, and it all was—green and lush beyond the glass. Out there where the trees were, with leaves that hug you tight.

Gas was sparked, leaking drip by little drip into my engine, fueling the rotations, fueling the air that was now pouring out. Humming and drumming, RPMs sitting gently at eight hundred. Drip by little drip, the lifeblood of my rocket ship was burning away—a one-way street leading straight back to another Oregon gas station, where another sideliner would have to pump my gas and be tipped for it. This stupid car. It can't run on water or piss, Just Powerade would rot the fuel lines. It's always leading to the same place, over and over—the gas station. More money out, more fuel in, more plummeting bank numbers, no other way than those one-way streets. The life of a digital nomad was supposed to be profitable, that's what those photos showed. That's the picture that those little Insta-squares painted. But I'm out here, and every day is evidence of that lie. Every time I check my bank account, there's no upward trend, no upward spike, no upward anomaly. Just down, down, cascading. I need to have some variation soon or my ticking time bomb is gonna go off. It's all one-way streets and anxious.

Money right now. Money right now, or this rocket ship will be grounded permanently. My car is idling and that isn't free. That has a cost, and it's one I don't feel so willing to pay. But this trip is temporary, this excursion into the great unknown and all its uncertainty is just where I am now, not where I will be next year. When I set out, I saw this existence as permanent, but it can't be, can it? This isn't how life will always be, and if it is, I'm going to need a lot more Powerade-porta-potty bottles. But it isn't, it can't be. This is a span of time, that moment between one thing ending and another beginning. A tiny stretch between the exhale and the next inhale. This isn't permanent. This rocket ship is gold and glowing, but it's still my car all the same. Back home, back on my graphing paper, this car would still take me to work, to the grocery store, the library, and the dog park. It wasn't transformed forever into a tent-on-wheels. It's just playing that center-stage part right now, and right now isn't permanent. But my money, my ticking time bomb is running out, my bank numbers plummet, and my detox hasn't run its course. That explosion, that zero-ticker detonation will be the death of me. No longer able to wheel the tires against the asphalt, no longer able to twist my car keys, no longer able to dump blankets of warm air across my face, no longer able to clear the muggy window fog gathering on the glass. I need to make money and I need to make it now. Or else it's tick-tick-boom.

I'm in my caesura, stuck in my caesura. Hovering at the top of a jump, living in this moment between moments. I'm not frozen in time, this is temporary, this will end someday. The actor playing the parts, playing the mountain man, playing the van-lifer, playing the zombie—the scene is set and my rocket is golden, built as a tent-on-wheels and it's playing its part. I'm leaping, just like Mom said, but I haven't landed yet. I can't even see the ground. I'm hovering, sitting, watching, waiting for the moment when things will be juuuust right. Waiting for the ground below me to be juuuust soft enough to cradle my fall. And my time bomb keeps on ticking, all the same. My RPMs keep humming, minute after minute, rotation after rotation, feeding away the fuel that livens up my rocket ship. Penny after penny, dime beyond dime, dollar bills out, dust and tortilla-turkey sandwiches, Mary-Jane pucks in crackpipes, and sitting and watching back in. Into my caesura. But I need money, and I need it now.

I pulled out my wallet, opening the leather fold. There were two dollars. I don't use cash all that often; it was my debit card that paved the way normally. A debit card that was on its way into overdraft fees if I'm not careful. Behind my debit card, was a bright orange rectangle of plastic that I had used sparingly. Forgotten about. My credit card. Credit cards are dangerous buggers, that's what I was always told. That's what I always believed. Dangerous and addictive—it's nice to spend money that you don't have. Money that's more of a figment of the imagination, a number on a screen somewhere, not an actual bill. It's easy to swipe through a card reader, then swipe it again, and suddenly a habit is forming. Just pay it off, just make sure you always pay it off, every single month. Or at least the minimum payment. The minimum payment, that didn't seem so bad. But none of this is permanent, so a little toe-dipping into my orange credit-keeper would be fine. A little flirting with questionable financial decisions wouldn't wreck me. None of this is permanent anyways, someday I will have an adult job with an adult income, and I'll pay off those accrued numbers then. Someday? That's awful. Someday doesn't exist. Someday doesn't even hover like me in my caesura. Someday is fake, it never comes. Not someday, I would pay those accrued numbers off when I got back. That wasn't someday, that was a real day on the horizon line. Because none of this is permanent. I'll be home again one day soon. But until then, gas station fill-ups and meal outings can be funded by my little orange I-O-U. A little debt for detox seems like a well enough trade. Money now? I've got it, right here in my wallet, just waiting to be swiped. How did I forget this before? Adults make appropriate use of their credit line and I'm an adult, so let's dive on in. No—not dive—let's dip in, wade in slowly. I'm aware, I have control. Control. I have that. I've thought about it enough, conceptualized it enough. Control. I have that. This would be enough.

I flipped to the next page of my little brown book. The morning was still chirping on, birds beeping and tweeting out proudly, drinking in the mountain air. I had scribbled on through box three and took up all of box four, too. I drew out a new square on the next clean page, and scrawled BOX NUMBER FOUR down the top pinstriped line.

Living. This question is the one that I truly have no fucking clue about.

In the months leading up to my graduation from college, I had constructed an idea that was now intermingling with my DNA. An idea that felt a part of me, no matter how much I tried to look away. I can't live in my perfect grid anymore, I can't stay on that graphing paper. I've been there for as long as I can remember. In fact, this little stunt away from home might be the longest amount of time that I've ever been abroad. And boy, am I feeling it. But I've committed, I've told myself that once college is done, I'm moving. Moving somewhere, because I've got to do something. What that something is, I'm not sure. Maybe it's writing. Maybe it's running for public office, maybe it's to start a non-profit organization. For all I know, maybe it's to wait tables. How many back-pats would I get if I picked up my shit and moved across the country somewhere just to wait tables? I don't think I would even pat my own back.

But I've got things to do, some life to accomplish. I've got a maze to solve, up from a thousand pieces to a million-and-one little odd-shaped cardboard bits. The winding and wishful problem of life is out there and it's not going to solve itself. Where do I put myself for all of this? The question that dances across my brain, teasing me with jests and jokes until I'm red in the face with fury. What if I choose wrong?

Before I committed to my tent-on-wheels, before I decided a road trip down the western tip of the continent was the way for me, I spent countless nights clicking through Google images of cities around the country. Seattle looked nice, with its rainy days and moderate seasons. They had kitschy little apartments that were tiny and everything was so cozy. Reno had a strange draw, with lax Nevada laws, no income tax and the mountains surrounding Lake Tahoe nearby. Boulder, Colorado had a cool vibe. All the pictures

Goldilocks

must have been snapped in the fall, as all the leaves were dying and explosive yellow and orange with red intertwined. Mountains all around, it seemed like a weed-friendly version of the grid-filled valley I already lived in back home. Nashville had a certain desirable aura. The land of music and starving artists. Culture, bucket loads of it, walking down the street, everywhere you looked. Who wouldn't want to live in a city with as cool a name as Nashville? That might work. Might be good enough. But Atlanta might be nice too. I went on a trip to Washington DC once, and it was incredible. That might fit the picture, living in the seat of the nation. That's where everything's happening, isn't it? What if it drove me mad, being around all the public servants who seem to only serve themselves. What if I became like them and forgot about the times when I sat in the front seat of my rocket ship in a stupor and watched my bank numbers blow out my exhaust pipe? There are thousands of cities to rifle through, and I've got to pick the right one. The right one. There *is* a right one.

Slow down.
Take a breath—deep and full into your chest.

I'm spilling everywhere. Asking the big questions. The only reason I'm trying to claw my way out of my perfect little grid in Utah is because my mom and my sister and a whole bunch of other people who I really want some back-pats and sideline trophies from have all told me that Utah has an illness. A self-centered disease that pumps through its veins. Filled to the brim with people who judge, comparing what they see against what they think they are or what they think they should be.

When you live in a perfect grid, you start thinking that ninety-degree angles are the normal way of life. You start seeing everyone as either inside the square or outside of it. Everyone's got right-angled halos hovering above their heads. They either hate it or love it and they don't leave much space in between. At least not for the people they see. They leave plenty of space for themselves to wiggle around. But if you like curvy lines, scribbles, and scratches—you lose your halo. No one comes and takes it, no one tells you you've lost it. But you convince yourself that you've lost it, that you're on the outside looking in. You've constructed an entire story about why you don't deserve your square-shaped halo, and you've told yourself that story a hundred-and-one times. Because this place is ninety-degree angles, so if you like curvy lines? You must be wrong. And I felt wrong, often enough. And never knew why.

When you live in a place that worships ninety-degree angles, you're forced to jump into one of two places of the box. You're either inside in the corner, sitting and watching your ninety-degree perfection, or you're on the outside, wallowing around in the two-hundred-and-seventy-degree cross-section. Any way you roll the dice, you are staring at that fucking corner—your nose is jammed in it like a child. Just as it should be. Children convince themselves that they're always right, that the world only exists as they see it. That the world is square and everyone is either on your team or against your team, and there's no curved lines in between. And if you think there might be some other teams, other players in the game of life, other ways of living, believing, experiencing, existing? You must be wrong. That's right-angle living, and Utah is infected with it. I was starting to know why.

It's not a conscious illness, not one that people talk about with each other. Often enough, it's not a disease that people corrupt one another with. It's one that you poison yourself on. It's one that slowly creeps up on you, one that you're never taught but always see. And before you know it, your nose is in the corner, and you're seeing things in nineties and two-seventies and you can't even help it. Before you know it, you're getting tattoos just to signal that you're not a saint. You're dying your hair bright pink just to show that you aren't like those folks who go to church on Sunday. You're getting fourteen piercings in your ears, eyebrows, and nose. You're filling your Tinder profile with your two-seventies—not religious, just so you know. Not one of those weirdos. Not one of those people who do those things. You're having sex with anything, attracted to everything because you've got two-hundred-and-seventy degrees of humanity to make up for. And ninety degrees to condemn everyone else on.

And if you're staring at your right-angle inside the box, your Tinder bio begins by addressing just how holy you are. That you aren't here for sex. You might be here for a good time, not a long time—but it better be good, wholesome fun. So you might go on a double-date, and the first question your right-angle grandparents ask is if the girl goes to church. What values does she have? If you're gonna date, gonna marry, gonna make that choice—it's best to do that with someone who's a right-angler too. Best to make sure all those metrics line up, can't have anyone who's living their life at ninety-one-and-a-half degrees. And I was starting to know why.

Everyone's signaling which angle bracket they play for, and they don't even mean to. And if you said this quiet part out loud, you'd be laughed out of the house by the common shallow response—these aren't smoke signals, they're just parts and parcels of identities! And how dare I tread on that.

The disease resides, growing and growing all the same. It's not spread like a virus, it's homegrown in the mind. It's not real. It's just a lie we tell ourselves in Utah, so we don't have to admit that every single person living in that state, in this country, on this planet—they're all having a three-hundred-and-sixty-degree experience. Every one of 'em.

But I still love my grid. I still love the place I call home. I may not live there, I might move to one of those other cities, or I might not—this isn't permanent. That's a can I'll kick down the road. Maybe my sister and my mom and all the people I want back-pats from are right. Maybe I do need to get out of Utah for a while, for a couple years, maybe forever. Maybe I'll live there again someday. Maybe not. Maybe it doesn't matter. I'm spending gas now, and not making money, and writing in my little brown book for my eyes only. My car is idling, and I've gone so far so fast, but when I look up, I'm sitting in the same place, staring at the same woodsy billboards with the same furry bears dipping their same furry paws in the same sticky honey.

But I'm spilling everywhere and feeling drained, and I haven't moved any muscles but the ones in my hand. It should be enough. Enough to see some upward spikes in bank account numbers, enough to rid me of all the poison I'm trying to detox, all the same. It should be enough to get a sideline trophy. It should be enough. Why isn't it ever enough?

Chapter 20

Bloodletting

Matthew peeled apart a folded strip of tinfoil. He had big fingers but handled the slice of shiny metal with intricate and gentle care. He was light with them and had to be. One fold opened into another, and into another, until finally, sitting on the metallic surface before us, were two little squares of paper. They were plain, with perforated edges where other squares might have been previously attached. These squares were flying solo, blanketed by bendy aluminum. He set the foil down on my food pantry bin we were using as an end table, clasped his hands together and raised his shoulders and vibrated a little. He looked over at me with a huge shit-eating grin.

"It's that time, boy-eee—how much do you want?" Matthew chirped and it was time, the bells were ringing and the times were now and present and his wide and white teeth were telling.

"I'll take a full one, I think. This is as good a place as any!" I chimed back, copying his hand rubbing and clasping motion, as we both ruminated in energetic anticipation. We were jittery like little kids on Christmas morning in the woods.

My belly was bubbling with vigor, nervous and ecstatic all at once. A little scared, a little surprised, a little frantic. This wasn't something new, I'd done it before. All the same, I knew it was a feeling that never got old, always familiar. He reached over the vacant firepit sitting between us, stretching out his hand, where on his thumb sat one of the pearly-white squares. I slowly used my finger and thumb like a pair of tweezers, securing the paper between them, only touching the square at the edges where the perforations were. Without a word, or time for a second thought, I opened my mouth, and plopped the paper atop the veiny meat under my tongue. My lips sealed. I smiled ear-to-ear and raised my eyebrows and all the skin on my forehead wrinkled up and smiled too. He followed my motions with the other slice of paper, reflecting back that same Joker-esque amusement. We were clowning and it was time.

"No going back now! And it really is the perfect spot, you weren't kidding. Look at this!" he exclaimed, turning his head around, using his arm like a circus ringmaster revealing the final act of the show. I'd been in these woods for a couple of days, but looked around at them like it was all new, just as he was. Time for my deep-woods trip.

Beyond our little camp was an endless forest of pine trees. Spaced similarly to the site in Mammoth Lakes, California—nearly perfect in their distance to one another, no big branches jutting out in the first ten or fifteen feet of the trunks. Huge girths of bark and wood and tree sap, and up above, crowding pine needles grating out the clear cyan sky. Through the scatter of emerald needles I could just barely make out the shapes of several billowed clouds. It wasn't too hot today, wasn't too cold. The sun snuck its way through the blanket of trees, providing the perfect amount of warmth. It was sweater weather, and I was well equipped. I leaned back in my everything chair, closed my eyes, and drank a deep breath in.

There are about thirty-five minutes between the time you slip LSD under your tongue and the time you start feeling weird. It's not always an abrupt hit, more of a slow onset of energy balling up in your tummy. As if you're growing an orb of electrical force inside your core. Before long, it starts sliding around, creeping its way out to your arms, your fingers, up the back of your neck, and down your legs. At some point, it crawls up your spine and slips through the back door of your brain. Once it does that, once it lets itself in, grabs the remote, and pulls up a chair to your prefrontal cortex, your channels start changing. And they change for at least twelve hours or more.

Those thirty-five minutes are exhilarating. Wondering if it's gonna work. Wondering if the papers are duds or if they'll be the strongest swatches you've ever had. Wondering if you just made a huge mistake, or if you are about to solve all your prying problems. Maybe you'll mentally achieve something, maybe you'll get that spiritual experience you always hope for. Maybe you'll get lost and wander through time cycles for ten hours straight before you realize you've done nothing but rock back and forth, weeping like a baby all day. It's a thirty-five-minute caesura transporting you from being blind to every seemingly insignificant thing to being amazed by the very dirt beneath your shoes. Thirty-five minutes before you leap off the cliff and speed back in time from twenty-four years old to six years young. When everything is fascinating, everything is simple, everything is laid bare, and you've got a twinkle in your eye, drunk on child-like wonder. We would be before long.

At forty minutes, you know if it's working. That's when the shakes start kicking in. All that energy buzzing like a conduit can't stay inside forever. You start shivering. You hold your hand up to your face and notice you can't keep the fingers and palm still. Shivering in the cold? It's not cold, it's juuuust right outside. Shivering, all the same. Then the jaw starts clenching. The back molars start biting down on nothing, and the muscles along the side of your face start bulging out from all that seizing. Maybe if you bite down hard enough you can stabilize the skull and not vibrate your brain into putty. Good thing I'm outside, I wouldn't want to clean my goo off the frilly carpet after it leaks out of my ears. But the pine trees are nice and this is as good a place as any. Fuck—I'm shivering.

"What time is it?" I said to Matthew, immediately realizing that I had already broken my own rule. I always time it. From paper insertion until bedtime. I always time it. I've got to know how long we've been floating. I always time it.

"Oh shit! You didn't start the timer did you?" he said with a cackle, reeling back and slapping his chest. I'd done this enough times with him that he knew—he liked it being timed, too. But he was never the timekeeper, that was always my job. I was the timekeeper, guardian of the passing second, relayer of finite knowledge. I was the one who says how far along we are. I always time it and I was already slacking on my duties.

"It's probably been, like, thirty or forty minutes. I'm feeling a little something. So I'll start the timer now, and every time we check it, I'll add forty minutes—just to be safe," I said with a nervous chuckle. Playing with time, the ultimate and godly time. That made me anxious, not something to take lightly. In charge of the past, pulling it into the present and naming it, and I was shivering. I pulled out my phone, thumbed over to the alarm application, and started the timer. The screen was wiggling in my hand.

Hundreds of pine trees speared out of the forest floor before me. Hundreds, thousands, there must have been millions of them. All so straight, all so perfectly straight up and down. They rose and bloomed from a bed of fallen needles. They climbed up out of their own deadfall. They were planted in their own waste. They sat in their own mess, their own graveyard, and they grew taller all the same. So many trees, rising straight up into the sky. Reaching, reaching their earthen needle-fingers up into the sky that I can't see. Can I see the sky? The sky is up there, past the jade and waving canopy. It's up there, and I can see little glimpses of it partitioned between all those needles. The green and lively ones. The needles that drank their water and held on for dear life. I'm walking on the bed of the fallen ones, the brown and lifeless husks that got dehydrated and fell far, far down to the floor. They're just carpet now, forest carpet, soft and squishy when rooted this way. Brown and dead, up into green and alive, up into blue and beautiful and vast. These trees are so straight, they don't waver in their stretching to the sun. But they wiggle and the canopy is waving. Is it windy? Are they flowing in the wind?

My finger is in my mouth. Out of my mouth. Tastes like barbecue—that's weird. Should have tasted like skin, like sweat, maybe like dirt. It tasted like barbecue. My thumb is in my mouth, rubbing against my tongue. It tastes like barbecue. Salt and seasoned barbecue. It shouldn't taste that way, but it does, and I don't mind. My middle finger, my ring finger is in my mouth. Barbecue, all of them taste like barbecue, and that tastes good. The canopy is waving, flushing out in the wind. Is it windy? My finger is wet and covered in spit—oh, yes. Out before me, is the wind rushing past my wet finger, is it cold on one of the sides? This is the trick they teach you when you're a little boy scout. Doesn't seem that way, not cold on one of the sides. The canopy might be waving, but I can't tell. Maybe my eyes are shivering. I'm shivering and my arms are vibrating, but it's not that cold out here.

The trees are so straight, up and down. There are red marks on some of them. Red gashes three feet up from the ground. Red slashes, red slices painted on some tree trunks, but not on others. Why do only some of the trunks get to wear crimson sashes? Only some trees have a showy line of scarlet jewelry, red and bright against the brown, bark pine trunk that's magnificently straight up and down. Only some were lucky enough to have the adornment. Why the lines? Why do only some have the paint? The paint, it's there for something. The red paint, red like blood. Bright like rose-colored blood against pearly-white skin, translucent skin, like the skin I have beneath my white tee-shirt. Blood, but on the outside. Why are only some of the trees bleeding? Three-foot-high marks, slashes—maybe they're gashes? Signs of what's to come? Oh no. It's a sea of winners and losers, a forest of some to be taken and some to be spared. Jewelry? Not so much, more like vibrant crimson lines, bloody lines that designate which straight up and down trees are gonna get their heads cut off. Oh no, no, no, no. Random trees, some trees gathered in families, some standing alone, the mommy tree here and the sister tree there—oh no. Brother tree is gonna get his neck cut in half, isn't he? But just look at all of 'em, they're so perfectly up and down, stretching out into the sunlight under the sparkling blue stratosphere. No, no, some of these are going to get their levers pulled, going to be sent beyond before they even have the chance to shed some brown needles, while their little pinpoint fingers are still green and lively. Then they'll all turn brown and die and cycle out of the world. Some are going to die, and some are going to watch.

What if this is how it's supposed to go? Maybe this is how it's supposed to go. Pruning. Trimming the fat of the forest. The red lines on trees, maybe they serve a great purpose. I'm breathing their air. I'm seeing them, walking among their fallen essence. The needles below my feet, the needles that once lived. I'm sitting on the needles, rubbing them between my fingers, snapping their little brown needle bones, feeling the sound, breathing the air. Maybe trimming the fat of the forest is necessary, maybe it's part of the cycle of life. Just as I'm breathing this air, just as I'm crunching and bending these needles, just as I'm sitting out here in the woods in the middle of winding Oregon, just as I took the magic paper. The paper that carried the keys, the paper—that paper was once a tree, just like all these ones standing straight up and down around me. The cycle of life continues. I'm breathing it, crunching it, feeling it. Maybe trimming the fat of the forest is part of it. Maybe the forest needs to detox so it can breathe better. Detox!

I'm detoxing. I'm out here detoxing, that's why I'm out here, isn't it? I'm spending time away, time with myself, time away from the same, detoxing. I'm trimming the fat of the forest inside. Me and this forest aren't so different. Both detoxing, both sitting and watching and breathing it all in, waving under the stratosphere. I've got red lines spray-painted all over different parts of me, detoxing away from the same. Those are the things that I'm chopping down. Those are the things that I plan to slice and dice out, remove from my woods. I've got red lines and some of these trees have red lines, crimson lines—the substance we intend to detox. Intending to detox. But I am detoxing, aren't I? I'm out here in the woods. Detoxing, breathing, feeling, hearing the sounds. Detoxing away from much of the same. Where's the lumberjack with his big, visceral axe, coming to chop down the red lines? What if he never comes, and me and the woods sit here and watch forever? The lumberjack will come, he's got to come. Why else would all the red lines be painted? He'll come, and until then, me and the woods will sit and watch for him. We'll cradle each other, the woods and I. Hold on, the lumberjack's coming. Someday he'll be here, and he'll swing wide and slice right down the red line and some of those chosen trees, some of the fat of the forest will come crashing down and the woods will breathe again. And I'll breathe again, and we'll be whole and beaming.

But what if he never comes? The lumberjack might never come. He might have spray painted the trees, might have colored some of them bright rosey-red, just intending to detox and that's just it. But that's what we're doing, we're out here, hand-in-hand, detoxing together. Me in the woods, the woods in me. We're sitting and watching and waiting for the lumberjack to come and do his best. Prune the fat of the forest. What if tomorrow we're still sitting here, waiting and watching? What about next month—oh no, no, no. He's gotta come, gotta chop these trees down. Gotta detox the woods. He has to. But what if he doesn't, what if he's lost, what if he's sitting at home, with his toes kicked up by the fire, and he forgot to move his feet out the front door? Oh no, no, no, no. He can't do that, he's got work to do, he has to chop these trees and they keep growing. Does he even know what it would mean to not start chopping? The woods might get bogged down, the woods can't breathe, the red lines are meaningless if he doesn't. The crimson lines will just be there, polluting the natural beauty of what the forest could be. Suffocating, fat, and weighted down. That motherfucker better show up—does he even know what it would mean if he didn't?

My eyes swelled, my eyes bulged, my eyes watered. Surface tension building, the water on the outer film of my eyes gathering and gathering. The woods are waving, wiggling, shaking back and forth, fast now—like watching the trees and the canopy through a water bottle. The tension broke and streams ran down my cheeks. Streams into rivers, my daily water intake is shifting into reverse and redirecting from my stomach up into my tear ducts and out onto my face. Rivers of saltwater, the red lines were squiggly lines now, not so straight, the trees aren't so straight up and down anymore. No screams, no wailing or shrieking, just rivers. The lumberjack's not coming, is he. It was all dawning and I shivered.

We're not detoxing, the woods and I. We're just sitting and watching. We're just painting red lines on the same things, on the things we think are problems, on anything. Just painting red lines, signaling which trunks are ripe for slicing, signaling, signaling, signaling—just sitting and watching and intending. And the lumberjack is not coming, is he? What's the use of the red lines if he isn't coming to wield his big axe against them?

I'm out here, out in the woods in the middle of emergent Oregon—I'm not detoxing. I'm out here, away from much of the same back home, breaking away from the routines back home. I'm out here, and I'm giving myself time to paint red lines, but the lumberjack is not coming, and I just keep painting. Oh no, no—painting. Just painting. Painting and sitting and watching and seeing what I painted and waiting. I'm not detoxing. I'm just painting red lines, red clown lines, red lipstick lines around the edges of my big fat fucking lips, smiling in the mirror like a clown and saying I'm detoxing, but I'm not. I'm just painting, just signaling, waiting for someone else to come and do the wretched work of cutting and trimming. Waiting for the time when the work will look easy, feel easy, be easy. And that time isn't coming, hasn't come yet, might not ever come, and I'm sitting here and watching and waiting for it like a damn clown. The trees are growing all the same, the trunks are getting wider, and I just keep painting new red lines and leaving all the old ones in place. The chopping is hard, the bark is tough, and I'm just watching it grow harder and tougher and crying all the while.

The lumberjack isn't coming because he's already here. Sitting on the ground, sitting among the deadfall of the woods, sitting, rocking back and forth, knees tucked so deep into his chest they're nearly popping out the back as angel wings. He's already here, shivering in the ice-cold reality that those shitty, red-lined trees aren't going to cut themselves down. What the fuck am I doing out here?

I leaned back in my everything chair, tears streaking down my cheeks. Matthew was sitting across the firepit with a tortilla draped over his knee, stacking a delicate little pile of barbecue chips in the middle. He had tears running down his cheeks, too. He was attempting to stifle the gut-wrenching laughter that was overtaking both of us, so the shakes wouldn't spill the precarious chip tower he was constructing. He had a brilliant idea but acted out loud, it just sounded like

the punchline of the funniest joke we'd ever heard. He put
another chip on top.

"Look, dude, a chip burrito—no, a barbecue chip
burrito—might sound strange, but let me fucking tell you!
No, stop laughing, you're gonna make me spill this. No, let
me tell you! It's good, the best even. I promise. You're gonna
take a bite of it, you son-of-a-bitch!" he cackled and spilled
one or two chips off the tortilla, tumbling down into the dirt.
Mia trotted over and snarfed up the crisps before either of us
could muster a word through our roaring laughter. Tears kept
coming, my cheeks were soaking wet. My guts hurt, my
mouth hurt, my jaw hurt—I was giving my stomach the
workout of the century, adding years to my life through
joyous howls. We hooted in the wilds and wept for it all. My
jaw locked and my veins bulged on my forehead and I broke
into an elated sweat.

"Stop, please—stop, you've gotta stop, dude! No more,
stop stacking them like that," I was trying to push the words
out, but the laughter was assaulting me. It was that brand of
laughter that grew silent from heaving, airy and convulsive.
The best kind.

"No! I'm fuckin' tellin' you, this is good! See, the
mayonnaise on the bottom acts like a cement foundation for
the lower few chips, but after that, you just have to stack them
carefully. I promise you it's good, dude. I mean, c'mon, it's
barbecue chips!" he said, shouting the instructions of how to
build a barbecue chip burrito out into the woods. I wasn't
taking notes, I was about to laugh myself in half, laugh myself
into vomiting up all the crisps I'd already eaten. They were
malding in my belly and I could feel them transfer from
seasoning into vibrations, shivering and clenching under the
weight of the woodland.

Matthew folded one side of the tortilla up over the top of the chip tower, pulled up the other side, tucked in the ends, and crunched the burrito down, smashing all the chips together amid the dough and mayonnaise that mixed inside. It was an abomination that Taco Bell scientists would have been proud of. Three ingredients, simple construction, capable of producing spectacular farts a few hours from now, and most importantly—it had that crunch. He drew the burrito up to his mouth, and before taking a bite, darted his eyes over to me, just to make sure I was watching.

Cackles and howls overtook us again, silent-laughing our way out of our chairs and into the dirt and dead pine needles. We were rolling around, clutching our stomachs, begging for each other to stop doing everything—any movement, comment, or eye-darting spurred more endless laughter. It was marvelous and we were like little boys, rolling around in the frills of the carpeted forest. I loved it down here, where the earth was warm and beating. We howled at the sun.

Through it all, he managed to cradle the burrito safely in his hand. I rose and replanted myself in my everything chair, burying my face in my arms so I wouldn't see anything, couldn't rub him any way that might bring back the gut-wrenching. It all hurt and reeled against me. Then I heard the crunch. He was doing it, eating it, shoving it in his mouth, chips, mayonnaise and all. I was helpless, choking on my own spit as I aired out more cackles into the crook of my arm. I still wasn't watching, still didn't want to see, still didn't want to screw up his biting process. Too late for that now, he spit the entire first bite out all across the dirt and fire pit, as the onslaught of laughter arrested him again. Helpless. We were both utterly and completely helpless and loving every minute of it.

Oftentimes, in the middle of intense drug-induced stupidity, I think about what it must look like to someone who just happened upon the scene, sober as a kite. What it must look like to see two grown men sitting in little chairs around an empty fire pit, one with snot and tears covering his face, sprawled out in the dirt; the other with bits of barbecue chip, mayonnaise, and tortilla strung about his beard and face. Not to mention the chunks of his first bite scattered about. Not to worry, Mia was doing her job at clearing that mess up. A hiker passing by might be confused, might get a little worried—and they might be right for feeling that way. But they'd get it, well enough, after I filled them in on the chronology of events. All I have to do is show them the burrito and they'd fall to the ground cackling like a hyena, too. Wouldn't they? Look at this burrito he made, with a tortilla, barbecue chips, and some mayonnaise, just look at it! Isn't that hilarious, doesn't all this make a little more sense now?

I stopped laughing. The cuffs were broken and my gut achieved its moment of respite. A stupid sober mind debunked the entire ordeal. That hiker would angle his eyebrows, and I'd be the one left feeling idiotic. A barbecue chip burrito? That's ridiculous. Maybe stupid, maybe dumb, maybe just a little funny—but bust-a-gut, piss-my-pants hilarious? Maybe not. Maybe we're just helpless, maybe we're just on drugs. And boy, were we ever.

"What's the timer say?" Matthew said, wiping bits of chip off his face with the back of his hand.

I shoved my hand in my hoodie pocket, pulled my phone out, and clicked the screen on. "Looks like three hours and twelve minutes. So if we add the forty minutes like we're supposed to, then we've been going for three hours and fifty-two minutes," I said, matter-of-factly. I'm scrambled eggs right now, but I can still do the math. We were going and going and went.

Smoke poured out of Matthew's mouth like a train engine steaming hot mist out its blast pipe. It kept coming, kept dumping like sheets of cotton across my body, across the blankets, across everything. It kept coming. How did he store this much inside? Where did it all go—he's pouring milk clouds from his wide-open lips and it just keeps coming. Look at his eyes though, just as wide open as his mouth. He's surprised just like I am, he's on the verge, the cough is rising, tickling the back of his throat. Look at his eyes, you can tell. He's making the groaning precursor to an onslaught of coughs, mouth filled with smoke, still surging from his windpipe. Eyes wide, bright eyes so wide. It just keeps coming, this quixotic beast.

He stifled the cough and shook his head. Reignited the lighter, drew the little crackpipe stuffed full of Mary-Jane up to his lips once more, and set the bowl aflame. Intake. Long intake. He's intaking, still breathing and sucking in, taking in all the essence of that green little puck, packed so tight and dense, just like the smoke he's gonna flood the tent with. Flooding the tent up, filling it like a fish tank with water. His eyes are bulging, just like fish eyes do, staring with those beady peepers. Bright eyes, so wide, his eyes are so big right now, so wide they might pop out of his sockets and roll down the front of his sweatshirt. Two more face-holes to exhale more smoke through, fill the fish tank up to the brim. And we were. And the little pipe is sitting in my hands now. Resting between my fingers again, for the second time. No, it must've been the… third time. Could be the first. Wouldn't be the last. My turn to fill the space with regurgitated smog. Deep inhale.

Long inhale. Eyes so wide, so bright, groaning the precursors, whites so scarlet red and veined with blood, and crystal blue, just like his are. We shivered and snickered and lit it all up and it was milk.

A grooving mallet started slamming. Something was pounding through the smoke, smashing around the tent, echoing off the vacant thoughts in my brain. Echoing off the walls of the fish tank, echoing off our hollowed skulls, echoing off the smoke itself. The tube. The little music tube was on, its tiny power lights emanating through the fog. It was on, it was spilling thoughts of its own into the fish tank, vibrating the smoggy water, vibrating it with bass.

A little airy voice started singing about white shirts and bloody noses. Vibrating with that pounding, booming, bass. Bass that's gyrating, waving, wiggling, shivering the little worms inside my head into a putty-mush—I'm gonna start leaking and this isn't dirt. I'm gonna have to clean this up if it gets on the floor of the tent. I can't even see the floor of the tent. I'm in a tent, a real tent, a tent that sits on the ground with no wheels attached. Where's the damn floor, the walls, the zipper. I can't see it, just my eyes and mouth are so wide, my jaw is cramped from clenching. Bass notes sleuthed through the tank and around our heads, and that little voice.

"No dude, you gotta start it over. Pleeeease! That was soooo good, start that one over. What *is* that? Yeah, start that one over for me," I quickly muttered to him through the pounding beats. His teeth are so white when he smiles back at me through the fog. I can see those, he's right by me and swimming in the success of a good tune.

"Ok, ok, I will. It's soooo good, isn't it? She's got the perfect music for this, right now."

Duhmmm duh duh dumm, duh duh duhuummm, mmmhuumm duh duh duh mhuummm. Oh, it was perfect. One after another, bass-infused drumbeats smashing against the sides of my head, perfectly spaced apart. One after another in perfect rhythm. I was nine seconds into the song and already about to orgasm from the mixture of a jive string line meshed with the slams, the pounds, the booms that were perfectly spaced apart. They were and I was swooning to it and my eyes were hearing it all. The voice broke in again and floated across the bass line like an ethereal ghost. White shirts dirtied up with bloody noses, again. And the creeping.

It's perfect! That little otherworldly voice, riding the golden river bass line. It was all highs and lows and enchanting. That voice that's speaking those words as if they are just popping into her brain in the perfect order and letting them spill from her lips like she doesn't even care. As if she doesn't even care. But she has to care, she's got to care, they're just falling from her lips and it's perfect and breezy and sleepy and... lovely. They're just falling out. Those words are just falling out in the perfect order with juuuust the right amount of... of what? What is that? She sounds like she doesn't even care. But she's got blood on her shirt, that's *it*, she's got blood and it's covering her white shirt, so she's gotta care. She's saying it all in the perfect order, the strings are plucking and dancing in the perfect order, the bass-beats hitting one after another in perfect, metrical timing. It was all chaos and order in the beginning, and I slouched closer to the speaker and leaned my ear against its casing and nourished myself on the notes.

"Who in the hell is singing this? Whose song is this?" The question burst out of me like a dam breaking. As if I was trying to get the courage to inquire, and finally, it was just too much. Too much to go on not knowing.

"Oh maaaan, you don't know? She's getting huge! It's Billie Eilish—she's killer, man. This is off her new album—song's called *Bad Guy*," Matthew said, eyes closed, leaning back against a pile of pillows and blankets in the corner of the tent.

She was getting big—getting huge. Gaining traction, becoming a big deal, and I knew it the second the song started. How could she not, with sounds like that? She didn't even care, she let the words spill out, soak into her shirt. Soak into her bright pearly-white shirt, all bloody and covered now. She wore it, let the words fall right out of her mouth, tumble right from her lips in perfect order, with the perfect bass line.

She kept airing out her voice, singing about creeping things, sleuthing things, and tippy toes and I wanted to crawl into the speaker tube and live there. She's not creeping around, she's making these music lines and putting them out there and now two guys in a smoke-filled, hot-boxed tent are breathing in Mary-Jane-musk like it's oxygen and floating, bobbing, breaking to the sounds of the sweet, un-caring vocal soup that's spilling from her lips. The perfect ingredients in the perfect order, one beat after another. You know what would be criminal? If she wrote this music, planned it all out, let it fall from her lips, and then left it in a journal somewhere. Left it as some audio file buried in her computer. Hid it behind several little manilla folders on her desktop, hid it away because it was bloody and weird. That would be the crime of the century. No, she didn't, though. She matched up the words and the beats, and now there's two guys head-bobbing in the middle of the woods in esoteric Oregon, having a spiritual experience in a foggy tent with no wheels.

We aren't going anywhere. I'm not about to, I just found out who Billie Eilish is.

"Oh dude, this part is so good. It's like she's singing through a fan—listen," Matthew suddenly perked up and said, eyes wide open now. He held his finger horizontal in between his lips and brushed it up and down, imitating the choppy sound produced by speaking through spinning fan blades. Just in unison with the voice spilling perfectly from the tube-speaker in the middle of the tent.

I missed something—she was chanting about being the bad guy. She's the bad guy, she's the bad guy—why is she the bad guy? She's putting this music in my tent. She doesn't even care, but she's saying and singing and playing all the perfect sounds in the perfect order, just like poetry. She's the bad guy for that? For bloodying up her white shirt, for spilling her feelings, her weird lyrics and fan-bladed refrains? She's the bad guy. The criminal creeping around on her tippy toes? But she's getting big, she's catching traction with the world—they love her bloody shirt, the un-caring way she spills the words from her mouth as if it doesn't matter what people think of them. She's spilling them, all the same. Blood and all. Like a gushing river, a golden river, a rapid-filled waterway. She's unleashing a dam of authenticity and she doesn't give a shit how anyone else feels about it—she's doing it anyway. And she's the bad guy? It was obvious to her and I missed something. Duh.

I can't feel my arms and legs and I'm shivering. I'm the bad guy. That's what she said, wasn't it? I'm the bad guy. Oh no, no. Maybe I'm the bad guy. What does the bad guy do, what part does he play? He creeps, stalks around thinking that no one knows, that no one sees him stalking. The bad guy thinks himself tough, thinks himself better than the bloody nose. The bad guy escapes and just can't get enough. Just can't get enough of the escape, the foggy tent, the bobbing. Oh no, no, no. I'm the bad guy.

The bad guy puffs his chest and thinks all the words always have to be in the perfect order, that they naturally spill in the perfect order and that should be good enough. The bad guy, this bad guy, this bad guy sitting in a stuffy tent, this bad guy, thinking these bad thoughts. This bad guy bleeds a gushing river from his running nose and hides it all in a little brown leather book. If you're reading this, don't. It's weird, and it's mine, and if anyone else's eyes catch sight of it, I'm ruined. I'm embarrassed because I give a fuck about what all the other guys think about me. How am I supposed to get my back-pats if my blood and guts are only painted down pinstriped lines?

I'm the bad guy, and she's the good one. She does what she wants when she's wanting to, because that's authentic living. She lays her head down in the crook of her arm and lets the notes and string-plucks and lyrics flow from her gray-matter like a big golden river and that's why she's catching traction with the world. That's why she's getting big and deserves her picture taken with her foot up on a stump in a history book. She's putting potential to the wheel, feet to the fire, always to the fire—and not giving a shit what everyone thinks about it. I'm the bad guy. I'm the puffed-up guy, the creeping around pretending no one knows guy. The sitting and watching and intending guy. Duh.

Her blood runs out her nose and onto her shirt and she wears it anyway. She's wearing it anyway. She's catching traction with the world, getting so many back-pats that she's gonna bruise. And when those people pat her back, they get some of that blood on their hands. Some of that gore that's leaking out of her head is getting on their hands, under their fingernails. But they love it, they crave it, they lick their palms clean. They drink it up like vampires, washing those bloody thumbs and fingers in their mouth, rubbing them against their tongues. My finger is in my mouth, and it tastes fake like barbecue. Like barbecue sauce? Seasoning, like barbecue seasoning, salted and specked all over my fingers and thumb. It doesn't taste like blood, doesn't taste like anything but artificial barbecue seasoning.

My crimson blood leaks out my head through my nose and eyes and ears, but I catch it on pinstriped lines and slam the book-spine shut before anyone can get any of it on them. My shirt keeps white, pearly white. My finger is in my mouth, my pinky finger even, and it, too, tastes like barbecue. Why do my fingers taste like barbecue? I can't feel my arms and legs, and I'm shivering, and my jaw is clenched, and it's not even cold. I have to stretch my mouth wide like my eyes when I'm inhaling my Mary-Jane-filled crackpipe, inhaling again, deep and deeper still. But not so deep that the fog dissipates in my guts. This fish tank still needs water, still needs to be filled up so I can't see to the other side of the tent-with-no-wheels. And I don't want to see the floor. It must be coated and gooey by now. So I keep on with the escapes, the Mary-Jane, the paper swatches, just to keep the space between my ears foggy enough—juuuust foggy enough—that I don't have to think about my fake-tasting fingers.

"Hey, will you restart the song one more time? Just one last time, I promise. It's just so good... I think I've got something off it."

Chapter 21

Trash in the Meadows

The remains of a maggot-fiend camp lay before the both of us. It was disgusting. We were slipping down the backside of our LSD-infused day and our guts hurt looking at the mess scattered between the trees like plaque on unflossed teeth. Matthew and I had been hiking and stumbling along in the fading light and found a litter of modern ruins. Piles of trash everywhere, boxes, empty milk cartons, cracked and moldy tupperware, a rubbermaid set of pull-out bin shelves, withdrawn and strewn about. A tent that was still staked into the soft dirt but flattened from aggressive storms and months of rainfall and wind. The poles were busted, snapped at every angle, zig-zagging across and through the nylon sheets that once framed a little shelter. It was a giant pile of pick-up sticks now, mingled with cloth and anchor ropes.

Off to the side, there was a bright blue grocery sack filled with used baby diapers. Shat-in, pissed-in, balled-up bundles of baby waste, collected neatly, tied shut, and thrown out into the woods. Pill bottles were scattered, adorning every pile of refuse around the scene. Little orange caps with white bodies, little white caps with orange bodies—every kind of pill, every kind of pellet that humans slip above their tongue and down their throat. Bottles everywhere, bottles that held medicine and drugs, bottles that held soda pop and beer, glass bottles shattered against rocks with their Heineken and Budweiser wrappers dispersed among the dirt. Piles of forest-green bottles, left to mingle with the dead pine needles, green gas bottles, propane bottles that fueled camp stoves, now left idle and spent, empty with stripped off labels from the weather of a hundred suns.

Beside one of the piles of trash, sat a blue cooler, lid thrown open wide to the elements. I have to see what's inside, what if there's something inside? Maybe papier-mache, like the stew that's simmering in the fossil-box in the front seat of my car. Maybe there would be nothing but a little gathered up rainwater. What if there's a head? What if there's a human head, or maybe some arms and fingers. Images from *Seven* started reeling across my mind—no, not a head. Not some arms, legs, toes, or fingers. No, they wouldn't be inside. I shuddered. I'm fragile right now, floating like a balloon, shivering in the good temperatures outside. I'm fragile right now, and a head in the cooler might set me off, might pop my skull into thin air. No, not a head, surely not a head. This trash has been here for months, maybe even years. A head would be reduced to bone by now. A skull in the cooler? No, not that, not finger bones, not femurs, not shoulder blades, or kneecaps. Just rainwater. It'll just be rainwater.

Dead needles and sticks crunched beneath the sole of my foot. One step. What's another? The trash can't come alive, can't slime together into a monstrous being that will devour me into the piles of garbage spread around. It can't, it's all dead. It's all inanimate. It's just garbage and there's no one out here looking at it but me and him.

Another crunch of needles, I was entering the ruins of the maggot-fiend camp. Trash on all sides, broken and decomposing boxes everywhere. No birds sang, no chipmunks chattered. The sun was resting low on the horizon as twilight set in through the trees. It was purple, gray, and dark green and brown everywhere, mixed together in a woodland mess. Another crunch, and the hairs on my neck rose. Jutting straight out from my skin, like a million little devil-worshiping elves were pulling each sprouting hair out, out of my skin, out of my blood, out of my being, my soul. Standing straight up, and another crunch. I hate it here. Glass everywhere, glass that would give you every disease known to mankind and beyond if it cut through my chilled and bumpy skin and into my blood. My blood, not here, no blood here. Keep that inside, inside and circulating fast and warm, disease-free—but I'm shivering, and I can hear my bones clicking off one another like I'm ancient. Another crunch. Trash on all sides, and I hate it here.

Another crunch, I stepped over a dirty tampon box, still stuffed with something. Stuffed with used ones, new ones, I wasn't about to check, not on my life. To the right, piles of trash, little plastic caps on syringes, little needles that weren't brown, weren't green, weren't bendy and natural. They were metal and hollow needles, shiny and glinting in the setting sunlight. Little metal needles that attached to the little plastic syringes, hundreds of them, could have been thousands. Everywhere, suddenly seeing their adornment on every pile of garbage—little needles, not so natural, not so friendly looking, scattered everywhere. The haystack became the anomaly, the needles, the metal needles, the man-made needles that poked and jabbed skin, rotten skin, rotting flesh, pores and open-bleeding wound-ridden skin. Those needles became the hay in the stack and I was the needle, the shiny and clean one, amid the trash. Another crunch. My boots are tied tight and my rubber soles are over an inch thick and no man-made needles, no maggot-juice is getting inside the soft surfaces of my feet tonight. I hate it here. Another crunch.

To the left, a folding end table, and on top of it, a wooden box, splitting and soaked with Oregonian woodland moisture. Moldy and wet, with rusted nails clamping in the sides and corners of the decaying box. Open on top, like a manger amid a sea of used and abused humanity. What's in the manger, what's in the box? Not a head, never a head. Why do I always have to see a head in the box, a severed, decapitated, sawed-off, gory head. Its eyes open wide, like my stretching out my jaw, like my own eyes, wide and red-veined and glazed. No, not a head, just nothing. Maybe an empty milk carton, maybe more papier-mache like the kind congealing in my science-experiment cooler. The manger would wait—the cooler, that blue cooler that's wide open comes first. Not a head inside it though, never a head. Just sap-flavored rainwater. Just water and another crunch and I'm shivering, skin so bumpy and perked-up I can hardly stand it here. I hate it here.

The cooler, here's the cooler. The bright blue cooler, lid left open to the world for God knows how long. Here it is, and hopefully there's nothing but dirty rainwater swirling around the bottom, but I have to look now. I can't go on not knowing, not seeing the end plot to *Seven*, the crime of the century.

Green water, green moldy and dreadful water, sickly and soupy. And sticks and a set of little eyes. A little button nose, and two little rosy cheeks. A jutting chin with a demonic little dimple right in the center. Golden little tufts of hardened hair spiraled around the faded forehead. I'm looking away, I'm shouting, yelling, and laughing, and screaming all at the same time. I'm fragile right now, and this is close to enough. The bumps on my skin, so close to bursting. Oh, come on. A head? There had to be a head, a little head, floating in the rainwater, there couldn't just be water, couldn't just be one thing. There had to be both.

Little plastic eyes, little blue plastic eyes, bright like the bag of baby shit, bright like the cooler, bright like his eyes. Bright like mine. Little plastic baby eyes, painted in the two little round divots, wide and full, framed in white. Staring up through the garbage, staring up and meeting my eyes. Just the head, no body. Just the little plastic head, popped off, yanked off, ripped off by a real baby somewhere else in the world. Screwed off, thrown around, left for days, months, maybe years in the growing green soupy science project of this woodland cooler. Eyes still wide, still blue, still so ocean blue. Floating in the box, face up. Just the head, just the doll's head. There had to be a head.

"Oh come on. There's a head in here, dude. You've gotta be kidding me, of course there'd be a head in here, why wouldn't there be a head in here," I said, half joking, half stunned from the fulfilling prophecy. Someone's successful end-plot, and I shuddered.

"No there's not—bullshit. Let me see, you're full of it," Matthew chimed back, stepping a bit quicker now across the maggot-camp. He had a contorted look on his face, like he wanted to laugh at the entire mess, while at the same time being deeply disturbed at the fact someone would leave all these rotting boxes and needles and defeated tents and bottles up here in the majestic woods of Oregon. And they were wonderful, the natural woods, the trees free from red marks, the verdant places of the woods, where the true Keebler-elves lived. Where they crawled inside the trunks of pine trees and drank tree-sap flavored beer, foamy and bubbly and magical. They belched little burps after a mug or two of their earthen guzzles, hearty and full and folk-like, a recipe passed down from one little elven generation to the next. No elves here, though. This was where the satanic ones came, where the evil elves came to worship the man-made needles and stir up the magic woodland with boxes, man-made boxes that were rotting under a thousand suns on purpose.

"I mean... come on. You really had me going for a minute. A head? Sure, I guess. You can't do that man, all this shit everywhere, and you're gonna just say there's a head in there? That's a doll's head!" he cried out, the contortion on his face transforming into genuine discomfort among the trash in the meadows. All this sin, one of the worst sins, acts flying in the face of mother nature, her elves, the good elves. Piles of garbage and death and metal needles, and baby-doll heads. I hate it here and I'm still shivering, peaking up on uncontrollable shivering and shaking, and this place is turning my brain into much of the same—piles of trash, piles of sin and evil. The trash piles don't need to congeal into a dumpster monster out here, it's already happening in my mind, hugging me, devouring me, yanking me out of the woods, out of the magical, emerald, cycle-of-life woods. I'm centerstage on a pentagram, each corner point dotted with its own moldy pile of waste. I hate it here.

"You're right. I'm sorry, that was careless, given the state of things," I said, looking at my feet, my boots, my legs shaking in my boots, standing in dead pine needles, standing atop a flattened, faded box. We were fragile. Glass shards to the right and further right still, a pile of empty plastic bottles. More bottles, bottles that stored liquor, Fireball and vodka so strong it might as well have been hand sanitizer. So many of those bottles. I hate it here and I'm fragile right now, a vase that's close to cracking, hairline fractures growing into boneline splits. I'm about to break apart at the seams. We both quivered under the weight of exile and malice.

"This place is disgusting, man. How could someone do this?" he said, turning his gaze away from the bright blue cooler box that cradled a plastic baby head, rocking it back and forth slightly in a pool of green, moldy water. The head smiled an ignorant grin and didn't know where it was. Matthew didn't want to look at it, not anymore. I didn't want to look at it anymore. Babies played with dolls, and there was an evil mixture of child's toys and intoxicants everywhere. Where was the baby? Where were the consumers of all that liquor, the ones who spent their days jamming those metal needles into the veins running down the crook of their arm? They weren't here, hadn't been here in weeks, months, maybe even years. They weren't here, but all their disgusting, putrid shit was. It was everywhere, and I hated it.

"I don't know how someone could leave all this out here. All these coolers, boxes of food, and drinks, and hygiene things—they were definitely living out here," I said, scanning each point of the evil garbage pentagram again.

"Yeah, they must have. Kids and parents, and look at all these beer and liquor bottles and needles. That doesn't seem like a good mix," he grumbled, kicking one of the plastic liquor bottles with the side of his foot. He shook his head.

"Nope. Not at all. It looks like they just up and left."

"But why is everything piled up like this?"

"That's a good point, they wouldn't have stored everything like this—in big piles. That doesn't make much sense. Some of these things belong in coolers, but they're out here, piled up with everything else."

"Yeah, I mean there's boxes of tampons next to a carton of rotten Lactaid."

"It's almost like the forest clean-up people came and piled everything up to burn it but never set the fire," I said, imagining each pentagram point being lit aflame—the final act to summon the sinful garbage monster into reality. I could see thousands of rebel devil-elves, hunched over on their knees, rocking forward and backward, waving their arms out in front of them, chanting some unintelligible sorcerer language with a lot of "s" sounds and grunts. And the fire, the burning fire of metal needles and man-made refuse reflecting off their little woodland eyes. Their wide eyes, bright and wide and watching for the embodiment of sin to come forth, summoned into the world to rule again.

"The clean-up crew wouldn't have left it like this, though. It's almost like the people who lived here were trying to burn it themselves, but got stopped before they could do it," Matthew said. He was imagining scenarios of his own, gears turning, replaying a hundred possibilities.

"Now there's definitely something to that, I think. What if they knew the police were coming and they were trying to pile all this up and burn it so there was no evidence?"

"But why would they try to do that, this is Oregon— damn near everything is legal. Plus, druggies don't usually panic or catch wind of things like that, do they?"

"I guess not, I wouldn't think so. I mean judging by all these needles and bottles, they were zonked out and probably dead-drunk, too." My gears were turning, trying to piece this disaster together. I turned back around, and locked eyes with the baby head floating in the green and murky water. It was the kids. The kids played with the dolls, there were kids here, children here, mingled with all this devil-worship. Mingled with all these boxes, these bottles, these crates and containers.

"I think it was the kids."

"You think the kids did all this, piled everything like this? No way," he retorted.

"No, they didn't pile all this up. It was the kids; the kids were the reason the adults tried to pile it all up and burn it. The police were coming, the parents knew. No state in the union lets parents keep their kids with this many needles, this much liquor and alcohol, this entire living situation. Those parents didn't have a chance in hell of keeping their kids with all this going on," I stated, motioning my hand to every point of the evil, trash-fueled pentagram.

"So the parents quickly piled up all the evidence, maybe intending to burn it, but didn't have the chance before the cops showed up and took everyone away," he replied, following the narrative we were constructing.

"I think so."

My eyes started stinging, burning from how wide they'd been pried open. Wide and bright and now filling with saltwater. I saw the kids, wandering around the middle of the pentagram, holding the plastic baby doll. It was dark, and parents were sprinting around, throwing their stuff into piles, screaming, shouting swears, attempting to find a sliver of sobriety to hang on to, to prove to the coming cops that they were well enough to parent children. But the kids didn't know any of that, they just saw their idols panicking, screaming, shrieking with worry. They were just being told to gather up their clothes, it was time to go. Everyone's eyes were wide and wielding fear and they all screamed like coyotes at the black moon.

Tears streamed down my cheeks, and I was shivering wildly and it wasn't cold outside. It was dark and getting darker. Cold and getting colder. But I saw the kids wandering around, baby dolls in hand, crying tears of their own down their little rosy cheeks. They were just kids, they just wanted to be kids. They just wanted to play with dolls in the woods, play make believe, play house. They just wanted to be kids, and their parents just wanted to escape back to those times, too. But the parent's toys were wrong, the parent's toys were metal needles and harsh chemicals, bottles of hand sanitizer, and boxes of cancer sticks. The parent's toys were all wrong. They were playing with adult toys, anything that could get them out of reality, escaped into much of the same. The parent's toys were all wrong, toys built to feed the feeling, obsessed with the feeling, always chasing that next feeling, that next high, that next needle jab into the crook of their arm. I hate it here, and I hate those parents—those careless, feeling-chasing, monkey-fuckers who brought kids into the wonderful woodland, among the Keebler-elves, and tarnished it all with the worst sin and vice they could foment. Among the children, too, among the kids who just want a chance to be young. My eyes stung, sodium-seasoned, wide still, unblinking, and terrified at the choices of these adults.

There was no time for baby-dolls during the chaotic scene that once played out here. I could see the kids, the one with the baby-doll, standing, crying, trying to understand. The dad approaches and tries to take the doll, tries to tell the kid that they need to leave, and they can't take the doll along for the escape. Another escape, always escaping. But the child wants the doll, can't part with the doll, the doll is the only thing, the very last thing they have to remind themselves that they are young. The last appropriate toy. And the dad pulls and the child pulls back, and they play tug-of-war for a moment—and pop! The head comes off, held in the dad's hand, in his palm, and he doesn't even care. He throws it behind him, into a wide-open cooler, a bright blue cooler. And the child stumbles backward into the dirt, onto their bum, holding the body, tears streaming down their face, holding a headless baby doll. And the dad doesn't even care, he turns, shakes his own head, still balled up and ballooned on two, three, four metal needles-worth of liquid death. He goes back to building devilish piles to burn before the police show up. Running around blind and ruinous to the little life sitting in the mud.

But this child is still there, holding their little doll—their headless doll. And they walk, stumble, and shuffle through the forming pentagram, crying, rocking the headless doll in their little arms, telling it to hush, everything will be okay. Telling it that maybe it didn't need a head after all, maybe it was better this way. Still crying, more tears staining their rosy cheeks, swollen eyes, the brightest eyes you can possibly imagine—those child eyes, luminous and twinkling and beautiful. Rocking their headless baby to sleep, wandering through the camp, to the other side of the human disaster their parents are scrambling around. Across the camp, across the forming pentagram, to a little end-table, with a little wooden manger sitting on top. Rocking the little headless baby doll to sleep, telling it that it would be comfortable here, it would be okay here, resting easy in its little wooden manger.

Another crunch sounded beneath my foot, another tear streaked down my cheek, and I shivered harder still. Another crunch, another, and I see the manger, that wooden, soaked-through, moldy box sitting on the edge of camp. Up beside it, I have to look inside it, and I'm not so fragile anymore, I already have the tears, I'm already cracked and splitting down my seams—I don't even care anymore. I have to see inside, I have to know. I can't go on not knowing.

Inside the manger, inside the decaying wooden box, laid the little plastic body of the baby doll. The body to the head floating in the green and malignant soup swishing around that bright blue cooler. The body was here, tucked in tight within the confines of the bed. Right where it belonged, right where it should be.

Another stinging tear made its way down my own rosy cheek, as I looked on at the final act a child made before they were forced to grow up. Forced to watch their parents get arrested, forced to live their youth in God knows how many foster homes, youth homes, parentless, careless, lifeless homes, that were more like houses than homes. More like places they resided than genuine homes filled with loving souls who cared, who hugged, who didn't rip the heads off their dolls. Away from real homes, living out their parent's wildest dreams in the mountains getting high and forgetting it all. They had to be in the mountains. This place, the last youthful moment in a child's history somewhere—a week ago, a month ago, a year ago, who knows. The last moment before this little baby, this real-life, real breathing baby had its childhood ripped from its grasp. The circumstances they were in didn't care how they felt, didn't care if they wanted to escape, didn't care what they thought—it was time to grow up, time to tuck the baby doll in one last time and grow up in the middle of a vice-ridden pentagram, in the middle of the deep, dark woods in broken Oregon.

I hate it here, where the worst things happened. In this air, between these trees, in the middle of this devil-star. The worst things. Horrible things. I hate it here, and I'm shivering and the sun has set. Those escaping parents, always trying to escape, always looking for the exit. Is this mess, this catastrophe littered all around me at the end of that road? The apex of escaping? The final move before you get the Mojave Desert jail bars slammed down around you?

Escaping, running away from the towns and cities, from the people—living in the woods, free to ram as many needles into the crook of your arm as you want, free to let your children run wild, free to drink bottle after plastic bottle of barely digestible zombifying vodka. Free to throw your trash into the trees, free to worship the devil as you see fit. Free to do anything but act in reality. Is this where that road leads? Escapism as an identity, as a way of life, as the very blood that runs through my veins, out my nose, onto my shirt. My veins, my golden, foam-flowing veins. The same ones that spill and catch in my leather-backed book.

I'm here, at the end of someone's escapism road, where the obsession with feeling, the obsession of finding that feeling, finding that high—where it all came to a close. Where nothing is ever enough. I'm here at the close, at the end, the abrupt and disastrous end of all things, where the victim is a child's bright and wide baby-blue eyes, where horrific and awful things happened. Where the boxes and cartons and bottles and needles of identity are proved as the wrong toys. Where soaking in the mess of idle mileage, drawing out re-penned boxes with shallow answers, thinking and drugging, and intoxicating and licking barbecue off my fingers and thumb is all mistaken as living. The wrong toys.

Here at the end of the road, here where everything is hated and darkness abounds. Here where I'm detoxing away from much of the same, begging for mountains, expecting sideline trophies and back-pats. Here, right here, where if I came up with a real reason to be out here, I might actually have to move my hands and feet and engage with life. Here where I'm writing in my little brown leather book down pinstriped lines so I don't have to write things that everyone can read because I'm not over myself. Because I've failed Bill. Here where I'll tell myself I don't give a shit how I feel, but I'm escaping all the same, always escaping. Here where I'm living on the road, where I'm sitting and watching, because I'm not willing to make a choice, not willing to leave my perfect grid, not willing to take a chance, not willing to do anything. Here where the caesuras stretch across the chasms of time and the outsets are all uphill climbs that are too steep. Because I'm Goldilocks and I only know how to engage with life and outset when the circumstances are juuuust right. And I hate that about me.

All the psychological snake oil—magic words, complacent wishes and whimsies, dreams and half-starts. All that conceptualization of a future and a past, all the aggressive thinking too fast while living too slow. What am I going to do after I graduate? Strip it all out, like the dotted lines in my book. What the fuck am I doing out here? Strip it all out, down to the base parts. Do. Doing. Lose the complicated forever questions, and just engage. Just do. I'm here, and reminding myself I'm here over and over because all it takes is a present moment to decide an outset for myself.

Maybe it's seeing the trash in the meadows that scares me into choice, away from idle habits. Maybe it's the slide-down of lysergic acid diethylamide that's drawing the poison out from the wound of my daydreamed life. Maybe I've hit the critical mass of over-thought juxtaposed with under-lived. Maybe it doesn't matter, because my power is born out of my ability to decide outsets—here and now. To engage with what's before me, regardless of its too-hotness or too-coldness. I don't give a shit how I feel, I'm gonna outset anyway. Fuck you, Goldilocks.

The bears come home. They always come home, kicking open the door and souring up life, and I've just been hiding under the bed shivering because it's too hard, too scary, too hot, too cold to do anything else. All the same, the bears always come home.

I've been standing still for so long, I haven't noticed I'm moving backward.

It was June now and bloody spring had set down the western sky. I closed my little brown leather book and slid my little silver pen in its stretchy loop, snug along the spine. It was the best book I never read—I was too busy living it.

ACKNOWLEDGEMENTS

There's a special moment when you set out to do something. It whiffs past your eyes and mind and you try to grab it, but it's slippery and snakes off into the backseat of your brain and becomes a brief memory. And your hands moved, your feet moved, and you try to pinpoint what changed, what energized those muscles and tendons to get up and go—but it's elusive. The reason *why*. And if you could just harness that moment, you might be able to use that outsetting power again and again forever.

The human experience craves rationality. Yearns to have all the lincoln-logs fall in perfect order, one stacked atop another. Our minds desire that sense, that sanity. So much, in fact, that they fill in the blanks with what we know. We want organized cabins of thought, built right and sturdy. We want sense, we want logic, we want a cohesive *why*. But the thing about the human experience? It's all too human. It's messy and disgusting, and it'll never make any kind of sense to a perfectly rational being. It varies, it changes, it grows and wanes. But through it all, it remains bright as a fire on a cold winter night. And that's just *it*.

The reason why you moved is in the past. It will always be in the past, and it matters—but not as much as it does to keep on moving. To keep on creating, producing—engaging with the gift, the warm blood that circulates around your body. The cycle of life demands it. The echelons of your very soul *demand it.*

In the spring of twenty-twenty-one, I received an email from a representative of a professor who worked at the University of Michigan. The subject line read: FEATURE OPPORTUNITY. I tilted my head, raised my eyebrows, and laughed at yet another scam email sent to flood my inbox. All the same, I clicked it and started reading.

The rep introduced a guy I'd never heard of named Richard E. Nisbett. She said he was a leading mind in the field of psychology. I scoffed a bit more but went on reading. Why would a "leading mind" want anything to do with me? Over the year-and-a-half prior, I had been trying my hand at podcasting, focusing on new psychological research released around the world. It was a fun little solo adventure, pouring through articles and peer-reviewed research on the subject I'm so obsessed with, then relaying that information out over the podcasting airwaves. Made me feel like I was in school again. And I loved that.

The representative told me that this Richard guy had just released a new book called *Thinking: A Memoir.* He wanted to join me on my podcast for an interview. I sat and stared at the pixels on my computer monitor and peeled at the decision to engage or not. Opportunity was knocking, and it seemed like a coin flip would decide if I'd answer. I told them yes and set the date and they mailed me a copy of his book.

I'm not a fast reader. I had about two weeks to read his book and formulate some good questions, and I was nervous and started adopting my old college habit of skimming. It felt wrong. Felt like he'd know, listeners would know, the world would know if I skimmed and didn't give the words a full run-down. So I figured out how many pages I needed to read every day to finish the book on time. And I did it. Our interview went off without a hitch.

One core tenet of Richard's book states that human beings are wildly incapable of attributing correct reasoning to why things happen, why they make certain decisions, or why they feel specific emotions. It's all reasoning errors. And in reading his book, I found liberation. Science stating that stewing in *whys* was a waste of time. Ruminating in idle moments was doing more harm than good. Because the reasons I'd find were more than likely wrong. But what's never wrong is action—the doing. *That* was the good stuff.

Maybe the stars lined up juuuust right. Maybe it doesn't matter, because without the help of people, none of this would've ever come into being. So I have more than gratitude for those that helped along the way. To Richard E. Nisbett, for taking a chance in time to sit and chat with some kid from Utah about brain stuff for a few hours one afternoon. For writing a book that bridged the gap between academic science and digestible nonfiction.

To my college professors—Bill, Cassady, and Lucy—for having faith in me. For believing in my ability even when I didn't myself. For telling me the hard things straight to my red face. For breathing your craft. For sparking my fire and nursing the flames.

To my friends, for always being there for me, even when I'm lost and strange. For all the jabs that keep me honest and not-so-serious. For all the times that left us gut-busted on the couch, laughing away the night. For the good times, the bad ones, and everything in between. For enduring it all together. Because we did it *together*. And we still do.

To my family. Mom and Dad for the unconditional love. For always believing in me and telling me it out loud. For accepting me for who I am and who I am trying to become. For being yourselves unabashedly, always. For being the listening ear, the warm hug from home, the people that have always lived for it, and have always cared for everyone else way before you care for yourselves. For being my idols. My heroes. And to my siblings—for giving me the chance to be myself. For laughing at my jokes, for telling your own. For always believing in family first. For the knowledge I have that you'll always be there. For not compromising who you are. For the example you set for me.

To my Grandma. For providing a roof over my head through college. For always trusting me. For digging up life with me, listening to my ideas, asking questions of your own. For helping me to see straight. For helping me to aspire.

To my Grandpa. For being a teacher, even from the grave. For giving me guidance, for providing sanctuary. For setting an example of someone who chases their dreams, even when all seems lost. Even when the cards are stacked against you. For being grateful and saying it, always.

To God above, for giving me the strength to push through my iniquities. The strength to overcome. The insight to learn from my mistakes, even when I like learning the hard way. For the desire to live in truth, and the strength to not be bitter.

And to everyone else that molded me into the person I am today. More importantly, the person I strive to become. The one ten years down the road. Thank you. It's with more love than I could ever profess that you have given me the ultimate gift: a full life of color and wonder.

Writing a book takes time. Takes energy, patience, resilience, and determination. None of which would have been possible without the help of other craftsmen I met along the way. Thank you to Amber, PJ, Yoanna, Jeff, Lili, Dinah, and Aunt Ruby for being the best editors I could ever ask for. To Regan Ferreira, for listening to my rants about the ideas in this book, as well as the incredible cover art. To my sister Whitney, for the perfect title art and design input. All the external ideas, directions, feedback, and care for my book made this whole thing possible. You all gave me the fuel to keep on going.

Thank you to the places that let me linger a little too long while I wrote this book. To the park benches and city picnic tables, the cafe in Harmons grocery store, the top of the Strat Hotel in Las Vegas, the Beans & Brews in Cottonwood Heights, Utah, Community Cup in Cumming, Georgia, and Because Coffee in Dawsonville, Georgia. Places that treat you like family. Places that made it possible for me to get up and out of the dungeon of my room. Places that juiced creativity and let me people-watch in peace.

And finally, thank you. For reading this book. For trading some time for the letters in these pages. For having the faith to get to the end. For loving it, for hating it, for being there with me. For stewing in the bloody mess of this story, allowing it to soak into your bones, if only just a little. I hope you move your hands and feet toward what you really want in this life. Afterall, it's the moving and doing—the outsetting—that will get you there.

And that's juuuust it.